Gender, Family and Society

Also by Faith Robertson Elliot

The Family: Change or Continuity?

Gender, Family and Society

Faith Robertson Elliot

Consultant Editor: Jo Campling

First published 1996 by
MACMILLAN PRESS LTD
Houndmills, Basingstoke, Hampshire RG21 6XS
and London
Companies and representatives
throughout the world

ISBN 0–333–52429–2 hardcover
ISBN 0–333–52430–6 paperback

A catalogue record for this book is available
from the British Library.

10   9   8   7   6   5   4   3   2   1
05   04   03   02   01   00   99   98   97   96

Printed in Malaysia

For my students

Contents

List of Tables and Figures

Tables

Figures

Acknowledgements

Pat Allatt, Sara Arber, Ken Blakemore, Jacqui Halson, Kathleen Kiernan and Jeffrey Weeks read early drafts of particular chapters of this book, while David Morgan and Nick Tilley read the penultimate draft of the whole. I am grateful to them all for their constructive and insightful comments, for their time and for their encouragement. I would also like to thank the staff of the Lanchester Library, Coventry University, and in particular Barbara Heaton and Geoffrey Stratford, for their exceptional helpfulness in my search for source materials for this book. Finally, I would like to thank Parbinder and Jaspreet Johal for all their assistance in obtaining books from, and returning books to, the Library on my behalf.

FAITH ROBERTSON ELLIOT

The author and publishers wish to thank those who have kindly given permission for the use of copyright material in charts and tables as follows: Cambridge University Press: Table 4.6; The Controller of Her Majesty's Stationery Office: Tables 1.2, 1.3, 1.5, 1.7, 2.1, 2.2, 3.1, 3.2, 3.3, 3.4, 4.1, 4.3 and 6.3 and Figures 1.1, 1.2 3.1, 6.2 and 6.3; Dartmouth Publishing Company Ltd: Tables 1.4 and 1.8; Guardian Newspapers Ltd: Figure 6.1; Indiana University Press: Table 5.6; Macmillan Press Ltd: Table 4.5; Middlesex University: Table 5.5; The National Council on Family Relations Minneapolis, MN 5421, USA: Tables 5.1 and 5.4; One Plus One: Table 1.1; The Office for Official Publications of the European Communities: Table 4.4: Elsevier Science Ltd: Table 5.2; The Policy Studies Institute: Table 2.3; Sage Publications: Figure 4.1; Taylor and Francis and the Controller of Her Majesty's Stationery Office: Table 6.4

1

Introduction

In contemporary Western societies, debates about 'the family' have taken on a resonance and direction that is markedly different from that of the 1960s and 1970s. The 1960s and 1970s were characterised by the emergence of wide-ranging critiques of the modern conjugal family as an oppressive and bankrupt institution, the development of a trenchant feminist analysis of male domination inside and outside 'the family' and pressure for the legitimation of alternative ways of ordering sexual and parental relationships. This ideological tendency was underpinned, on the one hand, by a decline in religious belief, collectivist values and moral absolutes and, on the other, by the progressive elaboration of individualism and cultural relativism. It was associated with the emergence of dual-worker families and delegated childrearing, the institutionalisation of divorce and serial monogamy, and the increasing acceptance of unmarried cohabitation, solo parenthood and gay and lesbian relationships.

These tendencies persist in the 1980s and 1990s. However, the societal framework within which sexual and parental relationships are negotiated has changed in significant ways. The liberationist movements of the 1960s and early 1970s took place against a backcloth of relative economic prosperity, expansionist welfare policies, the apparent diminution of class conflict, a new emphasis on leisure and the enjoyment of life and a new openness, egalitarianism and optimism in social relations. In contrast, the 1980s and 1990s are marked by the defensive protection of falling living standards, neo-conservatism and pessimism, and struggles over the ordering of sexual and parental relationships take place in the context of (i) increasing ethnic differentiation and conflict; (ii) economic restructuring, high levels of unemployment, tight monetary controls and welfare cuts; (iii) population ageing and the discovery of ageism; (iv) a new awareness of the pervasiveness of violence in family life and (v) the eruption of AIDS as a major health crisis. Each of these phenomena is

playing a significant part in structuring gender and family relationships. Thus, whereas key issues of the 1960s and early 1970s
were divorce law reform, the right to abortion, gay liberation,
non-married sex and the reworking of the domestic division of
labour, salient issues of the closing decades of the twentieth
century are the challenges to gender and family structures which
arise wherever different ethnic groups share a common territory; unemployment and the marginalisation of young men in
family life; pressures for, and resistance to, the reconstruction of
'the family' as a unit of care for older people; male violence
within the family; and the apparent destructiveness of 'liberated'
sexual ideologies.

Academic analysis and debate has also shifted in complex ways.
Ethnic differentiation has brought with it a new recognition of
contradictions, tensions and diversity among women and men of
different social groups. Recognition of these divisions is forcing a
rethinking of feminist theory to take account of ethnic and
national cleavages and of the crucial role of 'the black family' in
providing protection against the oppressions of racism. Unsettled
labour markets and high levels of male unemployment and sub-
employment are paralleled by debates about the sexual division of
labour, the crisis of masculinity, the marginalisation of young
people and the growth of an 'underclass'. The ageing of populations, combined with the contraction of state expenditure and the
development of community care, has fostered attempts to theo-
rise the position of older women and men and the role of women
in servicing not only children and men, but also older people.
'Patriarchy' is thus being reconceptualised and broken down to
take account of divisions of age as well as of ethnicity, class and
sexuality. Recognition of the pervasiveness and ubiquity of wife-
battering, rape and child sex abuse has moved the issue of men's
violence to a central place in feminist thought and action and has
fostered theories of male violence as a salient feature in the institutionalisation and reproduction of patriarchal domination.
Finally, the moral panic provoked by AIDS has led to a questioning of 'permissive' values. It is used by moral conservatives to urge
a more circumspect morality, has prompted a re-evaluation of 'liberated' gay ideology by gay men, and is seen by feminist writers as
providing an opportunity to reconstruct sexual scripts in ways that
would valorise women's sexual experience.

Gender, Family and Society is about the interrelationship between these key aspects of contemporary life and gender and family relationships. This introductory chapter outlines the major and often contradictory contours of gender and family relations in contemporary Western societies as a prelude to examining the way in which they shape and are being shaped by ethnic differentiation, high levels of unemployment and sub-employment, population ageing, male violence and the AIDS pandemic.

Chapter 2 examines, first, the differentiating features of British Afro-Caribbean and Asian gender and family structures and, second, the anxieties and conflicts surrounding ethnic difference as revealed by racist, anti-racist, 'black' feminist, ethnographic and marxist-feminist theories of 'race' and ethnicity.

Chapter 3 begins with an account of contemporary unemployment and sub-employment trends. It then examines debates about (i) the consequences of married men's unemployment for family living standards, stress in family life and change in the sexual division of labour; (ii) the loss of independence and psychological stress which unemployment brings to women; and (iii) the disruptive effect of youth unemployment on orderly transitions to adulthood and the formation of new family units. The concluding section of this chapter considers competing interpretations of the relationship between high levels of unemployment and sub-employment and the emergence of an underclass – a social category below or outside society at large.

Chapter 4 explores debates about the emergence of later life as a social problem by looking at the demographic ageing of populations, everyday images of later life as a period of biological decline and theories of the social construction, within the context of the ideologies and imperatives of contemporary capitalism, of later life as 'old age'. We then proceed to examine the role of family members in eldercare and its gendered nature by looking at (i) competing moral positions on the relationship between 'the family' and the state in eldercare, (ii) conceptualisations of the caring task, (iii) interpretations of the obligation to care in everyday thought, (iv) patterns of familial care and (v) images of the burdens of care. The chapter concludes with a brief examination of the politics of disability and the challenge to ageism.

Chapter 5 considers contemporary concerns over the apparent ubiquity and pervasiveness of male violence and sexual abuse in family life. It examines (i) debates about the definition of violence and abuse, (ii) evidence of the pervasiveness of parental violence, the sexual abuse of children and violence and sexual coercion in sexual partnerships and (iii) competing explanations of family violence as rooted in individual psychology; disadvantaged class position and/or the contradictions of family life; and the social construction of masculinity in a patriarchal world.

Chapter 6 delineates the moral panic over permissive ideologies and behaviours which AIDS has evoked. It outlines the epidemiology of AIDS, examines the sexual politics of AIDS by looking at representations of AIDS in conservative moral thought, gay thought and feminist thought, and considers prognostications of an end to the sexual revolution by examining research evidence on change in gay and heterosexual sexual behaviour patterns.

This text shows that ethnic differentiation, unsettled labour markets and high levels of male unemployment, population ageing, the apparent pervasiveness of violence and sexual abuse in family life and the perception of AIDS as constituting a major health crisis are changing the face of social life in contemporary Western societies and are the source of wide-ranging and deep-seated contradictions, conflicts and anxieties. Further, it shows that these phenomena are not only shaped by gender and family values but also challenge, in different ways, both 'traditional' and 'liberated' gender and familial values. Sexual, parental and gender relationships are thus revealed as subject to a wide range of cross-cutting pressures, anxieties and challenges. These competing pressures and challenges are summarised and highlighted in a short epilogue (Chapter 7).

Two caveats must be added. First, while the issues discussed in this book are relevant to all those societies commonly subsumed under the label 'Western society', every Western society has its own history. There are thus considerable cross-cultural variations, as well as similarities, between Western societies in their sexual, parental and gender structures and in their experience of, and discourses on, the issues with which we are concerned. This text focusses on Britain, but also makes reference to other Anglo-Saxon and northwest European societies by way of comparison and contrast. Second, there are issues other than those on which we focus which are changing the nature of social life in Western societies and/or are the source of public concern and alarm. The scope for debate over inclusions and exclusions and over distinctions between underlying trends and symptoms is great. However, the phenomena on which we focus are clearly of fundamental significance and have a particular resonance for family life. Considering them together reveals the intensity and scale of the contradictions, tensions and challenges that surround sexual, parental and gender relations in contemporary Western societies.

1.1 THE RELATIONSHIP REVOLUTION

In everyday thought, the decade of the 1960s stands for a key moment of change in family values and sexual mores. It is seen as marking a transition from general conformity with a sexual and family morality based on lifelong marriage and women's mothering to permissiveness and diversity. This view of the 1960s is questioned in academic thought. Weeks (1985, 1986) argues that the past was marked not by consensus on family values and sexual conventions but by change and dislocation, by social class, religious and ethnic variation and by marked differences between formal and informal standards. Moral consensus, Weeks maintains, is rare. Further, Weeks argues that many of the changes with which the 1960s are associated had a long gestation, while others post-dated the 1960s. Furthermore, he emphasises that the 1960s and 1970s saw the development of moral purity campaigns as well as the birth of permissive ideologies and were not monolithically revolutionary.

Yet, while the diversity of family patterns and the complexity of change make it difficult to delimit a 'mid-twentieth century family' and to identify the timing and direction of contemporary change, most sociologists believe that an ideal-typical model of 'the modern Western family' (that is, a model of a family form that may be said to be dominant in that there is an ideological emphasis on it or that most families belong to it or converge towards it) and of typical trends away from it can be constructed. This chapter looks first at ideal typical characterisations of the mid-twentieth century Western family. It then looks at the birth of 'permissiveness' in the 1960s, at contemporary changes in family life as revealed in demographic trends, public opinion surveys and sociological analysis, and finally at competing interpretations of the significance of these trends.

The Mid-Twentieth Century Western Family

In the mid-twentieth century, sociologists of all persuasions took it for granted that in Western societies sexual and parental relationships had traditionally been, and currently were, located in a nuclear family unit based on lifelong marriage and women's mothering. In addition, it was believed that the nuclear family had assumed a very specific form in modern times in that it had become relatively independent of kin and was marked by a new emphasis on the emotional closeness of husband and wife and parents and children. This family form was labelled 'the conjugal family' by Linton (1949) and Goode (1963) and 'the companionship family' by Burgess *et al.* (1963). It made its earliest appearance in England and reached its fullest development in the Anglo-Saxon world. Its dominance may be demonstrated in a number of ways.

First, there is evidence of cultural and ideological support for this family form, or for specific aspects of it, in a wide range of discourses. In Western societies, Christianity is very generally credited with having defined sexual relationships, procreation and childcare as properly taking place within the nuclear family, with constructing marriage as an indissoluble bond, and with sustaining women's mothering and men's authority. Further, a specific affinity between ascetic Protestantism and the development in modern times of the nuclear family as a sentimental reality has been asserted. A number of writers (among them Ariès, 1962; George, 1973; Hamilton, 1978; Hall, 1979) have argued that in the seventeenth century Puritanism, and in the late eighteenth and early nineteenth centuries the Evangelical Movement, placed a considerable emphasis on salvation through a Godly life and made the family central to the creation of a Godly society. Puritanism, these writers argue, defined socialisation within the family as important in bringing the child to God and invested marriage with the emotional content necessary to produce faithful husbands and stable non-adulterous marriages. Love was seen as purifying sexuality within marriage; mutual affection, trust and fidelity were extolled; and marriage was constructed as a partnership based upon common labour and love. A new value was thus placed on affection between family members and, it is argued, the family became a sentimental reality as well as the centre of morality. From the late nineteenth century onwards, this set of family values seems to have been refurbished and given renewed legitimation by sociobiological accounts of the naturalness of heterosexuality, the nuclear family and the sexual division of labour, and by psychological theories of the importance of stable, intimate family relationships to the emotional security of children and adults.

Second, sociological research provided evidence of widespread conformity with conjugal family norms. For example, Leonard's (1980) study of courtship and marriage showed that among Swansea couples in the early 1960s marriage and parenthood were regarded as inseparable, inevitable and desirable. Further, demographic data show that in the 1950s and early 1960s age at marriage was at historically low, and rates of marriage at historically high, levels, that fertility was 'buoyant' and that childbearing outside marriage was relatively low. Marriage, sex and childbearing, says Dormor (1992, p. 7), had rarely been so tightly bound together. Furthermore, a wide range of British and American studies (summarised by Elliot, 1986) point to the emergence at this time of a highly home-centred way of life. These studies suggested that rising living standards were associated with an increasing investment of resources, time and energy in the home and in family leisure. They provided evidence of the growing involvement of men in the daily routines of family life, delineated a new emphasis on mutual affection, psychological closeness and egalitarianism between husband and wife and parents and children, and pointed to the construction of the nuclear family as a primary source of personal happiness and self-fulfilment.

Third, functionalist sociology, then the dominant sociological approach to the family, seems to have reflected and reinforced beliefs in the ubiquity and eufunctionality of the nuclear family. For example, Murdock (1949) presented the nuclear family as a 'universal human grouping' and sought to explain its universality in terms of the efficacy with which it regulates sexual relationships, reproduces the species, socialises children and ensures economic cooperation between the sexes, 'functions' which, in Murdock's view, are necessary to the survival of the human species and the continuity of the social order. At the same time, some functionalist writers depicted the nuclear family as evolving in ways that 'fit' with changes in other parts of the social system. Talcott Parsons (1949, 1955), the most notable of early family theorists, claimed that the modern conjugal family contributes both to the efficient organisation of industrial economies and to the psychological needs of the individual. In Parsons' view, this family form makes it possible for the economic system to operate unhampered by wide-ranging kinship obligations and, at the same time, provides family members with a stable, if limited, set of primary relationships within which children may be socialised and adults may experience companionship and emotional support in an otherwise competitive, universalistic and mobile society.

There are accounts of family life in the mid-twentieth century which point to divergences from this conjugal family norm and doubts about its efficacy. For example, Kinsey's studies of sexual behaviour in the USA in the 1940s and early 1950s provide clear evidence of departures from conventional sexual morality (Kinsey *et al.*, 1948, 1953). Further, various community studies – such as Dennis *et al.*'s (1956) study of a mining community in northern England, Kerr's (1958) study of a Liverpool slum and Moynihan's (1965) account of poor African-American communities – point to occupational, class and ethnic variations in family patterns and suggest that the home-centred husband and father was by no means a universal feature of family life. Furthermore, as Fletcher (1962) shows, there were anxieties about the general direction of change in family life: anxieties that extended family ties were being weakened, that welfare responsibilities formerly entrusted to 'the family' were being usurped by the state, and that parental, and in particular paternal, authority was being eroded. Nevertheless, the general picture that emerges from contemporary accounts of mid-twentieth century family life is one of the dominance of a relatively autonomous and home-centred nuclear family based on the mutual affection and intimate association of husband and wife and parents and children. This trend was believed to be progressive and the prevailing mood, epitomised in a series of studies by Michael Young and Peter Willmott (Young and Willmott, 1957, 1973; Willmott and Young, 1960), was one of optimism.

Even so, a vigorous critique of the conjugal family, together with pressures for the legitimation of alternative lifestyles, emerged in the 1960s.

The Birth of Permissiveness

The impetus to the development of a permissive morality and of alternatives to the conventional family seems to have come from diverse groups of people and tendencies: from exponents of self-actualisation, propounders of sexual freedom and gay liberation, sections of socialism and sections of feminism. It was under-pinned by a common emphasis on equality, individual autonomy, and self-realisation and a shared perception of the conventional conjugal family as limiting freedom, impeding self-realisation and confining intimacy. 'Liberationists' sought to extend individual freedom to include the right to choose between a range of sexual and parental relationships. They celebrated non-binding commit-ments, asserted the viability of a social life based on the mutual negotiation of commitments rather than conformity with societal-ly-defined obligations, and sought to replace the emphases on procreational sex and the needs of the child, which had dominat-ed traditional family ideologies, with emphases on recreational sex and the rights of adults. In addition, feminist strands of alter-native lifestyle thought identified the conventional conjugal family with male domination and sought to restructure sexual and parental relationships in ways that would revolutionise gender roles.

Pressures for establishing alternative ways of ordering sexual and parental relationships seem to have arisen out of: (i) ideational change; (ii) structural contradiction and (iii) facilitat-ing social arrangements.

(i) Ideational change. Most accounts of alternative lifestyle trends locate their development in the divergent but mutually reinforc-ing revolutionary discourses and tendencies of the 1960s. According to Segal (1983), these tendencies included: the radical-isation of politics, as manifested in the emergence of the New Left, the growth of student protest and the development of civil rights movements; the birth of a hedonistic, permissive counter-culture of which the commune movement, self-actualising

lifestyles and hippy groups were expressions; the emergence of a succession of youth sub-cultures in which the work ethic, acquisitiveness, a disciplined way of life and conformity were rejected in favour of the pursuit of pleasure, 'doing your own thing' and self-fulfilment through leisure; and the rebirth of feminism and development of critiques of 'the family' as a central factor in women's oppression. These movements were anti-authoritarian and iconoclastic in their ideological orientations and, Segal argues, led to the questioning of traditional family values, an emphasis on sexual pleasure as the source of personal liberation, and pressure for the legitimation of new ways of ordering sexual, parental and gender relationships. Alternative lifestyle tendencies, Segal seems to suggest, are to be explained in part at least by a radical shift in ideas, values and attitudes.

This shift in values was accompanied by important shifts in academic discourse. In the social sciences, the functionalist theoretical perspective was subjected to extensive critique, rejected and superceded by Marxist, feminist and other critical theoretical perspectives. In these perspectives, the modern conjugal family may be depicted as a key instrument of capitalist domination and of the oppression of the working class, as a major site of patriarchal power and women's subordination and/or as stifling individuality and smothering self-awareness.

(ii) Structural contradiction. The notion that the modern conjugal family is permeated by a number of deep-rooted structural contradictions and tensions and, consequently, by pressures for change is found in all critical analyses of 'the family'.

First, the contemporary isolation of nuclear family members from kin and community ties is seen by some writers as leading not, as functionalist theorising had suggested, to mutually supportive relationships between husband and wife and parents and children, but to the claustrophobic and explosive intensification of family relationships. Contemporary family relationships, Leach (1967) argues, are overcharged and generate stress and conflict precisely because the family unit is isolated and segregated.

Second, non-feminist as well as feminist writers have suggested that the continuing identification of women with domesticity and motherhood is at odds with modern structural arrangements. Titmuss (1963) argues that small families have made motherhood a phase of life rather than a lifetime's activity, rendered mothers redundant in mid-life and necessitated change in women's roles. Oakley (1976) suggests that there is a disjuncture between women's domestication and modern emphases on occupational success as the mainspring of social status and personal identity. The feminist corpus as a whole maintains that the nuclear family denies women economic independence, gives men power over their fertility and sexuality and imprisons them in an oppressed gender identity (Elliot, 1986, pp. 126–31).

Third, Weeks (1989b), in a major and arresting argument, locates the sexual revolution in changes in class relations generated by the long period of economic expansion which followed the Second World War. Economic expansion, Weeks argues, was attended by the creation of new opportunities, the reshaping of class relations and political alliances, an explosion of youth cultures and the reorientation of the economy to domestic consumption. Following Hobsbawm (1969), he claims that a mass-consumption society is dominated by its biggest market, the working class, and that as the consumer society penetrated this market, styles of life were proletarianised. More speculatively, he suggests that economic expansion depended in part on a switch in moral attitudes away from the traditional bourgeois virtues of self-denial and prudence towards a compulsion to spend and the privileging of pleasure, including sexual pleasure.

Although connections between structural conditions and change in *mentalité* are not easily established, the notion that the discontents generated by these structural contradictions led to pressures for alternative ways of ordering sexual, parental and gender relationships seems a plausible one.

(iii) Facilitating processes. Much of the literature identifies various changes in the social environment as facilitating the implementation of alternative lifestyles. Most accounts pinpoint advances in contraceptive technology, and in particular the development of 'the pill', as making possible the separation of sexual gratification from procreation and marriage (see, for example, Weeks, 1989b, pp. 258–60). In addition, Elliot (1986, p. 180) suggests that population growth means that population control (rather than population replacement) has become a societal goal; procreation is therefore no longer seen as a universal obligation and the celebration of non-

reproductive sex is facilitated. Most writers also suggest that the increasing participation of women in the paid labour force, together with the mid-twentieth century expansion of state welfare, has reduced the importance of the nuclear family to the economic support of women and children and facilitated the development of alternatives. Finally, it has been suggested that the social and geographical mobility associated with modern life has freed many young people from encapsulation within the conventional value system and social controls of parents and neighbourhood groups. At the same time, the greater availability of higher education has exposed them to radical world views. The spokespersons of the new morality have in general come from the new, young, educated, mobile middle class created by these processes.

However, it must be noted that pressures for change are not universal and relentless throughout the Western world. They began, and appear to be at their most advanced, in Scandinavia and other Nordic countries. They have developed rapidly in northwest Europe and in the Anglo-Saxon world. They are, however, developing slowly in Ireland and southern Europe, where extended family ties appear to be more enduring, gender inequalities are marked, religious values play a significant part in public and private life and family life has historically been underpinned by collectivistic rather than individualistic values.

Contemporary Change in Family Patterns

Because change may occur in some aspects of family relations but not in others, may be in contradictory directions and may vary in timing and pace between social groups, and because there may be marked divergences between values and behaviour, the nature and scope of change in family life is not easily established. In addition, data on family patterns come from a variety of sources, are not easily comparable either over time or between societies and must therefore be interpreted with caution. Nevertheless, the literature suggests that in contemporary Anglo-Saxon and northwest European societies trends towards (i) the separation of sex from marriage; (ii) the reconstruction of marriage as a terminable arrangement; (iii) the separation of childbearing and childrearing from marriage, and (iv) the reworking of the sexual division of labour are now well established.

(i)   *The separation of sex from marriage*

Demographic and other data on the formation, acceptance and visibility of unmarried, extra-marital and homosexual relationships suggest that in contemporary Anglo-Saxon and northwest European societies sexual relationships are no longer firmly tied to lifelong and monogamous heterosexual marriage.

In the first place, sexual intercourse seems to have become an integral part of unmarried heterosexual relationships. All the available evidence suggests that it is now the norm in 'steady' relationships and that chastity tends to be ridiculed (*The Independent*, 21 December 1988). Further, studies of the sexual mores of young people show that, although informal norms limit intercourse to 'steady' relationships, these norms are more rigorously applied to women than to men (Lees, 1986a), friendships of quite short durations are defined as 'going steady' relationships (Abrams *et al.*, 1990), 'going steady relationships' are not necessarily and perhaps not usually defined as involving a commitment to marriage (Ford and Bowie, 1988) and monogamy is a minority pattern (Knox *et al.*, 1993; Wellings *et al.*, 1994, pp. 90–133).

More significantly, acceptance of unmarried sexual relationships seem to have evolved into acceptance of unmarried cohabitation. In Scandinavia, where this trend first appeared and is firmly established (Table 1.1), cohabitation before marriage is the norm, long-term cohabiting relationships are commonplace, age at marriage is relatively high and the proportions of women marrying relatively low (Table 1.2). In Britain (as Table 1.3 illustrates) unmarried cohabitation has also increased greatly and has become a common prelude to marriage and a common sequel to marital break-up. Further, age at marriage has risen and the ultimate proportion ever marrying is likely to be lower than in the past (Kiernan and Wicks, 1990). However, in Britain, as in other west European and Anglo-Saxon countries, cohabitation levels are modest and marriage levels high by Scandinavian standards (Tables 1.1 and 1.2).

Cohabitation in Britain and other Anglo-Saxon countries seems to be not only less common than in Scandinavia but to be different from Scandinavian cohabitation. Studies by Lewin (1982), Hoem and Hoem (1988), Kiernan and Estaugh (1993) and others suggest that in Scandinavia cohabitation is characterised by

Wellings *et al.* (1994) provide recent, comprehensive and apparently reliable national data on trends in unmarried sexual relations in Britain. They show that almost all young (16–24-year-old) women and men have their first experience of intercourse outside marriage (pp. 74–5). Moreover, 51 per cent of the young men and 32 per cent of the young women in their sample had their first experience of intercourse outside a committed (married, engaged, cohabiting or 'steady') relationship. Further, they find that pre-marital sex is normatively accepted by nearly all young people: only 5 per cent of the young men and 5 per cent of the young women in their sample believed sex before marriage to be 'mostly' or 'always wrong' (pp. 244–8). In addition, Wellings *et al.* point, on the one hand, to the erosion of monogamy and, on the other, to considerable variability in the number of partners people have (pp. 94–105). Overall, 27 per cent of men and 45 per cent of women reported being monogamous or (in a very small minority of cases) chaste, while 44 per cent of men and 20 per cent of women reported five or more partners. At ages 25–34 both women and men less often reported being monogamous and more often reported five or more partners than older people, despite the fact that older people had had more time in which to accumulate partners.

In the USA, researchers have also documented near universal participation in unmarried sex and increasing rates of partnership-turnover. However, attitudes seem to be more conservative than in Britain: 36 per cent of American people, compared with under 10 per cent of British people, believe pre-marital sex to be 'always' or 'mostly' wrong (Wellings *et al.*, 1994, pp. 244, 248).

marriage-like interaction patterns, is commonly accompanied by childbearing, is increasingly regulated by the principles of marriage law and may be regarded as a variation on marriage. In contrast, cohabiting relationships among young never-married people in Britain and the USA appear to be largely childfree, relatively short-lived and generally uncommitted arrangements. Studies conducted during the 1970s and early 1980s found that

Table 1.1 *Cohabitation in northwest Europe, Britain and the USA[1]*

Country	All adults 1990	Women Aged 20–4	25–9	Survey Year
	%	%	%	
Sweden	13	31	31	(1985)
Denmark	16	37	23	(1981)
Norway	10	28	16	(1986)
France	10	19	11	(1986)
Netherlands	7	19	16	(1988)
West Germany	7	14		(1982)
Belgium	7			
Great Britain	5	15	11	(1989)
USA		9[2]	16	(1989)

[1] Surveys of cohabitation have used different sample sizes, varied in their coverage and defined cohabitation in different ways. Comparisons between countries must therefore be regarded as tentative.

[2] Aged 16–24.

SOURCE Dormor, 1992, Table 4.

Table 1.2 *Proportion ever married and mean age at first marriage for women in selected northwest European countries, 1988*

Country	Proportion ever married by age 50[1]	Mean age at first marriage 1988[2]
England and Wales	78	24.6
Denmark	61	27.1
France	72	25.0
Germany (West)	72	25.5
Netherlands		25.0[3]
Norway	68	25.5
Sweden	55	27.9

[1] Estimate from age-specific first marriage rates for the 1960 birth cohort of women (incorporates projected trends).

[2] Age at marriage tends to correlate with overall propensity to marry and may be taken as an indication of the salience of marriage.

[3] For nearest available year.

SOURCE Haskey, 1992, Table 2.

they were characteristically based on the independence of each of the partners rather than their 'jointness' as a couple, were not usually seen as establishing long-term commitments and tended either to dissolve after a relatively short time or, if they lasted, to become married relationships (Cole, 1977; Macdonald and Mars, 1981; Macklin 1983). The demographic data for the late 1980s and early 1990s reveal a declining tendency for women to marry their first cohabiting partner (Schoen and Owens, 1992) and a lengthening of cohabitation durations among divorced people (Table 1.3), but provide little evidence either of the regular establishment of long-term unions (Haskey and Kiernan, 1989) or of

Table 1.3   *Cohabitation patterns among women aged 18–49 in Britain*

A. Proportion of women in cohabiting relationships	1979	1992
	%	%
All women	3.0	9.0
Never-married women	8.0	21.0
Separated women	17.0	12.0
Divorced women	20.0	28.0
Widowed women	nil	[9.0][1]

B. Proportion of women who cohabited before marriage by year of marriage	1975–9	1985–9
	%	%
First marriage of respondent, first or later marriage of partner	19.0	51.0
Second marriage of respondent, first or later marriage of partner	71.0	[86.0][1]

C. Median durations of cohabitation	1979	1987
	months	months
Never-married women	18	19
Divorced women	28	34

[1]   Base too small to be reliable.
SOURCE   A. *GHS*, 1992, Table 2.6; B; *GHS*, 1991, Table 11.10; C. Haskey and Kiernan, 1989.

the development of attitudes favourable to cohabitation as a life-long alternative to marriage (Table 1.4). In general, researchers have characterised cohabitation in Britain and the USA as representing, not a variation on marriage, but an expansion of the mate selection process, a variation on bachelor/spinster status or a transitional phase preceding marriage (Buunk and van Driel, 1989; Rindfuss and VandenHeuvel, 1992; Kiernan and Estaugh, 1993, p. 62).

In contrast with the widespread acceptance of unmarried sex, attitudes to extra-marital sexual activity appear to have remained conservative. American and British surveys show that most men and women disapprove of extra-marital sexual activity (Scott, 1990; Smith, 1990; Wellings *et al.*, 1994, pp. 249–52), that most young people marry in the hope and expectation of a faithful and lifelong union (Guy, 1983) and that fidelity is believed to be very important to successful marriage (Ashford, 1987). These expectations seem to hold for all age groups and all socio-economic levels. They also hold, but somewhat less strongly, for cohabiting relationships (Wellings *et al.*, 1994, p. 250).

Table 1.4 *Attitudes to unmarried cohabitation in selected Western countries*

	Britain	USA	Netherlands	West Germany
Advice respondents would give a young woman[1]:	%	%	%	%
Live with steady partner and then marry	43	26	45	50
Marry without living together first	37	46	24	19
Live alone without a steady partner	4	9	2	5
Live with steady partner without marrying	4	3	8	11
Can't choose	11	14	20	15

[1] The advice that would be given to a young man was substantially the same.
SOURCE Scott, 1990, p. 61; Scott *et al.*, 1993, p. 26.

However, attitudes and behaviour may diverge. One review of current research suggests that one quarter to one half of married women have at least one extra-marital relationship after marriage and that between 50 and 65 per cent of married men 'stray' before the age of 40 (Lawson, 1988, p. 75). Moreover, whereas early studies suggested that women 'strayed' less often than men, recent studies suggest that they 'stray' nearly as often as men (Richards and Elliott, 1991). However, married men and women are apparently much less likely to 'stray' than cohabiting men and women. Wellings *et al.* (1994, pp. 113–16) find that multiple relationships among cohabiting men and women approach the levels found among the unmarried and the divorced/separated rather than the married.

Finally, and perhaps most radically, conceptions of lesbian and gay relationships as 'abnormal' and 'sinful' have been challenged. In many Western societies, the idea that a lesbian or gay lifestyle can legitimately be chosen has gained ground, many legal sanctions against homosexuals have been removed, and gay women and men are increasingly coming out of the 'closet' and seeking to establish valid and distinctive homosexual identities and cultures. The United States, in particular, has played host to a spectacular growth of homosexual sub-cultures. In addition, lesbian women are establishing families through unmarried heterosexual relations, artificial insemination and single person adoption and as a result of a tentative modification of the prejudice against awarding custody to lesbian mothers on marital break-up (Elliot, 1986, p. 193). Nevertheless, homosexual behaviours remain legally circumscribed in a variety of ways, everyday attitudes to homosexuality have not changed substantially and few people believe that homosexual couples should have the right to marry (Scott *et al.*, 1993). Wellings *et al.* (1994, p. 253) report that in Britain 70 per cent of men and 58 per cent of women believe sex between two men to be 'always or mostly wrong'. Similar proportions see sex between women as wrong. In the USA, three-quarters of respondents in one survey said that homosexuality is always or mostly wrong (Smith, 1990).

In sum the data reviewed in this section suggest that, while attitudes towards unmarried cohabitation as a lifetime alternative to marriage, extra-marital sexual activity and homosexuality remain conservative, sexual relationships are no longer firmly located in marriage. Some writers have suggested that this change in sexual mores is underpinned by a fundamental shift in cultural images of sexuality – that whereas in traditional value systems sex was inextricably linked with procreation, profound emotional attachment and durable commitment, it is now linked with sensual pleasure and may be separated from procreation, love and commitment (Weeks, 1985; Lawson, 1988). Lawson (1988) points out that this reconstruction of sexuality is particularly significant in women's lives: it has, she argues, allowed women as well as men to claim that sex can be enjoyed separately from love and commitment and has thus liberated them from the constraints of the traditional double standard. The sexual revolution, says Lawson, is in reality a revolution in women's rather than in men's behaviour; like men, women are now not usually virgins at marriage, have a plurality of partners before marriage, conduct adulterous liaisons after marriage and engage in casual affairs and one-night stands.

However, the sexual revolution is a subject of considerable ambivalence for women. Feminist writers have welcomed the freedom from the constraints of traditional morality that it brought but they have also interpreted it as marketing as avant garde a sexual culture based on male notions of sexual pleasure and designed to benefit men. The sexual scripts of male liberationists, it has been argued, make 'macho' male patterns of diversity and casualness the norm for both sexes (Rossi, 1977), construct women as sex objects (Segal, 1983, p. 54), and are not intended to liberate women from 'anything but their common sense and instinct for self-protection' (Jeffreys, 1990, p. 93). Moreover, despite the greater freedom now available to women, it is clear that their reputations remain at risk in a way that men's are not. Lees (1986a, p. 30) shows that adolescent girls negotiate their sexual encounters in a social world in which 'if you don't like them [boys], then they'll call you a tight bitch. If you go with them they'll call you a slag afterwards.'

(ii)   The reconstruction of marriage

The reconstruction of marriage as a secular and terminable relationship represents a second major area of change in family structures.

In the 1960s and 1970s nearly all Western societies liberalised their divorce laws in ways which effectively gave couples the power to decide whether and when their marriage had ended (Mount, 1982, pp. 212–18; Weitzman, 1988). In England and Wales, for example, the irretrievable breakdown of marriage was made the basis of divorce under the Divorce Reform Act 1969 and seven years later this provision was extended to Scotland under the Divorce (Scotland) Act of 1976. Moreover, the redefinition of marriage as a terminable contract, which these Acts implied, was carried a stage further with changes to the post-divorce support obligations between spouses qua spouses under the Matrimonial and Family Proceedings Act, 1984. This Act retained the principle of parental support for children but based maintenance for former partners on the principle that self-sufficiency should be attained as soon as possible.

The 'liberalisation' of divorce law has in general been accompanied by marked rises in divorce rates and by trends towards divorcing at progressively earlier durations of marriage (Haskey, 1992; *Statistical Abstract of the United States*, 1992, Table 127; *Social Trends*, 1994, Tables 2.13, 2.14). In Britain, it is estimated that if present trends continue nearly four in every ten marriages will end in divorce (Haskey, 1989a) and one in four children will experience their parents' divorce before reaching their sixteenth birthday (Haskey, 1990). In the USA, an estimated three in five first marriages will end in divorce, if present trends continue (Scott *et al.*, 1993).

Marital break-up does not end the marital careers of most men and women. Although remarriage rates have fallen (*Social Trends*, 1994, Figure 2.12) in tandem with rising rates and durations of post-divorce cohabitation, most men and women remarry within a relatively short time of divorcing. In Britain, 56 per cent of women and 60 per cent of men who divorced during the period 1979–82 and who were under 35 when their marriages ended, remarried within six years (*GHS*, 1991, Tables 11.7, 11.8). According to one estimate, 25 per cent of women who marry will divorce and remarry at least once (Coleman, 1989). In the USA, an estimated one-third of those born between 1950 and 1954 will remarry at least once (Zinn and Eitzen, 1990, p. 374).

These developments are seen by some commentators as transforming the institution of marriage. The liberalisation of divorce, says Weitzman (1988), has placed the option to terminate a marriage in the hands of the partners and reconstructed marriage, hitherto a lifelong partnership, as a union contingent on the happiness of the partners. Further, Weitzman argues that divorce law reform has redefined the traditional support obligations of marriage as optional, time-limited, contingent, open to individual definition and terminable and, in addition, has made parenting terminable since its effect is to deprive children of one of their parents (usually the father).

This reconstruction of marriage is surrounded by considerable ambivalence. Social science commentators have in general interpreted it as a progressive development which banishes connotations of fault from divorce and facilitates the replacement of unsuccessful marriages by successful marriages (see, for example, Fletcher, 1988). At the same time, however, there is in most analyses of the divorce experience an overriding emphasis on its traumatic nature, on the economic difficulties experienced by divorced families and on the long-term emotional, educational and relational difficulties experienced by the children of divorce (see, for example, Wallerstein and Kelly, 1980; Maclean and Wadsworth, 1988; Weitzman, 1988; Wallerstein and Blakeslee, 1989). Further, public opinion surveys show that most people believe both that divorce is an appropriate solution to unhappy marriages and that marriage is treated too lightly and ought to be more effectively safeguarded (Ashford, 1987; Scott, 1990). A large minority believe that divorce should be less easily obtainable. In the USA, where in most states divorce may be obtained without having to prove marital breakdown, the proportion of people who believe that divorce should be less easily obtainable has increased over time from 42 per cent in 1974 to 51 per cent in 1989 (Airey, 1984, p. 139; Scott, 1990, p. 66). Finally, the belief that 'divorcing has got out of hand' permeates the policy statements of the political Right and has given rise to proposals for tightening up divorce. In Britain, reforms currently being discussed seek, on the one hand, to appease radical sentiment by abolishing the requirement that evidence of marital breakdown be provided and, on the other, to impose a year's waiting period on all divorcing couples. It is argued that this would enable couples to reflect on whether their marriages had in fact irretrievably broken down and, where they proposed going through with their divorce, to work out suitable arrangements – through mediation agencies rather than the courts – for their children and for the division of their economic resources.

(iii)   The separation of parenthood from marriage

The separation of parenthood from marriage and, linked with this, the separation of childrearing from biological fatherhood represent a third major area of change in the family structures of Western societies. This trend stems from rising levels of unmarried childbearing as well as increasing divorce and has given rise to one-parent, cohabiting and step-parent family units.

During the 1970s and 1980s, trends towards childbearing outside marriage emerged and developed at varying rates in all the major industrial countries of the Western world (Figure 1.1). In Sweden, where this trend is very 'advanced', one in two births take place outside marriage. In the United Kingdom, almost one in every three births now takes place outside marriage – compared with one in twenty throughout most of the first sixty years of this century (*Social Trends*, 1994, pp. 39–40).

Unmarried childbearing is the outcome not only of increased conception outside marriage but also of a declining tendency for such conceptions to be legitimated by marriage (Table 1.5) and of increasing childbearing within cohabiting unions. In Sweden, it is more common to have a first child in a cohabiting union than to marry before having had a child and most births outside marriage take place in cohabiting unions (Hoem and Hoem, 1988; Kiernan and Estaugh, 1993, p. 64). In England and Wales, approximately half of all unmarried births are to cohabiting women and half to unpartnered women (*Social Trends*, 1993, p. 32). About 27 per cent of never-married cohabitees have had a child (Kiernan and Estaugh, 1993, p. 11). However, evidence from Sweden (Hoem and Hoem, 1988) as well as Britain (Brown, 1986) suggests that cohabiting parents split up more readily than married parents, with the result that cohabiting childbearing considerably more frequently than married childbearing means the separation of children from one of their biological parents, usually the father, and their location in solo parent or step-parent family units. Brown (1986) finds that in Britain about 40 per cent of jointly registered extra-marital children under the age of 10

Percentages   0   10   20   30   40   50   60

[1] 1987
[2] 1990
[3] 1989
[4] 1988
[5] 1986
[6] Data for latest year is for Germany as constituted since 3 October 1990.

SOURCE   *Social Trends*, 1993, Figure 2.23.

FIGURE 1.1   *Live births outside marriage as a percentage of all births: international comparisons, 1960 and 1991*

(compared with 10 per cent of children born within marriage) are not living with both their natural parents.

The link between parenthood and marriage and between father and child has also been eroded by rising levels of divorce. In Britain, the *General Household Survey* for 1992 shows that the proportion of families headed by a divorced or separated mother more than doubled over the 1970s and 1980s and in 1992 stood at

Table 1.5   *Conceptions by marital status and outcome, England and Wales 1971 and 1991*

Conceptions	1971	1991
	%	%
Inside marriage		
Maternities	72.6	51.9
Legal abortions	5.2	4.4
Outside marriage		
Maternities inside marriage	8.1	3.7
Maternities outside marriage		
Joint registration	3.5	18.9
Sole registration	4.1	6.1
Legal abortions	6.7	15.0
All conceptions (numbers)	835.5	853.7

SOURCE   *Social Trends*, 1994, Table 2.17.

11 per cent of all families (*GHS*, 1992, Table 2.23). Over the same period, the proportion of families headed by a never-married mother rose from 1 per cent to 7 per cent. The proportion headed by a lone father fluctuated between 1 per cent and 2 per cent. Overall, British levels of solo parenthood are somewhat higher than in other northwest European countries but are lower than in the USA (Table 1.6).

Neither unmarried childbearing nor divorce necessarily mean the permanent separation of parenthood from marriage in the life of the individual. Unmarried parents may marry. In the study by Brown cited earlier, 62 per cent of the extra-marital children whose births were registered by both their parents, and 59 per cent of those whose births were registered by the mother only, were at ages 6–9 living in a married couple unit formed either by the marriage of the child's parents to each other or by the marriage of the child's mother to someone else. Similarly, as the data presented in the preceding section indicated, divorce may be followed by remarriage and the reconstitution of one-parent families as married two-parent families. In Britain, the median duration of solo parenthood appears to be about five years for women who become lone parents through marital break-up and three years

Table 1.6 *Proportion of families with children under 18, headed by a lone parent, in selected northwest European countries, 1989, and the USA, 1990*

Country	%
UK	17
Belgium	10
Denmark	15
France	11
Germany	12
Netherlands	12
USA	24

SOURCE   Roll, 1992, for European data; *Statistical Abstract of the United States*, 1992, Table 67, for USA data.

for those who do so through unmarried childbearing (Ermisch, 1989).

However, all the evidence suggests that trends towards divorce, unmarried childbearing (including in a small but ideologically significant proportion of cases childbearing by artificially inseminated lesbian/heterosexual women) and step-parenthood have weakened the bond between children and their biological fathers. A stream of research reports from the 1960s onwards has consistently shown that, on the break-up of parental relationships, fathers rarely have custody of their children, frequently have only limited contact with them and contribute only sporadically and minimally to their economic support (Elliot, 1986, pp. 157–62; Furstenberg and Harris, 1992). A recent British study by Bradshaw and Millar (1991) found that 43 per cent of absent parents have no contact with their children and, that of those who do, one-fourth see them less than once a month. Only 29 per cent of the lone parents in this study received regular maintenance from their former partners. Interaction between 'absent' fathers and their children appears to be weaker where they had not been married than where had been married (Bradshaw and Millar, 1991, p. 12). It tends to diminish where either parent remarries (Burgoyne and Clark, 1984).

In sum, trends towards divorce, serial monogamy and unmarried childbearing have led to the regular establishment of one-parent, step-parent and cohabiting family units. Kiernan and Wicks (1990) estimate that by the end of the century 50 per cent of British children will either not experience or not continuously experience conventional family life (defined as a family structure in which a child's parents are married at the time of his/her birth and remain married until the child achieves adulthood). In the USA, Bumpass and Sweet (1989) estimate that about half of all children born between 1970–84 will spend some time in a lone-mother family. While this trend involves the increasing separation of childrearing from marriage and of biological fathers from their children, the mother – child relationship remains intact. In Britain at the present time, 98 per cent of dependent children live with their mother, a proportion that has remained relatively unchanged over time (Kiernan and Wicks, 1990, p. 16).

As with divorce, the social response to these developments is a mixed one. It would appear that as their visibility has increased and as liberation ideologies have become established, alternative family forms have gained social acceptance. Old stereotypes, say Crow and Hardey (1992), have been eroded and stigmatising labels such as 'the unmarried mother', 'deserted wives', 'broken homes' and 'fatherless families' have been replaced by terms such as 'lone-parent families' and 'solo parenthood'. The removal of virtually all differences in the legal status of children born inside and outside marriage and the abandonment of the term 'illegitimate' in legal documents is a further manifestation of the acceptance of childbearing and rearing outside marriage. At the same time, however, negative images of these family forms persist in conservative moral and political ideologies while the social science literature contains an overwhelming emphasis on their vulnerability to poverty, emotional stress and breakdown.

Men's role in family life is a critical element in these ambivalences. On the one hand, there is the concern of the political Right over the dependence of fatherless families on public funds, the concern of the Left over their poverty and of women over the feminisation of poverty, the concern of men over women's apparent potential for parenting without them, and a more general concern (fuelled by rising anxieties over crime among young people) over children who are without a father figure or who experience a succession of father figures. On the other hand, emphases on the importance of fathers is seen by some feminist writers as denying legitimacy and autonomy to women who want to make a complete break with their former partner or to have and rear children without paternal involvement (Itzin, 1980; Segal, 1990, pp. 49–57).

These concerns have had as an outcome two major new policy initiatives. First, in Britain, Europe, the USA and elsewhere, a variety of measures to enlarge and enforce the support obligations of 'absent' fathers have been introduced. Second, the rights of divorced 'absent' parents have been strengthened. In the USA and in many European countries, the use of joint custody orders and split orders have become a popular device for reaffirming the bond between a child and the 'absent' parent. In Britain, the Children Act 1989 has replaced custody and access orders with residence and contact orders and asserted the principle that parental responsibility continues to rest with both parents after divorce. Yet more radically, the Scottish Law Commission has proposed that parental rights should be automatically vested in unmarried fathers – whereas at present they must be acquired by a parental responsibility agreement with the mother or by means of a court order (*The Independent*, 5 January 1993). Measures such as these represent attempts to affirm parent – child relationships in the context of the breakdown of sexual partnerships. They have also evoked considerable controversy. Thus, in Britain, measures to enlarge and enforce parental support obligations (introduced under the Child Support Act, 1991) have won some support from lone-parent pressure groups but are opposed by the Left because the deduction of maintenance from income support means that lone-parent family poverty is not alleviated; by many lone mothers because it keeps alive links with former partners which they may wish to sever; by feminists because women are not compensated for the costs they bear as a consequence of inequalities in marriage and childrearing; and by men on the grounds that the way in which their obligations are calculated sweeps aside clean break settlements, jeopardises the financial viability of their second families, and takes no account of 'blame', of their possible entrapment into fatherhood and of their limited access rights (Millar, 1992; Toynbee, 1994).

(iv)   The challenge to the sexual division of labour

Women's challenge to the sexual division of family labour, responsibility and authority represents the fourth significant area of change in family life.

A major stream of feminist theorising seeks to show that the identification of women with domestic labour and motherhood does not, as traditional family ideologies maintain, arise almost naturally out of the conditions of human reproduction, but is the product of specific cultural, political and economic arrangements. Further, feminism asserts that the domination of women's lives by the housewife-mothering role makes women economically dependent on men and gives men power and authority over their lives – in the private world of the family as well as in the public world. The reordering of the conventional division of familial labour is therefore seen by many feminists as essential to the liberation of women.

This feminist discourse represents an attempt to rework the way in which women's and men's place within the social world has been constructed. Its impact at the ideological level has been considerable (Segal, 1987b). However, the extent to which the status and roles of women and men have in fact changed is contested. This debate may be illustrated by focussing on two issues: women's participation in the labour force and men's involvement in domestic labour and childrearing.

In many Western societies, the proportion of married women who are in the labour force has increased markedly. In Britain, for example, 70 per cent of married women were economically active in 1992 compared with just under 50 per cent in 1971 (*Social Trends*, 1991, p. 66; *Social Trends*, 1993, pp. 52–3). Dual-earner families are thus commonplace. More significantly, researchers have found that although, as in the past, most mothers withdraw from waged work following the birth of a child, each successive post-war generation of mothers has returned to waged work more quickly than the preceding generation had done (Martin and Roberts, 1984; McRae, 1991, pp. 195–9). Women are thus increasingly combining waged work with motherhood, even when their children are very young, and are spending an increasing proportion of their lives in the labour force.

The involvement of women in paid employment has been interpreted as bringing women economic independence, enhanced status and equality with men (see for example, Blood and Wolfe, 1960; Young and Willmott, 1973; Blumstein and Schwartz, 1983). However, feminist analysis suggests that women's labour force participation is in fact severely limited by their familial roles. Studies such as those carried out by Beechey and Perkins (1987), Yeandle (1984) and Martin and Roberts (1984) show that, on the one hand, women believe that they should assume only those occupational commitments that mesh with their family responsibilities and search for work accordingly and, on the other hand, employers and male employees have clear ideas of what is appropriate work for women and structure their employment opportunities accordingly. Thus, in Britain, only 4 per cent of mothers adopt the 'male pattern' of continuous participation in the labour market (Martin and Roberts, 1984). Further, though the proportion who work full-time is increasing, most economically active women with dependent children are in part-time employment (Table 1.7). In addition, feminist analysis emphasises that the labour market is segregated horizontally and vertically by sex: horizontally in that women are concentrated in typically women's occupations – occupations such as teaching, office work, nursing, catering and cleaning which are in some sense an extension of their familial roles – and vertically in that women are concentrated at the lower levels of occupational hierarchies (Hakim, 1979; Arber and Gilbert, 1992; Kiernan, 1992a; Lonsdale, 1992).

In sum, the evidence seems to suggest that in entering the labour force, the majority of women with children have entered a specifically female labour market of part-time, low-status jobs. Consequently, though gender differentials in earnings have narrowed over the last twenty years, women's earnings are in general less than men's (Figure 1.2). Furthermore, though opinion surveys document some growth in attitudes favourable to women working outside the home, they also show that approval tends to diminish when respondents are asked to take family commitments into account (Witherspoon, 1988; Kiernan, 1992a, 1992b; Scott *et al.*, 1993). Importantly, full-time paid work by mothers of dependent children commands little support (Table 1.8).

In the 1950s and 1960s sociological studies of family life in the United States and in Britain highlighted men's growing involve-

Table 1.7   *Women aged 16–59 in employment by age of youngest child, Great Britain, 1973–92*

Age of youngest dependent child and economic activity	1973	1992
	%	%
Youngest child aged 0–4		
Working full-time	7	11
Working part-time	18	31
All working	25	43
Unemployed	2	7
Youngest child aged 5–9		
Working full-time	18	20
Working part-time	42	44
All working	61	64
Unemployed	2	8
Youngest child aged 10 or over		
Working full-time	30	31
Working part-time	37	45
All working	67	76
Unemployed	1	4
All with dependent children		
Working full-time	17	20
Working part-time	30	39
All working	47	59
Unemployed	2	6
No dependent children		
Working full-time	52	47
Working part-time	17	24
All working	69	72
Unemployed	2	6
Total		
Working full-time	34	35
Working part-time	23	30
All working	58	66
Unemployed	2	6

SOURCE   *General Household Survey*, 1992, Table 7.8.

Table 1.8 *Attitudes towards women with dependent children working*

| | Britain | | USA | | West Germany | |
	Men	Women	Men	Women	Men	Women
	%	%	%	%	%	%
Should a woman work when her children are under school age?						
No, stay at home	67	61	54	44	70	68
Yes, work part-time	23	29	25	34	18	22
Yes, work full-time	2	3	9	10	2	2
after the youngest child starts school						
No, stay at home	13	10	14	9	45	43
Yes, work part-time	65	70	45	45	40	43
Yes, work full-time	12	14	27	33	4	4

SOURCE Scott *et al.*, 1993.

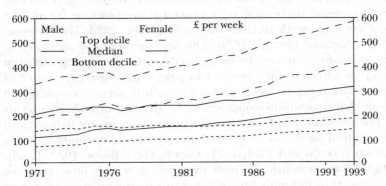

[1] Adjusted to April 1993 prices by using the retail prices index.

SOURCE *Social Trends*, 1994, Figure 5.5.

FIGURE 1.2 *Real weekly earnings by sex, Great Britain, 1971–93*[1]

ment in domestic labour and childrearing and pointed to a new psychological closeness and egalitarianism in marital relationships (see, for example, Bott, 1957; Young and Willmott, 1957, 1973; Blood and Wolfe, 1960). More recently, the media have identified emergence of 'the new man', the caring male who turned his back on the traditional images and pursuits of 'macho man'. Moreover, in all Western societies opinion surveys report the emergence, particularly among the young, the educated, the unmarried, women in full-time work and men whose partners are in full-time work, of attitudes favourable to task sharing in at least some areas of domestic life (Airey, 1984; Witherspoon, 1988; Kiernan, 1992a).

In contrast, the feminist and feminist-influenced research of the 1970s and 1980s emphasises the elusiveness of the 'new man'. In Britain, the USA and elsewhere, feminist studies have shown that men's participation in childrearing and domestic tasks tends to be low and highly selective, that it may increase where wives are in full-time employment (though not where they are in part-time employment), but that even in these circumstances women have primary responsibility for the children and the home and men 'help out' (Oakley, 1974; Martin and Roberts, 1984; Hochschild, 1990). These data are complemented by public opinion surveys which show that, while attitudes are broadly favourable to shared domestic labour and childrearing, behaviour is, in general, traditional: most women are responsible for most of the everyday work of the household (Airey, 1984; Witherspoon 1988; Kiernan 1992a, 1992b). This arrangement appears to be at its most pronounced in households with very young children and/or where women are not in paid work. Further, studies of the relationship between work and family in men's lives show not only that masculinity continues to be defined primarily in terms of breadwinning but that male occupational roles are defined and structured on the assumption that men's primary commitment is to work (Pahl and Pahl, 1971; Edgell, 1980; Elliot, 1982; Finch, 1983). Consequently, the male work role may leave little scope for involvement in family life and presents men who are desirous of greater participation in family life with major dilemmas (Elliot, 1982; Segal, 1990, pp. 30–8). According to Finch and Morgan (1991), the 'men's studies' which began to appear in the latter part of the 1980s and which seek to understand the position of men in modern society from the perspective of men have come to much the same conclusion. Finally, trends towards cohabitation do not seem to be accompanied by any significant reordering of the domestic division of labour. Kiernan and Estaugh (1993, p. 20) find that, although childless cohabiting couples are markedly less traditional in their attitudes and behaviour than childless married couples, cohabiting couples with children have as conventional a division of labour as married couples with children.

The broad picture that emerges from all these data is one of the resilience of traditional patterns. They show that responsibility for breadwinning usually remains with men, while everyday and ultimate responsibility for childrearing and the management of the household usually remains with women. Men's occupational role continues to be seen as their primary commitment, while women's occupational role continues to be seen as secondary to their familial roles. Moreover, it would seem that perceptions of women's breadwinning activities and men's familial involvements are heavily influenced by traditional conceptions of the roles of women and men. Thompson and Walker (1989), in a review of the American literature, find that partners tend to view women's substantial help with economic provision as minimal and men's minimal help with raising children as substantial. Finally, accounts of men's defensive action against change (Faludi, 1991), of the sexual politics of the Right (Eisenstein, 1982; Abbott and Wallace, 1992), of the complex and contradictory meanings which the reordering of gender relations has for women (Neustatter, 1989; Segal 1990, pp. 46–59; Coward, 1992) and of a return to full-time mothering in the USA (Robson-Scott, 1993) are evidence of deep-rooted resistances to, and ambivalences about, radical change in the sexual division of labour.

Nevertheless, it would be an oversimplification to say that nothing has changed. Women are more often and more continuously in the labour force than in the past. Men are more involved parents, and more often than in the past 'help out', particularly with the pleasant side of childrearing and with non-routine, creative domestic tasks (Segal, 1990; Gershuny, 1992). Attitudes have shifted even where behaviour has not. In everyday images of family life and in psychological perspectives on parenting, there is a greater emphasis on the positive value of fatherhood and a new 'open-endedness' to fathering (Segal, 1990, pp. 30–7, 57–9; Finch and Morgan, 1991, p. 66).

How Much Change?

The trends of the past three decades have been interpreted in three important ways: they have been seen as representing the emergence of a neo-conventional family, as constituting the revolutionary transformation of family structures and as embodying both change and continuity, ambivalence and contradiction.

Chester (1985) provides an example of the 'emergence of the neo-conventional family' argument. Chester recognises that change has occurred, but argues that change must be set in the context of major continuities in family life. He makes three points. First, he maintains that unmarried sexual relationships and cohabitation are a temporary and transitional phase in the life course and constitute the postponement, rather than the rejection, of marriage. Second, arguing (a) that the disruption divorce occasions is no greater than that occasioned by high mortality in the nineteenth century and (b) that high rates of marriage and remarriage indicate the continued 'popularity' of marriage as a social institution, he claims that the institutionalisation of divorce matters less than is generally supposed. Third, he argues that women's return to paid work is scarcely a drastic reordering of the conventional nuclear family. Thus, in Chester's view, contemporary trends represent not the abandonment of family life but the rise of the 'neo-conventional family', a different but not greatly changed version of the conventional family.

Explanations of the persistence, relatively unchanged, of 'the family' have been advanced from both pro-family and anti-family stances and on the basis of two broadly opposing arguments. The pro-family stance provides us with contemporary reinterpretations of the traditionalist argument that 'the family' is inextricably bound up with reproduction and socialisation, and attributes its persistence to its unique capacity to meet fundamental and ubiquitous human needs (see, for example, Mount, 1982; Berger and Berger, 1983). In contrast, many Marxist and feminist scholars, writing from a broadly anti-family stance, attribute the persistence of 'the family' to its utility to capitalism and/or patriarchy. From this point of view, alternative family forms remain marginal because capitalist and/or patriarchal processes privilege the conventional conjugal family and seek to reproduce it through, for example, family laws and welfare policies which assume nuclear family responsibility for children (Wilson, 1977; McIntosh, 1978; Smart, 1984). Other relationships, say Barrett and McIntosh (1982), seem pale and unsatisfactory because 'the family' is so massively privileged.

Interpretations of contemporary changes in sexual, parental and gender relationships as constituting the revolutionary transformation of family life have been advanced by traditionalists for whom departures from the conjugal family represent the disintegration of social order, by radicals who view the conjugal family as an oppressive and bankrupt institution and welcome its demise, and by liberals for whom diversity in family forms is a pathway to choice and self-determination. This argument tends to assert that there is now no dominant family form in the Western world, but a growing pluralism. Thus, Laslett (1982, p. xii) argues that '"The British family" is not the phrase to use, but a phrase consciously to abandon for there is now no single British family, but a rich variety of forms ... a plurality'.

Arguments for diversity are frequently based on household composition data which show that nuclear family households composed of a married couple and dependent children constitute only a minority of households. This argument is misconceived. It fails to take account of family life-cycle processes and thus ignores the fact that most 'married couple, no children households' and 'one person households' are in either the pre-childbearing or the post-childbearing stage of the life cycle and either will become or have been 'married couple, dependent children households'. Further, it conflates households (groups of persons bound to a place) with families (groups of persons bound together by sexual and reproductive ties). Information about the former does not by itself enable us to draw conclusions about the latter.

A more convincing argument for significant change is presented by Scanzoni *et al.* (1989, ch. 1). Scanzoni and his colleagues argue that the ideals of exclusivity and permanence which have been fundamental to conventional family life have been replaced by non-binding commitments and the serialisation of relationships. In contradistinction to Chester, they maintain that repetitions of cohabitation, marriage and divorce have radically altered our life experiences in that we now live out our lives in a number of different family types and have widely varying life histories. Further, they are critical of arguments that maintain that there is continued support for ideals of sexual exclusivity and permanence in marriage. They maintain that ideals of exclusivity are meaningless in the context of widespread departure therefrom. They further argue that, although permanence in marriage may be a professed ideal, most people lean towards the notion that a relationship should be continued only as long as it serves the individual's interests. In practice, they say, the ideal of permanence for its own sake is not now an institutionalised feature of marriage. Instead, divorce has become an intrinsic part of the family system, one option in an increasingly varied sexual career. Finally, Scanzoni and his colleagues maintain that to argue that the fact that most couples have children demonstrates the persistence of the conventional family obscures the reality that marriage and childrearing are increasingly disconnected. In short, Scanzoni and his colleagues maintain that contemporary sexual and parental relations are based on principles that are radically different from those of the past. They propose that the very term 'family' should be abandoned and replaced by the concept of 'close' or 'primary relations'.

The first of these interpretations of contemporary trends suggests that present-day sexual and parental patterns represent variations on a traditional theme, the second that different themes are being played. The first emphasises structural continuities and similarities, the second change and diversity. We are thus presented with sharply opposing interpretations of change. However, there are a number of considerations which suggest that the first interpretation understates change while the second overstates change and that both obscure the dualism, ambiguities and ambivalences which permeate contemporary sexual, parental and gender relationships. First, both interpretations seem to assume the homogeneity of past patterns. Yet, as indicated earlier (p. 5), moral consensus is rare. Second, neither model delimits with any care the time period with which the present is being compared. Third, some continuities or changes in family life may reasonably be assumed to be more important than others but no clear criteria have been established for assessing their relative importance.

Fourth, neither of these interpretations of contemporary trends valorise the deep-seated ambivalences, ambiguities and contradictions with which they appear to be permeated.

These considerations lead us to a third model of family change in which dualism – the co-existence of 'traditional' and 'liberated' values and patterns of behaviour – is emphasised and ambiguity, ambivalence and contradiction highlighted. This model is implicit in the commentary of Jeffrey Weeks and Lynne Segal.

Weeks (1986, ch. 5, 1989b, chs 13–15) maintains that it is vital to recognise both trends and counter trends. On the one hand, he argues, 'the permissive moment' represented a historic shift in the regulation of sexuality and family life away from public determination and towards individual determination and from absolutism to the legal acceptance of moral pluralism. Further, he claims that diversity in family forms is a growing reality. On the other hand, Weeks argues, most people are still born into a conventional family unit, live most of their lives in one and aspire to found one; our culture, he says, remains suffused by familial values and the language of family continues to provide the only vocabulary of lasting relatedness that we have. The result is paradoxical: on the one hand, there are many for whom the traditional family is in decline; on the other hand, those who live in non-conventional relationships find that the ideology of 'the family' so dominates that there is no real alternative legitimation to that of the family itself. Further, Weeks shows that 'the permissive revolution' has produced counter-revolutionary movements which have as their central concern the restoration of absolutist moral values and the stability of 'the family', and as immediate targets the modification of the legislative 'reforms' of the 1960s. Campaigns against abortion, the availability of contraception to young women, pornography and the 'promotion' of the acceptability of homosexuality in sex education are, in part at least, the product of this counter-revolutionary movement. Pluralism, Weeks suggests, is a growing reality but is still far from being accepted.

Segal (1983, 1987b, 1990), writing in particular of women's experiences, highlights both the counter-revolutionary tendencies of the 1980s and the irreversibility of change in women's roles. She delineates Thatcherism's emphasis on women's role in the family and its fit with conservative economic policies, the retreat of feminist and other scholars from their radical views, the growth of vigorous pro-family movements in the USA, the pervasiveness of conventional models of 'the family', and the limited scope of change in women's situation. At the same time, Segal emphasises the extent of change in sexual mores, fertility behaviour and marriage patterns, the irreversibility of women's assumption of paid employment, the development of a new, if variable and limited, open-endedness in men's commitment to fatherhood and the impact of feminism at an ideological level. Like Weeks', Segal's analysis suggests that change is never smooth, uniform nor free from contradiction. The very fact of diversity, Segal (1990, p. 35) says, makes it difficult to assess change and continuity in family life.

These accounts of the coexistence of 'traditional' and 'liberated' tendencies 'fit' with the evidence presented in the preceding section of ambivalence and ambiguity in everyday attitudes. As that discussion indicated, pre-marital sex is generally accepted, but extra-marital sex is not, though it is common. Cohabitation before marriage is accepted but cohabitation as a lifelong alternative to marriage is not. Gay and lesbian relationships are more visible but, although legal sanctions against them have been ameliorated, they are not generally accepted. Childbearing outside marriage is increasing but it continues to be believed that childbearing should take place within marriage (Scott *et al.*, 1993). The proportions marrying are expected to fall, yet marriage and parenthood seem to be valued (Dormor, 1992, Table 7; Scott *et al.*, 1993) and remain the focus of women's lives (Martin and Roberts, 1984). Serial monogamy is widespread, yet permanence is seen as desirable. Solo parenthood is commonplace and is defended (Itzin, 1980), but it is not generally believed that a lone parent can bring up her (or his) child as well as a married couple (Scott *et al.*, 1993) and on both the political Right and Left the increase in solo parenthood is seen as a drain on public resources, as leading to the marginalisation of men and as a threat to social order. Women's participation in the labour force is increasing, their right to compete on equal terms with men is vigorously asserted and formally recognised in various legislative measures, and the importance of paid work to women is acknowledged. Yet it is believed, though more often by men than women, that women's employment conflicts with the interests of their families (Witherspoon,

1988; Scott *et al.*, 1993). Broadly speaking, values support the sharing of domestic tasks but tasks are not shared. Persistence and change, ambiguity and contradiction thus seem to be central to contemporary sexual, parental and gender structures.

It is against this background that the concerns of the late 1980s and the 1990s – over ethnic differentiation, unemployment, the ageing of populations, violence and sexual abuse and AIDS – must be viewed.

2
Ethnic Differentiation, Gender and Family Life

Over the past forty years, ethnic divisions have assumed heightened salience in national and international politics – as conflicts surrounding migration movements in Britain, Europe and the USA, the break up of the Soviet Union and Yugoslavia, and the growth in Britain, the USA and South Africa of 'black' challenges to the hegemony of 'white' peoples demonstrate. These divisions involve cultural differences and allegiances, are in general associated with marked inequalities of power and wealth and tend to be at their sharpest wherever they coincide with racial and/or religious distinctions. At their centre lie differences in gender and family structures. Gender and family patterns may reflect long-standing cultural traditions, are frequently governed by deeply held religious beliefs and are integral to a people's identity. However, they are inevitably challenged, and become the source of intense anxieties, wherever ethnic groups share a common territory and must negotiate a shared way of life.

This chapter examines the anxieties and conflicts surrounding the ethnic diversification of contemporary British society. Section 2.1 focusses on Afro-Caribbean and Asian communities, and examines the way in which their 'traditional' gender and family structures are persisting or changing. Section 2.2 examines the discourses which have arisen out of, and inform, ethnic divisions and conflicts and the images of gender and family which appear in these discourses.

2.1 THE EVOLUTION OF AFRO-CARIBBEAN AND ASIAN GENDER AND FAMILY STRUCTURES IN BRITAIN

Between the 1950s and 1970s, various New Commonwealth as well as Old Commonwealth and European peoples migrated to, and

40

settled in, Britain. As a result, non-European communities have become a significant element in British society. This is not a new phenomenon (Fryer, 1984). However, the migrant groups of the past were relatively small, were largely restricted to London and to seaport towns and tended either to merge with the indigenous population or to remain hidden in their own communities. In contrast, the migration of the 1950s–1970s was *relatively* large and highly visible. At the present time, non-European peoples constitute 5.5 per cent of the non-European population of Great Britain (OPCS, 1993). People of Asian origin constitute just over one half, and people of Afro-Caribbean and African origin about 30 per cent, of the non-European population. Further, the non-European population is a young population, and is likely to grow substantially. Ballard and Kalra (1994) estimate that it may stabilise at around 9 per cent of the total population.

Early discussions of the ethnic diversification of British society were informed by what has become known as the 'host – immigrant' model of ethnic relations. This theoretical model assumed that the host society is culturally homogeneous, depicted ethnic minority groups as immigrants, strangers and bearers of alien cultural traditions and envisaged the disruption of the cultural consensus of the 'host' society. Differences in gender and family values were seen as critical elements in this cultural dissonance, the source of problems for both minority and majority groups. However, the host – immigrant thesis assumed that ethnic minorities would gradually adopt the values and customs of the 'host' society and shed their distinctive cultural identities. Consensus and equilibrium would thus ultimately be restored.

This thesis, most sociologists now maintain, did not take sufficient account either of the enduring significance of ethnic bonds or of the pervasiveness of discrimination by the 'host' society and, as a result, misinterpreted the direction of change. Recent studies in the USA and Britain suggest that the gender and family structures of minority ethnic groups change as a result of the interplay of majority and minority cultures, but in ways that are consistent with their own traditions. They thus remain distinctively different from the family structures of Anglo-British peoples. Moreover, 'black' writers and political leaders are increasingly contesting the ideological hegemony of 'white' family values, asserting the integrity of 'black' family life and arguing for a social order based on the distinct but equal status of different cultures. The general direction of change would therefore seem to be one of cultural pluralism rather than cultural assimilation.

This section examines in ideal typical terms the evolution of Afro-Caribbean and Asian gender and family structures in Britain. In each case, we begin with a description of the gender and family patterns which were dominant in the Caribbean working class and in rural South Asia (the populations from which most migrants came) in the 1950s and 1960s. We then provide an account of dominant trends in the family life of working class Afro-Caribbean and Asian peoples in Britain. This account is not to be seen as depicting the family life of all Afro-Caribbeans or Asians in Britain. Minority patterns, like majority patterns, are marked by sub-cultural variation and class differentiation. Ideal typical models therefore provide only a generalised model of dominant and differentiating tendencies.

Afro-Caribbean Gender and Family Structures

Accounts of Caribbean family values suggest that marriage is widely perceived as 'the correct and respectable form of mating relationship' (R. T. Smith, 1963). Nevertheless, Caribbean society seems to be characterised by a range of sexual unions and varied sexual careers rather than by conformity with a married nuclear-family ideal. In Afro-Caribbean lower-status groups, says R. T. Smith (1988), maleness is equated with a propensity to 'wander', and marriage tends to take place in mid-life after men have had a chance to play out their 'natural' desires and are ready to renounce 'sporting'. Moreover, Smith maintains that in the middle classes cultural emphases on marriage as an essential prelude to childbearing and intrinsic to an 'orderly life' coexist with a pervasive pattern of male sexual licence. Ambivalence about the possibility of monogamous marriage for men, Smith claims, exists at all levels of Caribbean society.

The range of sexual unions associated with this ethos have been defined, categorised and labelled in different ways. However, there seems to be general agreement that they fall into three broad categories: (i) marriage; (ii) consensual unions – co-residential, non-legal unions which take the form either of 'faithful concubinage' or of short-term 'housekeeper unions'; and (iii) visiting unions – non-residential but established relationships.

The household forms with which these mating patterns are associated have been categorised as: (i) nuclear family households based on marriage; (ii) common-law family households based on unmarried cohabitation and including the children of the couple and/or children of one or both of the partners from earlier relationships; and (iii) women-headed households. In some woman-headed households, a grandmother or other female relative heads the household and takes on many of the mother's child-rearing functions while the mother assumes the provider role. In other households, the mother heads the household and fulfils breadwinning as well as childrearing functions. Finally, the evidence suggests that in non-married unions gender relationships are characterised by the diminution of the father–child relationship, women's breadwinning and active participation in the labour market and the salience of mother–daughter bonds.

In sum, the research literature suggests that the institutional weakness of marriage, the prevalence of woman-headed households, the relative strength of matrilineal kin relations and the diminution of the husband-father role are important and interconnected features of Afro-Caribbean working-class family life. This Afro-Caribbean family pattern, like the African-American woman-headed family with which it has broad similarities, has been explained in three broad ways.

First, it has been seen as 'the legacy of slavery'. This thesis, of which the African-American scholar, E. Franklin Frazier (Frazier, 1939), is the most notable exponent, suggests that enslavement broke up families, destabilised sexual unions, eroded male authority and created woman-headed families. Further, it attributes the persistence of these phenomena in the post-slavery period to the socio-economic deprivation which African peoples in the Americas continue to experience and which, it is argued, leaves Afro-Caribbean/African-American men without the means of fulfilling a husband-provider role. The woman-headed family is thus portrayed as the product of social disorganisation and as a pathological family form that is not only different from the conventional Western conjugal family but is discontinuous with African traditions. In early academic thought, it was frequently cited as a rare instance of deviation from the 'normal' nuclear-family.

Second, in the 'retentionist' thesis of Herskovits (1941) and the culturally variant theories of contemporary African-American 'black' writers (such as Sudarkasa, 1988), the relative strength of matrilineal relationships, the prevalence of woman-headed families and multiple sexual relationships are seen as survivals of the polygamous, extended West African family. This thesis suggests that West African family traditions were not obliterated by enslavement but survived, albeit in an altered form, and shaped responses first to enslavement and then to the socio-economic deprivations of modern times. In 'black' political thought, the primacy of consanguineal relationships and the independence of women are 'strengths' which enable African peoples to survive.

The third explanatory model focusses on contemporary socio-economic conditions, directs our attention to variability in the prevalence of woman-headed families and seeks to demonstrate connections between variability in household patterns, on the one hand, and social, economic, occupational and community structures on the other. Orlando Patterson (1982), for example, points out that, in the Caribbean, visiting unions and unstable common-law unions are the dominant pattern among the urban poor and on the sugar plantations, but married households are the dominant pattern among the established rural peasantry.

Change and continuity in British Afro-Caribbean family patterns

In the 1960s, studies of Afro-Caribbean life in Britain depicted Afro-Caribbeans as adopting conventional Western nuclear family norms. For example, comparisons of marriage data from the 1970 Jamaican census and the 1981 British census showed that marriage was significantly more common, and occurred at a younger age, than had been customary in the Caribbean (Venner, 1985). Further, sociological studies of Afro-Caribbean communities found that many Afro-Caribbeans married within a relatively short time of arrival in Britain (Davison, 1966; Bell, 1969) and that acceptance of cohabitation was being replaced by disapproval of it and the perception of illegitimate children as an embarassment (Foner, 1977). Furthermore, these and other studies found that men were more involved in domestic labour, childrearing and family leisure than in the Caribbean, a finding which was interpreted as indicating a trend to companionate conjugal relationships (S. Patterson, 1965; Foner, 1977, 1986). Finally, much of the early research emphasised that migration broke up kinship groups, leaving women without the traditional support of their kin in childrearing and men without access to the domestic services of their female relatives (S. Patterson, 1965; Foner, 1977; Driver, 1982).

Recent studies suggest that although generation depth has increased the availability of kin, extended family units have not reappeared. For example, Haskey (1989b) shows that households only infrequently contain members of the extended family. More significantly, Griffiths (1983) finds that less than 1 per cent of children are cared for by grandmothers. These data, though slender, seem to point to the virtual disappearance of the 'grand-mother family'. In contrast, trends towards conventional marriage appear to have been short-lived and modest. Labour Force Survey data for 1986–8 show that only 33 per cent of the Afro-Caribbean population is married (Table 2.1). Further, analyses of trends in solo parenting reveal that one in two Afro-Caribbean families with

Table 2.1   *Marital status by ethnic group, Great Britain, 1986–8*

Ethnic group	Single	Married	Separated/ Divorced	Widowed	All
	%	%	%	%	%
West Indian/ Guyanese	58	33	7	2	100
Indian[1]	45	51	2	3	100
Pakistani[1]	55	42	–	1	100
Bangladeshi[1]	58	40	–	1	100
Chinese	49	47	–	3	100
African	54	38	7	2	100
Arab	42	52	4	2	100
Mixed[1]	75	21	3	1	100
Other	47	48	3	2	100
White	38	51	4	8	100
Not stated	49	42	3	6	100
All groups	38	51	4	7	100

[1]   The high proportion of single people in these ethnic groups reflects their age structure: they contain a high proportion of children. The proportion of children in the Afro-Caribbean population is not very different from that of the 'white' population.

SOURCE   *Social Trends*, 1991, Table 1.4.

dependent children is a lone-parent family (Table 2.2). As Tables
2.1 and 2.2 indicate, marriage is markedly less, and divorce and
solo parenthood markedly more, prevalent among Afro-
Caribbeans than among other ethnic groups.

Most writers locate the trends towards and then away from marriage in the changing socio-economic circumstances of Afro-
Caribbean life in Britain. Foner (1977), for example, attributes
the tendency of first-generation Afro-Caribbeans to marry to three
sets of circumstances: access to economic opportunities which
facilitated male breadwinning, the isolation consequent on separation from kin and location in an alien environment, and pressures to conform to British nuclear family norms. Conversely, it

Table 2.2   *One-parent families with dependent children[1] as a proportion of all families, by ethnic group, Great Britain, 1987–9*

	Type of family with dependent children				
Ethnic group of head of family	Lone Mothers	Lone Fathers	All Lone Parents	Married Couples[2]	All
	%	%	%	%	%
West Indian	44	5	49	51	100
African	27	(2)	30	70	100
Indian	6	(1)	6	94	100
Pakistani	6	(2)	8	92	100
Bangladeshi	(5)	(3)	(8)	92	100
Chinese	(1)	(0)	(2)	98	100
Arab	(4)	(1)	(5)	95	100
Mixed	33	(3)	36	64	100
Other	(16)	(0)	(16)	84	100
All Ethnic Minority Groups	16	2	18	82	100
'White'	13	2	15	85	100
Not stated	19	(3)	22	78	100
All Groups	13	2	15	85	100

[1]   Children under 16 or aged 16–18 and in full-time education.
[2]   Includes cohabiting couples.
Bracketed estimates are based on sample sizes of 30 or under.
SOURCE   Haskey, 1991, Table 4,

has been argued that the economic changes of the 1980s resulted in the vulnerability of young 'black' men to unemployment and may have given rise to post-migration forms of male marginality (Driver, 1982) and that racism has fostered 'black pride' movements and the deliberate rejection of British cultural patterns (Cashmore, 1979). In any case, the emergence in Britain of 'liberated' sexual ideologies has eroded pressures to conformity with a married-nuclear-family ideal.

The reassertion of 'traditional' patterns of sexual unions seems to have been paralleled by the persistence of male marginality in family life. Foner (1986) maintains that men, although more involved in family life than in the Caribbean, resent doing 'women's work', devote much of their time and money to leisure activities outside the home, may have a tenuous relationship with their children and tend to be viewed with a deep-rooted distrust by women as having a propensity to 'wander'. Foner emphasises that men are not entirely absent from family life: bonds with sons and other male relatives are often strong and couples may be bound together by affection and a shared struggle for advancement. Nevertheless, she finds that in Britain, as in the Caribbean, the household is primarily women's domain and the mother – child relationship is the cornerstone of family life.

Furthermore, it seems that, as in the Caribbean, motherhood routinely includes financial provision for the family. Official statistics show that Afro-Caribbean women are more likely to be economically active than women of other ethnic groups (Table 2.3) and more often have an occupational status that is higher than that of their partner (Mirza, 1992). Further, a substantial body of evidence suggests that their orientation to work is distinctive. Afro-Caribbean girls, Mirza (1992) finds, are more likely to aspire to high status occupations, are more certain of their occupational aspirations and are more confident that their aspirations will be realised than Afro-Caribbean boys, 'white' British boys and 'white' British girls. They are also more likely to choose non-gendered occupations (Mirza, 1992), to be employment-oriented rather than marriage-oriented (Dex, 1983) and to be strongly committed to economic independence (Stone, 1983; Mirza, 1992). Stone (1983) reports that, whereas Asian and 'white' British women see waged work as an essential contribution to the household economy, the majority of Afro-Caribbean women value waged work for the financial independence it provides

Table 2.3   *Labour force participation rates of women, aged 16–59 by ethnic group, Great Britain, 1988–90*

	%
Afro-Caribbean	76
African Asian	69
Indian	57
Pakistani[1]	23
Bangladeshi[1]	23
Chinese	55
African	61
Other/mixed	61
All ethnic minority	57
'White'	71
All women	71

[1]   Participation in the informal economy is usually invisible in official statistics. These data therefore tend to understate the overall economic activity of women – and in particular that of Pakistani and Bangladeshi women who frequently work as outworkers or in family businesses.
SOURCE   Jones, 1993, Table 4.1.

and are likely to control their own earnings – whereas 'white' British couples tend to pool their resources, and in Asian households income is controlled and managed by husbands or parents-in-law. In addition, Stone finds that Afro-Caribbean women less often than Asian or 'white' British women believe that the biological mother is always the best person to care for a pre-school child. Stone suggests that the Caribbean tradition of shared childcare makes the decision to work less guilt-ridden for Afro-Caribbean mothers than for 'white' British mothers.

Asian Gender and Family Structures

Asian migrants to Britain came from India, Pakistan, Bangladesh and East Africa, spoke different languages, belonged to different religions and varied in their ways of life, including their family and gender structures. However, their family and gender structures appear to have been characterised by certain underlying similarities.

Roger Ballard (1982) maintains that in the 1950s and early 1960s the ideal-typical rural South Asian family was characterised by patri-lineality (that is, the tracing of descent, inheritance and succession through the father's line), the formation of three-generation patri-local households (consisting of a man, his sons and grandsons, their wives and unmarried daughters), and the hierarchic organisation of relationships between the sexes, the generations and older and younger members of the same generation. Further, Ballard shows that family life was governed by ideals of corporate loyalty which assert the priority of family obligations over personal self-interest. He maintains that the three-generation family unit is bound to-gether by this value system and constitutes the core of Asian family structures. Further, Ballard claims that families who are related through males constitute locality-based descent groups (variously referred to as *biraderi, bhaichara,* or *khandan*) and are bound togeth-er by ideas of brotherhood and family loyalty. Furthermore, he sug-gests that marriage is a contract between two families rather than a union of two individuals, is arranged by families and is concerned with the maintenance and advancement of family honour. Primary emotional bonds are therefore with parents, siblings and children rather than between marital partners (Shaw, 1988).

Ballard's analysis suggests that in the village societies of rural South Asia, the individual is at the centre of a complex network of rights and duties which extend outwards from the immediate family to kin and fellow villagers and are determined by gender, stage in the family life cycle and birth order. Ballard emphasises that there is variation around these basic principles, that family loyalty is tempered by conflict, competition and self-interest and that extra-familial kinship obligations are less comprehensive than intra-familial obligations. Further, his observations cannot be gen-eralised to urban life where gender and family structures articulate with a different set of material and social realities and may be subject to Westernising influences. Nevertheless, Ballard shows that the prototypical rural Asian family is constructed around an ideolo-gy of patrilineal cooperation. This 'traditional Asian family' is fre-quently cited as epitomising the classical extended family believed to be characteristic of subsistence societies. It stands in sharp con-trast with the conventional Western conjugal family and in even sharper contrast with 'liberated' Western sexual and family values.

Most early accounts of the reworking of Asian family life in Britain emphasised change and disruption. They pointed to dislocations occasioned by the migration process, emphasised the readjustments demanded by life in an urban-industrial environment and anticipated the gradual adoption of British values. In the late 1970s and early 1980s, images of change and dislocation gave way to images of continuity, to the identification of various elements in Asian life – such as the collectivism of "the Asian family', the strength of religious tradition and the integrity of Asian cultures – as having a particular capacity to perpetuate traditional ways, and to an emphasis on the role of racism in renewing pride in Asian-ness. By the late 1980s and early 1990s, researchers were again emphasising change, but now tended to see change as involving, on the one hand, positive adaptations to the economic, political and ideological conditions of life in Britain and, on the other, as underpinned by Asian cultural values and thus as continuous with Asian traditions. These different emphases – which are to be found in media as well as social science accounts of Asian family life – seem to be not so much competing interpretations of change in Asian family life as accounts of different phases in the evolution of British Asian-ness and of contradictory tendencies to change and continuity. These issues are examined by focussing on (i) kinship (ii) gender and (iii) intergenerational relations.

(i)   Change and continuity in British Asian kinship patterns

All the evidence suggests that the traditional reciprocities of Asian kinship structures were severely disrupted by migration to Britain and the exigencies of urban-industrial life. The ethnographic literature shows that migration, together with immigration controls, separated family members from each other, that location in a wage-based urban economy made sons economically independent of fathers and deprived older people of an economic role, and that the small size of British houses inhibited the formation of three-generation households (C. Ballard, 1979; Saifullah Kahn, 1979; R. Ballard, 1982; Shaw, 1988). This literature also suggests that the dislocation of kinship bonds had specific and contradictory consequences for women. It brought women independence of their mothers-in-law, control over their households and the socialisation of their children and closer emotional relationships with their husbands, but it also left them without the support of other women in the household, without access to the sanctions which male kinsmen had traditionally exercised over recalcitrant husbands and without the option of returning to their natal home on marital breakdown. The research literature paints a vivid picture of an abrupt transition from a village life in which women were supported by other women to a life in which they were imprisoned in their homes, saddled with lone responsibility for their households, fearful of racist attacks and prone to loneliness, anxiety and depression.

Nevertheless, the salience of kinship bonds in Asian culture represented an important resource in the reworking of Asian life in Britain. The ethnographic literature shows that patterns of chain migration (in which brothers join brothers, sons their fathers and villagers their wider kin group) re-created communities based on the proximity of kin. Further, though social mobility has sometimes resulted in the residential dispersal of kin (Blakemore and Boneham, 1993, p. 80) and though preferences for nuclear-family households are emerging (Stopes-Roe and Cochrane, 1990a), Asian households remain larger and are more likely to contain extended family members than either 'white' British or British Afro-Caribbean households (Haskey, 1989b; Ballard and Kalra, 1994). In addition, the research literature suggests that kinship ties remain an important source of mutual aid. Ethnographic and other studies show that kin ties may be mobilised in the search for employment and accommodation, that financial resources may be pooled as a means of facilitating home-ownership and the acquisition of consumer durables, that kin in positions of authority may be enlisted in dealings with state bureaucracies – for example, in handling social security claims, sorting out court cases and negotiating rights of entry to Britain for relatives – and that entrepreneurial activity tends to be facilitated by using kin ties as a source of capital and of cheap labour (Rex and Moore, 1967; R. Ballard, 1982; Shaw, 1988, pp. 33–5, 81, 138–9). Finally, the work of Catherine Ballard (1979), Roger Ballard (1982) and Shaw (1988) suggests that the kin group re-emerged as a culturally and psychologically important unit. These writers argue that the kin group provides a cultural environment in which Asian people feel at home, is important as a source of personal identity and plays a critical role in the reproduction of Asian cultural values by socialising children into Asian norms and sanctioning Westernising kinsmen and women. Further, they maintain that family unity is at one and the same time an ideal and a defence against Westernisation on the one hand and racism on the other. They find that English family life is perceived to be morally bankrupt, and that racism has produced a reactive pride in Asian culture, but they also find that the concept of being part of a large kinship group with its concomittant loyalties and obligations is valued in itself and is a powerful force in the construction of Asian community life.

However, the accounts of gender and intergenerational relationships to which we now turn suggest that kinship bonds and loyalties are being reforged in ways that are significantly different from the past.

(ii)   Change and continuity in Asian gender relationships

Studies of gender divisions in rural Pakistan, Bangladesh and India show that women play key roles in the subsistence activities of the household. Moreover, Parmar (1982) argues that, contrary to popular belief, significant proportions of South Asian women are in paid (usually agrarian) employment. Nevertheless, most researchers maintain that in rural Asia women's economic activity is for the most part centred on the home, family farm or business. As such it is unpaid and tends to be regarded as an extension of their domestic roles (Shaw, 1988). In Britain, in contrast, most Asian women are in paid work.

Some commentators have suggested that the labour force activity of Asian women poses the possibility of a fundamental reworking of traditional gender hierarchies. Access to a regular wage, it has been argued, enables Asian women to be resource procurers as well as resource managers, makes possible the achievement of an independent economic identity and enhances women's status (Dhanjal, 1976; Banton, 1979; R. Ballard, 1982). However, change seems to vary between East African Asian, Indian, Pakistani and Bangladeshi communities in ways that reflect specific cultural interpretations of gender.

In the first place, Labour Force Surveys reveal that participation in paid employment outside the home differs sharply between East African Asian women and Indian women on the one hand and Pakistani and Bangladeshi women on the other (Table 2.3). This pattern of economic activity, says Stone (1983), demonstrates the impact of cultural norms on women's lives. She argues that Pakistani and Bangladeshi families confront the same kind of economic pressures which propel Indian and Afro-Caribbean women, as well as 'white' working class women, into the labour market but that the labour force activity of Pakistani and Bangladeshi women is limited by Islamic norms which prescribe women's seclusion from unrelated men. Economic necessity, she argues, is overridden by cultural norms.

In the second place, studies of the experiences of Sikh and Pakistani women suggest that the reworking of conjugal relationships is mediated by cultural differences in Asian interpretations of femininity and masculinity. Parminder Bhachu's studies of Sikh communities in London and the Midlands suggest that in the Sikh community paid employment is leading to the renegotiation of authority patterns within the kin group and between husband and wife. In contrast, Alison Shaw's and Haleh Afshar's studies of Pakistani communities in Oxford and West Yorkshire, respectively, point to the Pakistani woman's continuing acceptance of home-based segregated work and commitment to motherhood and family life.

Bhachu (1985, 1988) finds that in Sikh communities women's earnings have facilitated home-ownership and the establishment of separate nuclear-family households. As a result the household has become couple-focussed rather than kin-focussed, women have come to manage household expenditure and the gift exchange system before reaching seniority and the authority of elders, which had accrued from their command over productive resources, has been dented. Further, Bhachu finds that paid employment makes it possible for women to be more assertive about their own areas of operation and personal rights, reduces the dominance of their husbands as key decision-makers and controllers of economic resources and increases men's involvement in domestic tasks and childcare.

Bhachu emphasises that shifts in the construction of Sikh masculinity and femininity are not radical. Nevertheless, she maintains that women, in becoming resource procurers as well as resource managers, are negotiating a power base from which they may exercise greater control over cultural patterns. Bhachu argues that the 'empowerment' of Sikh women is aided by Sikh religious traditions which, she maintains, emphasise equality for all and give Sikh women a measure of independence not available to other Asian women. She points out that Sikh women, unlike Muslim women, are not in purdah and differ from Gujarati women in that their group ethos is less strong. The empowerment of Sikh women, Bhachu seems to suggest, is the product of the articulation of economic opportunity with a relatively 'liberal' cultural tradition.

The empowerment of Sikh women described by Bhachu contrasts with the particularly disadvantaged position of Pakistani and Bangladeshi women as revealed by Shaw (1988) and Afshar (1989). These researchers show that Pakistani women, though absent from the formal economy, work in family businesses or as outworkers for local shops and factories. However, they are subject to what Afshar terms 'the moral economy of kin'. Afshar finds that outworkers work long hours for a pittance, that they risk their health and that their earnings are subject to male control. Further, these and other studies suggest that employment in family businesses reproduces the dependence of domestic labour and operates in terms of male-defined goals. Second-generation women may break with tradition and obtain professional qualifications and/or take full-time employment outside the Pakistani community. However, both Afshar and Shaw report that breaches of tradition are the source of family conflict, may be dependent on acquiescence in an arranged marriage and usually involve the subordination of career aspirations to commitments to the extended kin group as well as to children and husbands.

These and other studies show that the ethnic economy is a gendered economy in which women's labour is the mainstay of cheap labour costs and male entrepreneurial success. At the same time, they emphasise that Pakistani women see it as natural that they should contribute their labour and their income to the family and take it for granted that the individual should be subordinate to the family unit as a whole. They thus suggest that 'the moral economy of kin' has proved remarkably firm over the generations.

It must not, however, be assumed that Pakistani women are passive victims of male domination. Both Shaw and Afshar emphasise that women actively accept their family obligations and are committed to motherhood. Further, Werbner's (1988) account of a Manchester Pakistani community shows that Pakistani women can manipulate their social environment to their advantage and may influence the social world of men. Werbner finds that neighbourhood networks are sustained by women and that husbands are incorporated into these networks on the basis of statuses built up by their wives. Neighbourhood networks, says Werbner, can be described as women-centred without denying the patriarchal status of men as the 'guardians' of women and the representatives of the family in the public world. In addition, Werbner shows that, although Pakistani women are in general confined to the domestic domain, male control over women's movements has lessened over time, women are assertive and influential in family decision-making, domestic activities are not entirely sex-segregated and purdah has been radically modified among second-generation women.

(iii)   The reworking of parent–child relationships

The notion that young Asians are caught between the opposing values of Asian and Anglo-Saxon cultures – in particular between the Asian emphasis on cooperation and familial loyalty and the Anglo-Saxon emphasis on individual self-determination – is a recurrent theme in everyday thought. Media reportage, political rhetoric and the professional ideologies of social workers and others, says Catherine Ballard (1979), emphasise differences between Asian and Anglo-Saxon cultures and present young Asians as actively challenging the authoritarian repressiveness of their parents. Everyday thought thus sets young Asians apart as a 'problem' category, locates their problems in cultural conflicts and treats cultures as static. In contrast, the ethnographic literature emphasises the malleability of cultural forms. Broadly speaking, this literature presents young Asians not as facing a bleak choice between Anglo-Saxon and Asian values, but as making compromises that enable them to move between parallel cultural worlds and/or to develop a lifestyle that is a synthesis of Anglo-Saxon and Asian values (C. Ballard, 1979; R. Ballard, 1982; Bhachu, 1985; Shaw, 1988). Further, parents may themselves make compromises. Drury (1991), for example, finds that Sikh parents do not necessarily seek to transmit all aspects of Sikh culture to children and Stopes-Roe and Cochrane (1989) say that Asian parents are conscious of the impracticality of attempting to enforce 'the old ways'.

The literature points to four major areas of change in the familial values of young Asians: their more active involvement in family decision-making, a questioning of the value of extra-familial kinship networks, a trend towards closer and more autonomous marriage relationships and increased access to higher education and careers for young women. Thus, the family support networks of young Asians tend to be restricted to the nuclear family, whereas the support networks of the older generation tend to include wider kin (Stopes-Roe and Cochrane, 1990b), their notions of family obligation are less rigorous than their parents' (Stopes-Roe and Cochrane, 1989) and their consumption and leisure patterns are influenced by the mass media and by the youth and class cultures with which they interact in their localities (Bhachu, 1991).

However, although the research evidence shows that young Asians do not wish to remain entirely within the family, it also shows that they have a stronger sense of family obligation than their Anglo-Saxon peers and value the corporateness of Asian family life (Stopes-Roe and Cochrane, 1989, 1990b). Shaw's account of the values of young Pakistani women and men emphasises this (Shaw, 1988, pp. 157–61). Shaw finds that young Pakistani women identify with their culture, take on family responsibilities on leaving school and, where they enter higher education or take employment outside the Pakistani community, continue to fulfil *biraderi* obligations, accept arranged marriages and participate in family, community and religious events. Shaw also finds that young men, whether they have a social status that is similar to, or different from, that of their fathers, spend their leisure with their family and peers within the community, contribute their earnings to the family budget and accept arranged marriages.

Generational continuities and discontinuities are epitomised in the reworking of the arranged marriage. The literature under review shows that marriages continue to be arranged, that caste, status and economic interests continue to play a part in the selection of spouses and that the arranged marriage reinforces kin controls and obliges the individual to make a clear public statement about where his/her loyalties lie. However, it also suggests that young Asians are more fully involved in the arrangement of their marriages (C. Ballard, 1979, p. 125; R. Ballard, 1982, p. 197), that young women are being allowed to defer marriage so as to go into higher education (Shaw, 1988) and that instances of young people having clandestine relationships or rejecting their parents' plans for them and entering into relationships of their own choosing are not uncommon (Shaw, 1988 pp. 167–80; Afshar, 1989; Drury, 1991). Drury (1991) finds that, although nearly all the young Nottingham Sikh women in her sample anticipate an arranged marriage, two-thirds do not support it and nearly one-quarter meet boyfriends clandestinely.

Summary

The data under review suggest that the gender and family structures of ethnic minority groups are subject to change and continuity.

They show that in Afro-Caribbean communities, extended family relationships are weaker than they were in the Caribbean, that the grandmother family is virtually non-existent and that there may be tendencies towards higher rates of marriage and more symmetrical conjugal role relationships. Nevertheless, Afro-Caribbean family patterns remain distinctive in terms of the institutional weakness of marriage, the prevalence of woman-headed families, the marginality of men and the orientation of women to economic independence. This seems to be so even though, as we saw in Chapter 1, Anglo-Saxon gender and family structures are moving in these directions.

In Asian communities, extra-nuclear family loyalties are less extensive, women are more often in the labour force, the arranged marriage is becoming more flexible and married relationships are in general closer than was customary in rural South Asia in the 1950s and 1960s. However, the evidence suggests that Asian ideals of family loyalty and obligation, of the primacy of mothering in women's lives and of male authority are being reproduced. The low rates of unmarried cohabitation, divorce and solo parenthood among Asian peoples (illustrated in Tables 2.1 and 2.2), together with their low rate of inter-marriage with people of other ethnicities (Jones, 1993, Table 2.8), are evidence of the continuing integrity of Asian family values.

In sum, it appears that the gender and family structures of Afro-Caribbean and Asian groups have changed in the context of the cultural, economic and political opportunities and constraints of life in Britain but in ways that are shaped by their own cultural logic. They remain distinctively different from Anglo-Saxon gender and family structures. The gender and family structures of other ethnic minority groups (including European minority groups) can also be expected to display their own cultural specificities. Afro-Caribbean and Asian patterns are thus indicative of the ethnic diversification of British society in the latter part of the twentieth century.

2.2   THE DISCOURSES OF 'RACE' AND ETHNICITY

In Britain, as elsewhere, ethnic diversification has given rise to intense anxieties within both majority and minority populations, and to conflicts between them, in which differences in ways of organising gender and family relations play a central part. This section considers these antagonisms by focussing on the ideological and theoretical positions of the major protagonists in ethnic relations debates. We look at (i) racist and nationalist, (ii) 'black' radical and anti-racist, (iii) 'black' feminist, (iv) ethnicity, and (v) Marxist discourses.

Each of these bodies of thought exists at commonsense and academic levels and each has informed political activism, social policy-making and professional practice. Each gives priority to a particular aspect of 'black–white' relations and is distinctive. At the same time, each is constantly being reworked in the light of changing circumstances and counter-argument and, in each case, argument and counter-argument have led to the development of relatively open-ended positions which continue to prioritise a particular aspect of social reality, but which nevertheless recognise that a range of social forces interact to shape ethnic relations. We focus on the prototypical or 'pure' versions of these arguments so as to highlight their distinctive features.

'Racist' and 'Nationalist' Discourses

Most academic analyses of the ethnic differentiation of Western societies presume that relationships between, on the one hand, Anglo-Saxon and European peoples and, on the other hand, peoples of colour are characterised by a deep-rooted and un-wavering racism. Racism, though defined in different ways, is in general seen as the construction of social boundaries on the basis of variations in phenotypical characteristics, such as skin colour, and as including all those ideologies and social processes which stigmatise, marginalise and discriminate against others on the basis of their putatively different racial group membership (Solomos, 1993, p. 9).

The prevalence in nineteenth and early twentieth century thought of the belief that human beings are divided into 'races' (distinctive biological groups) that share naturally given aptitudes, behaviour patterns and levels of achievement and can be ranked in some sort of hierarchy of superiority and inferiority has been amply documented. This biological racism, as it has been called, was in part drawn from, and appeared to be given legitimacy by, Darwinian theories of human evolution. However, modern genetic theory shows that people cannot be divided into distinct genotypical groups (Richardson and Lambert, 1985). Further, sociological analysis suggests, first, that physical differentiation is not necessarily paralleled by cultural difference and, second, that whether or not physical characteristics become the basis for social divisions is highly variable and socially determined (Richardson and Lambert, 1985). In other words, notions of biologically-determined group boundaries and inferiorities have been discredited. Nevertheless, they linger on, notably in the thinking of Far Right groups such as the National Front, and give rise to attempts to marginalise ethnic minority groups, and in particular people of colour.

Further, a number of writers have argued that a new 'cultural racism', which mobilises not around notions of 'race' and biological inferiority but around notions of culture and nationhood, has emerged. This cultural racism has as its dominant theme the threat which peoples of a different ethnicity pose to the cultural, religious and political hegemony of the British peoples. Its prevalence in the commonsense thought of everyday life, as evidenced by recurring images of Afro-Caribbean and Asian peoples as 'immigrants', 'outsiders' and 'the enemy within', has been extensively documented (see Barker, 1981; CCCS, 1982; Solomos, 1993). Further, it appears on the academic and political New Right where its notable exponents include the philosophers, Roger Scruton and John Casey and the former Conservative MP,

Enoch Powell. According to Solomos (1993, ch. 8), the protagonists of the New Right see national identity as defined by the
cohesion and historical 'rootedness' of a people's cultural, religious and political traditions, and as inevitably undermined by an
influx of 'alien' cultures. They therefore advocate, as strategies
for containing the threat to 'the British way of life', rigorous
immigration control, social policies that facilitate assimilation to
'the British way of life' and repatriation.

In the view of most commentators, the construction of gender
and family structures as symbols of national identity and cultural
alienness is a core element in racist discourses. On the one hand,
says Lawrence (1982), the conventional nuclear family is perceived as an important element in Britishness, as the building
block from which the national community is constructed. On the
other hand, the different family structures of ethnic minority
groups are seen as epitomising their alienness and as reproducing
alien ways of life. Lawrence maintains that British culture is permeated by stereotyped images of the Asian family as an extended
family group characterised by hierarchic and authoritarian relationships, arranged marriages, large families and the submissive-
ness and isolation of women. Similarly, he claims that images of
Afro-Caribbean family life as characterised by authoritarian but
ultimately ineffective childrearing practices, woman-headed families and unmarried childbearing are commonplace. Further,
Lawrence maintains that the alien family structures of minority
groups are seen as the source of the manifold problems which
they are believed to experience in adjusting to British society and
to present to British society. Minority family structures, says
Lawrence, are seen as the source of crime, violence and poverty,
and are constantly pathologised.

In sum, it is very generally argued that ethnic minority communities are widely perceived as 'alien wedges' which are destroying
'the British way of life'. In media reportage, political debate and
everyday thought, says Lawrence (1982), ethnic minority groups
appear as communities that are not just different but so foreign
that they cannot readily be assimilated into British society.

This 'cultural racism' is not concerned only with the role and
characteristics of minority communities; it is also an attempt to
reaffirm understandings of Englishness or Britishness (Solomos,
1993, ch. 8). Further, its New Right protagonists deny the charge

of racism, claiming that they assert, not the biological difference and inferiority of Asian and Afro-Caribbean peoples, but their cultural difference. However, anti-racist writers argue that notions of nationhood, like older 'biological racisms', interpret skin colour as signalling cultural differences and alienness, assume the 'naturalness' of a preference for one's own kind, blame 'black' people for a range of social problems and deny ethnic minority groups the right to maintain their own cultural identities (Barker, 1981; Lawrence, 1982; Gilroy, 1992; Solomos, 1993).

This debate raises complex conceptual questions as to what constitutes racism and nationalism and how they interact (see Miles, 1993, ch. 2). These questions cannot be explored here. However, whether they are interpreted as racist, nationalist or both, perceptions of ethnic diversification as transforming and destroying British society signal deep dismay over changes in 'the British way of life'. They rest on assumptions of the homogeneity, distinctiveness and stability over time of British culture. Yet this essentialist view of the British way of life seems to be mistaken. Sociological analysis suggests that cultures are rarely homogeneous and never fixed, final and complete (Gilroy, 1992) and shows that 'the British way of life' embraces long-standing regional and class variations and is constantly being remade. Importantly, the image of 'the British family' found in racist/nationalist discourses harks back to the conjugal family of the mid-twentieth century and bears little resemblance to the patterns of family life which the 'sexual revolution' of the 1960s brought into being (see Chapter 1).

However, images of an unwavering, unambiguous and all pervasive hostility to 'alien' cultures also slide into presenting us with a monolithic image of reactions to the ethnic diversification of British society and are similarly misconceived. They obscure beliefs in the essential equality of all people (Worsley, 1987, p. 360), respect for religious difference (Parekh, 1982), perceptions of the cohesiveness of Asian family life as potentially enabling as well as potentially oppressive, evidence of the incorporation of some aspects of ethnic minority cultures into mainstream youth cultures (Parekh, 1982; Bhachu, 1991) and differences in responses to different ethnic groups. These competing tendencies suggest that responses to the diversification of British society are varied and cannot be reduced to a monolithic racism.

'Black' Radical and Anti-racist Perspectives

'Black' radical and anti-racist discourses challenge the cultural and biological racisms of Western societies. These ideological positions first came to the fore among 'black power' leaders in the USA in the 1960s and have become a major tendency in 'black' and Left-wing political thought in the USA and Britain. They contain a significant ideological shift from the aspirations of older generations of 'people of colour' for integration into 'white' society to aspirations for an independent but equal position within a multi-racial and multi-cultural society (Wilson, 1987).

In these discourses the relationship between Asian and African peoples on the one hand and European peoples on the other is conceptualised as a 'black–white' relationship. That is, over-arching 'pan-black' and 'pan-white' identities which reach beyond particular ethnic differences to embrace all 'people of colour' (including people of 'mixed-race') and all Anglo-Saxon and European peoples, respectively, are constructed. Further, the oppression of 'black' people, as 'black' people, is asserted and located in 'white' political and economic domination and the ideological force of 'racism'. 'Racism' is portrayed as the exclusive property of 'white' people, seen as relatively autonomous and given a long history.

In these discourses, as in 'racist' discourses, 'the family' becomes an important symbol of 'black' identity. Thus, the pathologisation of 'black' family life in the ideology of the state, the welfare professions, the media and elsewhere is critiqued and its deleterious consequences elaborated. Critiques of immigration controls as breaking up Asian families by separating husbands from wives and parents from children (Amos and Parmar, 1984; Sondhi, 1987) and of social workers as breaking up Afro-Caribbean families by over-hastily taking their children into care on the basis of stereotyped images of their childrearing practices (Gibson, 1980; CARF, 1983; Barn, 1990) are illustrative of this tendency. The effect of racism on the labour force position of 'black' men and women, and consequently on the living standards of 'black' families, is also a recurring theme in this literature (Parmar, 1982; Malveaux, 1987, 1988; Bhat *et al.*, 1988).

At the same time, 'black' radical thought tends to assert the strengths of 'the black family' and to define it as a primary source of political and cultural resistance to racism. For example, some African-American writers see woman-headed families and bread-winning by women as evidence of a flexibility in the distribution of family maintenance responsibilities that compensates for the disadvantaged labour force position of African-American men (Billingsley, 1968; Hill, 1971). Similarly, the relative strength of kinship ties among poor African-Americans has been interpreted as an arrangement through which women gain assistance in child-rearing, resources are shared and physical, emotional and economic needs are met (Dodson, 1988).

Debates over transracial fostering and adoption epitomise the importance which anti-racist/radical 'black' discourses attach to 'the black family'. 'Black' radicalism, say Tizard and Phoenix (1989), maintains that 'black' couples are the only appropriate foster or adoptive parents for Afro-Caribbean, Asian and 'mixed-race' children on three grounds, namely (i) that 'black' children living in white families will be unable to develop a positive 'black' identity, (ii) will grow up unable to relate to 'black' people and (iii) will not be equipped with the skills necessary to survival in a 'racist' society. Tizard and Phoenix show that these contentions are not supported by the available evidence. None the less, advocacy of 'same-race' adoption has had such outcomes as the placement of a child who had been fostered since birth by a 'white' and would-be adoptive mother with 'black' adoptive parents (*The Guardian*, 2 February 1990), the placement of a child whose mother was 'white' and father Asian with an Afro-Caribbean family (*New Society*, 30 June 1983) and the proposed placement of a child whose only 'black' parent was a great-grandparent and who looked 'white' with 'black' adoptive parents (*The Daily Telegraph*, 17 March 1990). In these debates, says Gilroy (1992), 'the black family' is idealised as the only authentic repository of 'black culture' and elevated into a guaranteed means of transmitting all the skills that children need to survive in a 'racist' society.

This 'black' radicalism/anti-racism expresses and informs resistance to racism. Whereas 'racist' projects advocate the assimilation of ethnic minority groups to 'the British way of life' and/or their expulsion from British society, 'black' radicalism advocates a multi-racial, multi-cultural society. Whereas 'racist' discourses define 'the black family' as reproducing an alien way of life, 'black' radical and anti-racist discourses define it as an important site of resistance to 'racism'. Notions of 'race' are incorporated into 'black' radical and anti-racist discourses but are transformed into a discourse of resistance. 'Black' peoples, Miles (1989, pp. 72–3) observes, may accept their designation as a separate 'race', but they invert negative evaluations of their capacities [as in the slogan 'black is beautiful'] and use 'blackness' to signify a common experience as an excluded population. 'Black' identity then becomes a strategy for unifying otherwise diverse minorities and the basis of political mobilisations intended to reverse the disadvantaged position of 'black' peoples.

However, in seeking to assert a distinctive 'black' identity and contest the hegemony of 'white' culture, 'black' radicalism tends to drift towards a belief in the fixed nature of ethnic categories that replicates New Right notions of a close relationship between culture, nation and 'race'. Counter-arguments, similar to those which it has itself directed against 'racism', have been levelled against it from anti-anti-racist, marxist and ethnicity perspectives. It has been argued: (i) that the concept of a fundamental 'black–white' division homogenises and polarises 'black' and 'white' peoples and obscures their ethnic diversity (Anthias and Yuval-Davis, 1983) as well as significant differences between ethnic groups in their socio-economic position (Brown, 1984; Jones, 1993; Ballard and Kalra, 1994); (ii) that the emphasis on racism as the determining factor in 'black' life obscures the role of underlying structural conditions – such as capitalism's demand for cheap labour – in shaping the material conditions of 'black' family life and suppresses class divisions within both 'black' and 'white' populations (Wilson, 1987; Miles 1989); (iii) that the construction of 'racism' as the exclusive property of 'white' people and of 'black' people as its exclusive victims obscures the racialisation of 'white' minority groups, such as the Irish and Jews, and the intensity of ethnic conflicts between peoples of colour and so fails to recognise that any ethnic group may be imbued with a fixed essential difference, categorised as a separate 'race' and inferiorised (Anthias, 1992; Miles, 1993); (iv) that 'white/black' categories are not fixed but are socially constructed and historically variable as evidenced by the varying self-identification and classification of people of 'mixedparentage' as 'black', 'white' or 'mixed race', and the ambiguous status of Asian peoples as 'black' (Modood, 1988; Tizard and Phoenix, 1993); and (v) that attempts to defend and sustain a distinctive 'black' culture imply an immutable 'black' cultural pattern – even an intimate connection between phenotypical difference and culture – and thus parallel racist discourses (Gilroy, 1992). Anti-racist thought, Gilroy (1992) argues, reduces the struggle for 'black' advancement to a struggle against 'white racism', isolates 'racism' from other political processes, including class conflicts and conflicts between women and men, and obscures the complexity of 'black–white' relationships.

Many 'black' scholars and political spokespersons are now seeking to resolve these dilemmas by moving beyond a narrowly constituted racism to consider interconnections between racial categorisations, class, ethnicity, nationality and patriarchy (see pp. 72–3). However, whatever its conceptual limitations, anti-racist thought reflects the way in which some sections of ethnic minority populations define their situation and is an important element in contemporary political debates and activity. It has evoked an anti-anti-racist backlash, but it has also been effective in placing such issues as the education of 'black' children and 'black' unemployment on political agendas, in moderating the public expression of racism and in securing some concessions by public bureaucracies to ethnic minority ways of life.

'Black' Feminist Perspectives

In the 1970s and 1980s 'black' women were doubly marginalised: they were in general invisible in 'black' radical thought and in feminist thought. As a result, the question of whether or not 'black' women experience sexism in different ways from 'white' women and 'racism' in different ways from 'black' men was not addressed. 'Black feminism' attempts to redress this.

Most 'black' feminist writers recognise the need to address the double oppressions of 'race' and gender (as in Hooks, 1982) and some seek to address the triple oppressions of class, 'race' and gender (as in Davis, 1982). Nevertheless, 'black feminism', like male 'black' political thought, tends to assert the priority and autonomy of 'racial' oppression (see, for example, Carby, 1982; Bryan *et al.*, 1985; Ramazanoglu, 1989). 'Racism', Ramazanoglu

(1989) argues, has given 'black' women a specific historical experience of enslavement, indentured labour, enforced migration, imperial conquest and genocide, creates power relationships between 'black' and 'white' women, subjects 'black' women to forms of sexual oppression unknown to 'white' women and evokes strategies and responses that are unique to 'black' women.

This position contains four important and interrelated sets of arguments. First, the radical-feminist notion of universal sisterhood is rejected in favour of the argument that women are divided by racial distinctions, ethnicity and nationality and the power relations which are embedded in these distinctions. Divisions among women, says Ramazanoglu (1989, pp. 116–37), mean that they not only have different histories and contend with different oppressions, but that they also stand in power relationships to each other.

Second and relatedly, the priority of patriarchal oppression is called in question. Male violence, control of sexuality and reproduction and domination of the public world are recognised as problems for 'black' women, but tend to be regarded as less immediate than racial oppression (Ramazanoglu, 1989), the devaluation of 'black' womanhood in 'white' cultures tends to be unproblematically attributed to 'racism' rather than sexism, and 'black' male sexism is rarely challenged (Nain, 1991). Thus, Carby (1982) argues that the relative powerlessness of 'black' men means that the concept of patriarchy is not applicable to 'black' people in the same way as it is to 'white' people. Similarly, Ramazanoglu (1989) emphasises the struggle which 'black' women and men share against 'racism' and *seems* to suggest that their shared racial oppression overrides divisions of gender.

Third, 'black' feminist writers have argued that radical-feminist and marxist-feminist understandings of 'the family', motherhood, reproduction and sexuality are based on the 'white' woman's experience and betray the interests of 'black' women. Amos and Parmar (1984), for example, argue that whereas 'white' women struggle for the right to abortion, 'black' women struggle against the use of abortion, sterilisation and contraception to limit the reproduction of 'black' people. Similarly, a number of writers have argued that accounts of 'the family' as the primary site of women's oppression are insensitive to the differences between 'black' and 'white' family forms, and fail to recognise that for 'black' women (and men) the family is a source of support and resistance in their struggle against 'white' oppression (Carby, 1982; Amos and Parmar, 1984). 'White' feminist debates about such issues as abortion, female circumcision, purdah conventions, the superiority of individually chosen marriages over arranged marriages and the oppressiveness of 'the family', say Amos and Parmar (1984), measure the 'black' woman's experience against that of the 'white' woman, find it in some way wanting and deny the validity of struggles and aspirations which have their origin in non-Western philosophical traditions.

Fourth and relatedly, feminism is defined as 'white feminism' and labelled 'racist' (Hooks, 1982, 1986; Carby, 1982; Amos and Parmar, 1984). This argument rests on the assertion that notions of universal womanhood are in reality grounded in the specific experience of 'white' middle-class women. This, it is argued, has had two consequences. 'Black' women may be made invisible, the specificity of their culture denied and the oppressive force of 'racism' ignored. Alternatively, when their specific experience is recognised, their culture is devalued and liberation is construed in terms of entry into Western culture.

This overwhelming emphasis on racial oppression tends, as in male 'black' radicalism, to slide into essentialism – and has evoked counter-arguments similar to those levelled against male 'black' radicalism (see p. 64). In addition, the 'downgrading' of sexism has been vigorously criticised. Lees (1986b), for example, points out that, given the diversity of 'black' cultures, the defence of 'black' communities against racial oppression does not of necessity entail the defence of any particular set of cultural practices. In her view, arguments for cultural pluralism treat cultures as static, fall into the absurdity of moral relativism and protect patriarchal practices from critique. Further, Nain (1991) argues that the 'downgrading' of sexism leads to ambivalence and uncertainty as to where 'black' feminism stands in relation to 'mainstream' feminism: as to whether it is part of the women's movement, part of the 'black' movement, or part of both movements and, relatedly, as to whether it speaks for all women or on behalf of 'black' women only.

However, 'black' feminism, like male 'black' radicalism, is a diverse enterprise and patriarchal processes are valorised by some 'black' feminist writers. Nain (1991) demonstrates the importance of male domination in the lives of 'black' women by pointing to the role of 'black' women in providing domestic services for 'black' men, the disadvantaged labour market position of 'black' and 'white' women relative to 'black' as well as 'white' men and the prevalence of sexism in 'black' cultures. Hooks (1982) provides a vivid account of the pervasiveness of patriarchal attitudes in African-American culture. She argues that in the final analysis 'white' men's assault on 'black' women is governed by sexism rather than 'racism'. Men of all 'races', she argues, bond on the basis of a shared belief that a patriarchal social order is the only viable social foundation for society.

Ethnicity Perspectives

The concept of ethnicity underpins a long and diverse ethnographic research tradition. This concept stems from the notion that ethnic groups (collectivities with a strong sense of peoplehood) develop around shared cultural values, common historical experiences and/or common kinship, regional or national bonds and are an important element in social life.

The study of relations between 'black' and 'white' peoples as ethnic relations emphasises cultural differences and allegiances and sees ethnic boundaries as defined by culture. It categorises people not primarily as 'black' or 'white' but in terms of their specific ethnic identity (that is, as African-Americans, Afro-Caribbeans, Indians, Pakistanis, English, Welsh, Scots and so on). It thus conceptualises 'black' and 'white' peoples not as monolithic and polarised 'racial' groups but as a series of ethnic groups. Discriminations based on phenotypical distinctions may then be seen as a specific form of ethnic differentiation and exclusion. Further, and importantly, ethnic boundaries are seen not as fixed and single-stranded but as flexible, multi-layered and operating at different levels according to situation and context (Saifullah Kahn, 1981; Anthias, 1992).

This research tradition, though it recognises the importance of material conditions, valorises cultural values. For example, Ballard and Ballard (1977, p. 53) argue that:

> ... external constraints, such as the migrant's position in the labour and housing markets, or the discrimination he [*sic*] faces, are ultimately prior to the internal preferences of the group ... It is the external constraints of discrimination which

set the limits within which South Asians and West Indians in Britain may operate. But the particular behaviour of different groups can only be finally explained in terms of the culturally determined choices made within these limits as well as the various ethnic strategies used to counteract, circumvent or overthrow those constraints.

Further, the ethnicity perspective forefronts gender and familial structures as central elements in a people's culture and in the definition of group boundaries. As the studies of ethnic minority family life reviewed in Section 2.1 illustrate, it tends to see gender and family structures as evolving in terms of their own cultural logic, though in ways that are shaped by interaction with other cultures and by material conditions. It contains a number of competing propositions as to the consequences and functions of a group's adherence to its traditions. A group's traditions have been seen as: (i) a lifestyle that is chosen, created and preserved as a valued symbol of peoplehood; (ii) a resource which may be mobilised in the pursuit of material and non-material goals (as demonstrated in accounts of the salience of Asian kinship bonds – see p. 51); (iii) a 'deviation' from mainstream culture which, because it is out of step with mainstream culture or because it is seen by the majority as containing inherent 'cultural deficiencies', gives rise to economic disadvantage, social isolation, intergenerational conflict and a range of other problems; and (iv) a source of inter-group conflict, given the jealous protection by minority and majority groups of their distinctive cultural identities.

The ethnicity perspective is not linked with political activism, but like all research traditions it contains political implications. These have been severely criticised by radicals of various persuasions. First, it has been argued that it reproduces stereotyped images of ethnic minority gender and family structures. For example, Morokvasic (1983) says that the ethnographic literature locates women in a family framework, conceptualises them as wives and mothers, and portrays them as dependent, unproductive and isolated, the bearers of many children and conservative upholders of traditional norms.

Second, it has been suggested that its emphasis on the cultural values and practices of minorities obscures the power relationship between majority and minority groups. The ethnicity perspective, it is argued, fails to address either the ideological force of 'white' racism or the capitalist processes which determine the class position of minorities. According to this critique, the ethnicity perspective locates the economic and social problems of minorities in their gender and family structures rather than in the exploitative power structures of 'white' capitalist societies; consequently, solutions to their dilemmas are seen as lying in the reworking of their cultures rather than in the transformation of an exploitative and oppressive society.

This critique has in turn been challenged. First, it has been argued that it caricatures the ethnographic tradition. Most ethnographic studies, say Richardson and Lambert (1985, pp. 66–7), do not pathologise ethnic minority groups. Richardson and Lambert further argue that, in emphasising the strength of cultural allegiances, the ethnographic literature presents ethnic minority peoples as active subjects whose experiences are shaped by their aspirations and consciousness. It thus provides a useful corrective to images of ethnic minority peoples as helpless victims of capitalist and/or racial oppression.

In the second place, some scholars have sought to rework the ethnicity concept so as to give greater weight to material conditions and power relations. For example, Saifullah Kahn (1981) maintains that ethnic divisions involve not only cultural difference but also a power relation, including the power successfully to label 'outsider' groups as 'inferior'. In her view, racism is an element in dominant ethnicities. Again, Anthias (1992) suggests that ethnicity is more than a question of cultural identity. It involves the sharing of the material conditions of existence of the group, the pursuit of economic, territorial and political as well as cultural goals, and relations of domination and subordination. Like Saifullah Kahn, Anthias locates racism in ethnic relations. Ethnic difference, says Anthias, is the essential building block of racism – that is of discourses and practices whereby ethnic groups (of any skin colour) are imbued with a fixed essential difference, categorised as a separate 'race' and inferiorised.

Marxist and Marxist-Feminist Approaches

Marxist discourses locate 'black–white' relationships in capitalist imperatives and class conflicts. They thus swing the debate away from its familiar preoccupations with cultural and phenotypical distinctions and valorise underlying structural conditions.

This tradition asserts the expansionist tendencies of capitalism and focusses on its labour needs. It maintains that both in the colonial past and in modern times labour shortages in socially devalued sectors of the economy are met through the exploitation of migrant labour from less developed nations. Capitalism, it is argued, uses 'black' and other ethnic minority people as a source of cheap labour, slots them into menial jobs and thus constitutes, and subsequently reproduces, them as a specific and disadvantaged class category within the proletariat. It is further argued by some marxist writers that capitalism generates and sustains racist ideologies and practices as a means of legitimating the exploitation of 'black' workers, dividing the working class and/or providing a scapegoat for structurally created problems, such as unemployment. In early versions of this argument, capitalism was seen as the seedbed of 'racism' and ethnic relations were reduced to class relations (see, for example, Cox, 1948; Castles and Kosack, 1973). This line of analysis tended to be crudely economistic and has been criticised on a number of grounds. It has been argued that (i) the fact that racism may serve capitalist interests does not mean that its origins are located in capitalism (Richardson and Lambert, 1985); (ii) racism is not in any case unambiguously useful to capitalism – it may generate disruptive social conflicts (Richardson and Lambert, 1985); (iii) notions of the usefulness of 'black' migrant labour rest on dubious assumptions of its relative cheapness; (iv) ethnic identities are reduced to some form of false consciousness and the cultural allegiances and values of ethnic groups are denied independent causal power (Anthias and Yuval-Davis, 1983; Richardson and Lambert, 1985); and (v) 'black' subordination is portrayed as the unfolding of an inevitable plan directed by the logic of capital with the result that conflicts, struggles and contradictions within both the capitalist and working classes are obscured (Richardson and Lambert, 1985).

Marxist accounts of ethnic relations are therefore being reworked and have become more open-ended. In this neo-marxist discourse, racism may be seen as independent of, but interacting with, class relations (see, for example, Miles, 1982, 1989, 1993) or as having specific historical origins but as now entrenched within class divisions (Hall *et al.*, 1978).

Further and importantly, marxist-feminist writers are seeking to expand marxist accounts of 'black – white' relationships – and their own earlier 'race-blind' theory – to take account of the specific position of ethnic minority women in capitalist economies. Broadly speaking, marxist–feminist writers accept the proposition that people of colour are constituted as a racialised labour force and are deployed in socially devalued sectors of the economy. However, they have as their distinctive theoretical concern the interaction of class, racism and ethnicity with gender, and as a major substantive concern the articulation of the labour force position of ethnic minority women with their domestic roles. They have shown that ethnic minority women enter a labour market that is sex-segregated as well as racialised and compete with men on terms that are influenced by their responsibility for childbearing and the personal servicing of men (see, for example, Phizacklea, 1983).

In effect, marxist-feminist accounts of the position of 'black' women in the labour force recognise 'racial' and/or ethnic distinctions as well as gender and class divisions. At the same time, some ethnic minority feminist writers are seeking to rework 'black' feminist theory to take account of capitalist processes and class relations (see, for example, Brewer, 1993). These endeavours seem to be driving feminism towards an open-ended, multi-dimensional theoretical framework (exemplified in a recent collection of readings edited by Westwood and Bhachu, 1988) in which class, racism, ethnicity and gender are seen as inextricably intertwined. This theoretical tendency may either not specify the precise nature of the interrelationship between racial distinctions, class, ethnicity and gender or assume it to be specifiable only in particular historical conditions. It may be analytically evasive or gender, racial/ethnic distinctions and class may be tagged on to each other in a mechanical way. However, this mode of analysis avoids the difficulties that confront mono-causal explanations. It leaves us with a conception of modern societies as comprised of cross-cutting social divisions, volatile alliances and shifts in power relations. It recognises not only that women's experience is specific to their class, ethnic and 'racial' positions in particular historical periods, but that women, because they are located in a range of social divisions, have a range of identities. Moreover, research in this vein points not only to division and conflict but also to commonalities between 'black' and 'white' women based on a shared class position. For example, commonalities of class and gender are demonstrated in Westwood's (1988) account of the incorporation of Gujarati women into a vigorous 'white' woman's shopfloor culture on the basis of their shared interests in resisting the capitalist labour process and in celebrating the life cycle events of women's lives as brides, wives and mothers.

Summary

In sum, the diversification of ways of life associated with the development of non-European communities in Britain has been accompanied, not by the celebration of diversity, but by intense anxiety and conflicts. These anxieties have given rise to, and are informed by, a range of competing discourses.

The racisms of the Far Right and the New Right define ethnic minority groups as 'alien wedges' that are destroying 'the British way of life'. They construct the conjugal family as the building block of British national identity, perceive the family and gender structures of minority groups as the primary site of alienness and may advocate, as strategies for preserving 'the British way of life', immigration control, repatriation and/or the assimilation of minority groups to British ways of life through socialisation. They are underpinned by essentialist views of British and minority cultures as fixed, clearly bounded and relatively homogeneous.

Racist ideologies are countered by the anti-racist ideologies of 'black' radicalism and some sections of the political Left. These ideologies maintain that the position of 'people of colour' is determined by the construction of social boundaries based on skin colour categorisations, contest the hegemony of Anglo-Saxon cultural values and have as a political goal the establishment of a multi-racial, multi-cultural society in which diverse family structures and ways of life have equality of recognition. In these discourses, 'the black family' becomes the site of resistance to racism and an arena within which 'black' ways of life are reproduced and 'black' people equipped with the skills necessary to survival in a 'racist' society. Like racist ideologies, anti-racist ideologies tend to rest on essentialist notions of culture and to reproduce minorities as distinct and separate ethnic communities.

The ethnographic research tradition, marxism and feminism provide alternative understandings of ethnic divisions. The ethno-

graphic perspective emphasises the importance of cultural allegiances in defining group boundaries and shaping ways of life,
points to the malleability of culture and the permeability of group
boundaries and presents 'black' and 'white' peoples not as monolithic racial groupings but as a series of ethnic groups. Gender
and family structures again appear as a central factor in the life of
a group and its reproduction. Marxist thought sees the class position of ethnic minority groups as structured by the labour force
needs of capitalism and as in turn determining the living standards of their families and their interactions with other groups.
'Black' feminism has put the oppression of 'black' women on
political and theoretical agendas and shown that racism alters the
form and significance of sexism, on the one hand, and women's
struggles on the other. Its core argument – that notions of the
universality of women's oppression by men must be replaced by
the specificity of the forms of oppression experienced by different
'races', ethnic groups and classes – has profoundly influenced
feminist thought. It has been a potent (though not the only)
force in the reworking of feminist theory and practice in the late
1980s and 1990s. In this reworking, the diversity of womanhood
rather than the commonality of women's experience is valorised
and divisions of 'race', ethnicity, nationality, class, sexuality and
gender are conceptualised as interlocking oppressions.

These bodies of thought represent different perceptions of
'black' and 'white' relationships and provide the ideological bases
from which different sections of the 'black' and 'white' populations are struggling to affirm or renegotiate their relationships
and shape the nature of the society in which they live. They are
not, however, static discourses but are constantly being reworked
in the context of argument and counter-argument and changing
material conditions. Importantly, grand generalisations appear to
be crumbling in the face of a growing awareness of the complexity
of majority – minority relations and of the importance of class,
ethnicity and gender as well as racism in shaping relationships
between majority and minority groups.

3

Economic Restructuring and Unemployment: A Crisis for Masculinity?

Over the past thirty years, Western societies have experienced the development of labour-intensive technologies, increasing competition from the expanding economies of the Third World, the decline of traditional heavy manufacturing industry and the growth of service sector activity. This massive restructuring of the economy has had as a major outcome the contraction and increasing casualisation of labour markets. At the same time, married women are increasingly economically active and the labour force has grown in size. These processes have produced a shift from full-time, secure and pensionable employment to part-time and casual employment, from male labour to female labour and from full or nearly full employment conditions to high levels of unemployment and sub-employment.

The consequences of these changed labour market conditions are far reaching and corrosive. Unemployment and sub-employment undermine the economic status of individuals and their families and, in the view of some authorities, have increased poverty, widened the gap between the financially comfortable and the poor and contributed to the growth of an underclass. Further, these employment conditions are widely perceived as threatening the traditional organisation of masculinity, disrupting expected transitions from dependent childhood to independent adulthood, putting at risk the independence women have achieved through increasing economic activity, challenging the work ethic and undermining everyday understandings of what is fair and just. They may lead not only to physical and psychological ill-health and conflict between family members but also to lawlessness and self-destructive deviance.

These far-reaching changes in labour market conditions and their consequences have taken place in the context of, and are mediated by, deep-seated political change: by the decline of socialism, the rise of the New Right, the replacement of Keynesian economics by monetarism and the erosion of the Butskellite consensus on state welfare. Within this political context, unemployment may be interpreted as the unfortunate but necessary consequence of curbing inflation, the unemployed tend to be defined as 'scroungers' and are marginalised, and social security support for the unemployed has been circumscribed.

This chapter explores the consequences of these labour market conditions for gender and family relations. Section 3.1 delineates trends in unemployment. Section 3.2 examines the consequences of unemployment for men, women and young people. Section 3.3 looks at debates about the growth of an underclass and its relationship to unemployment.

3.1 UNEMPLOYMENT TRENDS AND PATTERNS

In Britain, government agencies produce two different estimates of unemployment. The first, 'the claimant count', is arrived at by counting the unemployed claimants of social security benefits. This measure is available monthly and is the estimate of unemployment levels given most prominence in the media. However, as academic writers have frequently pointed out, successive changes in the way in which claimants are defined and counted mean that this measure is an unreliable guide to changes in unemployment levels over time. Further, it does not take account of those who, because they are not entitled to benefits or for some other reason, do not register with government agencies as unemployed. It therefore not only underestimates the 'real' overall level of unemployment but also obscures differences between different categories of people. Feminist and non-feminist analysis emphasises that married women, whose eligibility for benefits may be circumscribed by their employment histories or discounted because their childcare arrangements are interpreted as placing unreasonable restrictions on their availability for employment, are significantly under-represented in claimant counts (Martin and Roberts, 1984; Daniel, 1990, pp. 14–15; Callender, 1992). The introduction of a succession of restrictions on the eligibility of young people and of people over 60 to benefits means that these groups are also under-represented in claimant counts.

The second measure of unemployment, a population count, is arrived at by conducting surveys in which people are asked whether or not they are in work and, if not, whether they are seeking work. In Britain, survey data are provided by the quarterly *Labour Force Survey* and the annual *General Household Survey*. In general, these surveys seem to provide the more accurate measure of unemployment levels and are the data sources used in this text.

However, changes in the questions used by researchers to identify the unemployed mean that comparisons over time are again difficult. Further, much unemployment – particularly among the young, people approaching retirement and married women – may be masked by the way in which boundaries between unemployment and economic inactivity are constructed. Muncie (1984) and others have argued that in Britain attempts to deal with the 'problem' of youth unemployment through youth training schemes such as the Youth Opportunities Programme and the Youth Training Scheme do not provide genuine training opportunities and serve only to disguise unemployment. Similarly, Laczko *et al.* (1988) maintain that early retirement schemes artificially remove older workers from the labour market. Further, feminist analysis suggests that married women may not define themselves as unemployed even when they want employment because they regard domestic labour as work in its own right (Martin and Roberts, 1984; Callender, 1992). Alternatively, they may leave the labour market because they believe they are unlikely to get employment or because they perceive men as having a greater claim to available jobs (Callender, 1992).

In sum, it is generally agreed that employment and unemployment categorisations are problematic, that unemployment statistics are uncertain guides to unemployment trends and that their overall effect is to mask the extent of unemployment. Nevertheless, it is clear that unemployment levels have risen markedly.

The available data show that, during the early post-war period of economic expansion, all the major industrial societies of the Western world enjoyed full or nearly full employment. In Britain, for example, unemployment rates stood at less than 2 per cent of the labour force throughout most of the 1950s and 1960s. However, in the 1970s and 1980s the development of labour-intensive technologies, competition from the expanding economies of the Third World and the decline of traditional manufacturing industries combined,as has already been indicated, to produce contracting and casualised labour markets. Table 3.1 shows that unemployment rose sharply in most industrial societies during the late 1970s and early 1980s, fell back in the late 1980s, but rose again at the beginning at the 1990s. This Table also demonstrates considerable variation between countries in unemployment levels: at one extreme, Spain had an unemployment rate of 18.1 per cent in 1992; at the other extreme Japan had an unemployment rate of 2.2 per cent. The United Kingdom had an unemployment rate roughly midway between these extremes: in 1992, 9.9 per cent of its labour force were unemployed.

These data identify the proportions of people who are unemployed at a particular point in time. They do not tell us about movement in and out of employment and are therefore not

Table 3.1   *Unemployment rates[1] in selected industrial countries: 1976–92*

	1976	1981	1983	1988	1990	1992
United Kingdom	5.6	9.8	12.4	8.5	6.8	9.9
Belgium	6.4	10.8	12.1	9.7	7.2	7.9
France	4.4	7.4	8.3	10.0	8.9	10.3
Germany[2]	3.7	4.4	8.0	6.2	4.8	4.6
Netherlands	5.5	8.5	12.0	9.2	7.5	6.8
Spain	4.6	13.9	17.2	19.1	15.9	18.1
Australia	4.7	5.7	9.9	7.2	6.9	10.7
Canada	7.1	7.5	11.8	7.7	8.1	11.2
Japan	2.0	2.2	2.6	2.5	2.1	2.2
Sweden	1.6	2.5	3.5	1.6	1.5	4.8
United States	7.6	7.5	9.5	5.4	5.4	7.3

[1]   Based on OECD definitions.
[2]   As constituted since 3 October, 1990.
SOURCE   *Social Trends*, 1994, Table 4.19.

indicative of the total proportion of people who experience unemployment during the course of their working life. However, in-depth studies suggest that most families now experience the unemployment or sub-employment (part-time and/or casual employment), at some point in their life course, of one or more of their members. For example, in Allatt and Yeandle's study of youth unemployment in Newcastle in the early 1980s only seven of forty young people had been in continuous employment since leaving school and only seventeen had had only one job (Allatt and Yeandle, 1992, pp. 49–57). Thirteen had never had a job and ten had had twenty-six jobs between them. In addition, many new jobs are part-time jobs and increasingly men, like women, are in part-time employment. In the United Kingdom, the number of men and women in part-time employment increased by 55 per cent and 16 per cent, respectively, between 1984 and 1993 (*Social Trends,* 1994, p. 60). Nearly one in every fifteen men and one in every two women is now in part-time employment.

Unemployment and sub-employment are not evenly distributed across the population but vary in four major ways. First, it has been consistently found that class disadvantage is associated with increased vulnerability to unemployment. As Table 3.2 shows,

Table 3.2 *Unemployment rates by socio-economic group[1] and sex, Great Britain, 1992*

Socio-economic group	Men	Women	All
	%	%	%
Professional	4	4	4
Employers and managers	6	5	6
Intermediate and junior non-manual	7	6	7
Skilled manual and own account professional	12	8	12
Semi-skilled manual and personal service	19	12	15
Unskilled manual	31	11	18
Total	11	8	10

[1] Socio-economic group is based on the informant's last job.
SOURCE *General Household Survey,* 1992, Table 7.5.

manual workers are more likely to experience unemployment than white-collar workers and, within these broad occupational categories, semi-skilled and unskilled workers are more likely to be unemployed than skilled workers and junior intermediate workers than professional workers. Second, differences between ethnic groups in the incidence of unemployment have been extensively documented. In Britain, the 1991 Census shows not only that unemployment rates are considerably higher in ethnic minority populations than in the 'white' population, but that there is variation between ethnic minority groups. Levels are significantly higher among Pakistani, Bangladeshi, Black African and Afro-Caribbean men than among men in other ethnic minority groups (Figure 3.1). Third, levels of unemployment among young people are higher than in older age groups and have increased at a faster rate. In Britain in 1992, nearly one in four young men aged 16–19 and one in six young men aged 20–29 were unemployed (Table 3.3). The comparable figures for young women were approximately one in six and one in ten respectively. Further, part-time and temporary work and recurrent unemployment have increased proportionately more among young people than among older workers (Allatt and Yeandle,

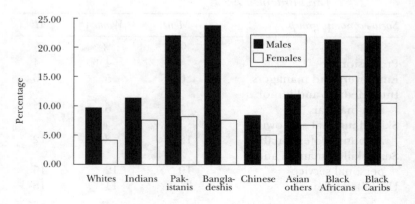

SOURCE   Ballard and Kalra, 1994, Figure 5.13 (derived from 1991 Census data, Crown Copyright).

FIGURE 3.1   *Unemployment by ethnicity, Great Britain, 1991*

Table 3.3 *Unemployment rates[1] by sex and age, United Kingdom, 1993*

Age	Men	Women
	%	%
16–19	22.0	16.0
20–29	16.4	10.2
30–39	10.3	7.0
40–49	8.8	4.7
50–64 for men 50–59 for women	11.9	5.6
65 and over for men 60 and over for women	4.6	3.9
All aged 16 and over	12.4	7.5

[1] Based on the ILO definition.
SOURCE *Social Trends*, 1994, Table 4.20.

1992, pp. 18–19). On the other hand, unemployed young people seem to have a better chance of obtaining employment than unemployed older people and are less likely to experience long-term unemployment (Payne and Payne, 1994). Fourth, as Tables 3.2, 3.3 and 3.4 and Figure 3.1 demonstrate, unemployment rates are higher and durations of unemployment longer among men than women. These gender differences are particularly marked among unskilled and semi-skilled workers (Table 3.2). They reflect the fact that the sectors of the economy in which men were heavily concentrated (namely heavy manufacturing industries) have contracted sharply, whereas the service sector of the economy, in which women have conventionally been concentrated, expanded in the 1970s and, though also subject to recessionary troughs, continues to offer more employment opportunities than manufacturing industry.

3.2 UNEMPLOYMENT AND FAMILY LIFE

Contemporary Western images of unemployment and sub-employment are based on the belief that employment plays a criti-

Table 3.4   *Duration of unemployment[1] by sex and age, United Kingdom, 1993*

	Duration of unemployment				
	Up to 13 weeks	Over 13, up to 26 weeks	Over 26, up to 52 weeks	Over 52 weeks	Total[2]
	%	%	%	%	thousands
Men aged					
16–19	26.8	19.9	26.6	25.8	192
20–29	18.5	17.0	20.0	44.2	666
30–39	15.2	14.9	18.5	51.3	404
40–49	17.3	14.5	15.5	52.5	317
50–64	13.5	14.1	18.9	53.5	377
All over 16[3]	17.6	15.8	19.4	47.1	1967
Women aged					
16–19	32.9	19.4	24.6	18.4	126
20–29	29.9	18.1	23.5	28.5	321
30–39	24.9	20.0	22.4	32.6	207
40–49	27.0	13.7	21.3	38.1	142
50–59	20.3	10.8	21.6	47.2	106
All over 16[3]	27.6	17.0	22.7	32.7	924

[1]   Based on the ILO definition.
[2]   Includes those who did not state their duration.
[3]   Includes men aged 65 and over and women aged 60 and over.
SOURCE   *Social Trends*, 1994, Table 4.22.

cal and positive role in structuring social life. In a now classic analysis, Jahoda (1982, pp. 22–6) argues that employment does not provide the individual only with a livelihood. Employment, she maintains, provides a time structure for the day, the week and the year, enforces regular activity, establishes structured social networks outside the family, links the individual to goals and purposes that transcend his/her own, and is the basis of personal identity and status. Conversely, unemployment brings not only poverty, dependence and powerlessness; it places the unemployed and their families outside the taken-for-granted structures of everyday life.

However, images of the deleterious consequences of unemploy-ment and sub-employment are largely concerned with the fractur-ing of men's lives. In the dominant strands of academic and everyday thought, family breadwinning is presumed to be of sec-ondary importance in women's lives, but to be men's primary responsibility, to be the basis of masculine identity and to be central to men's status and authority in family life and the wider society. Contracting and unsettled labour market conditions thus tend to be interpreted as a crisis for masculinity, but not for fem-ininity. Moreover, the unemployment of young men is the source of considerable concern and alarm. It is widely seen as jeopardis-ing an orderly transition to adulthood, undermining the work ethic and creating a lawless and aggressive masculinity. It has been linked with vandalism, theft, violence, racial conflict and self-destructive deviance and with the emergence of an impover-ished, marginalised and nihilistic underclass.

Feminist analysis provides a different perspective on unemploy-ment. It suggests that employment is significant for women as well as men and seeks to show that unemployment denies women an independent source of income and an occupational identity. Further, many feminist writers construe men's unemployment as presenting opportunities for reworking the conventional sexual division of labour through role sharing and role reversal, an opportunity which, it is argued, is not being realised.

This section examines these issues by looking at accounts of the consequences of unemployment and sub-employment for (i) men, (ii) women and (iii) young people.

Married Men, Unemployment and Family Life

Most studies of male unemployment are studies of unemployment among the 'white' working class. They have focussed on three sets of issues: (i) the erosion of family living standards; (ii) the erosion of a work-based masculine identity and the psychological and rela-tionship problems of unemployed men and their families; and (iii) disruptions to, and the possibility of renegotiating, the con-ventional sexual division of labour. The first issue has in general been discussed from Left-wing political perspectives and tends to be linked with a critique of state income support policies. Discussion of the second issue is dominated by individualistic social psychological perspectives. Discussions of the third issue reflect feminist concerns and are based on critiques of the conventional sexual division of labour.

(i)   *The erosion of family living standards*

Male unemployment deprives families of their primary means of economic support, the male wage, and leaves them with redundancy payments, the earnings of their partners and sometimes their children, unemployment insurance benefits and various forms of means-tested state benefits as their major alternative sources of income. However, these income sources are, in the view of most observers, poor substitutes for the male wage.

The research literature shows that only a small proportion of unemployed men have substantial redundancy payments (Daniel, 1990, pp. 41–4), that women's earnings are low relative to men's (see p. 31) and that unemployment insurance benefits are lower than earnings, are available only for a limited period, have been cut back as high unemployment levels persisted and, in any case, are available only to those who have been in employment long enough to have built up sufficient national insurance contributions. Means-tested benefits, the fourth source of income, are intended only to enable those whose income falls below an officially-defined poverty level to have a basic income. Yet, with the persistence of high levels of unemployment and the reduction of unemployment insurance benefits, the families of unemployed men have become increasingly dependent on this meagre income source. In Britain, official data show that the proportion of unemployed men who are either wholly or partly dependent on means-tested supplementary benefit/income support rose from 31 per cent in 1961 to 70 per cent in 1992 (*Social Trends,* 1994, Table 5.8). Official data also demonstrate the sharpness with which incomes fall following unemployment. A Department of Social Security survey shows that the average disposable income of families in which the household head is unemployed (and had been in full-time work) is only 59 per cent of what it had been during employment (Heady and Smyth, 1989).

Moreover, some of the research literature suggests that any period of unemployment has long-term disadvantaging effects on family life. It has been found that men who experience unemployment typically take a pay cut in order to return to employment (Daniel, 1990, p. 232), when they return to employment are more likely to be in low status, part-time or temporary jobs than men of comparable skill levels who have not experienced unemployment (Payne and Payne, 1993), are at risk of subsequent spells of unemployment (Daniel, 1990, p. 232; Gershuny and Marsh, 1993) and lose out on derivative forms of welfare such as occupational pensions and health insurance (Rodger, 1992). However, the severity of its long-term consequences seems to depend on the stage in the life course at which unemployment occurs. Gershuny and Marsh (1993) suggest that early unemployment damages immediate career prospects and may have persistent small effects over the life course, but does not dominate the entire careers of most people. On the other hand, men who become unemployed in late middle age tend to be more or less permanently excluded from the labour market (Payne and Payne, 1994).

Predictably, researchers have found that the material hardship experienced during unemployment varies with its duration, stage in the life course, number of dependants, availability of supportive kin networks and class position. However, and again predictably, the living standards of both long-term and short-term unemployed men and their families are in general lower than the living standards of the poorest families in work (Bradshaw *et al.*, 1983). Studies of their expenditure patterns show that they economise on all the major components of everyday living – food, clothing and social activity – as well as on consumer durables and holidays (Heady and Smyth, 1989; Gallie and Vogler, 1993), are more likely than the employed to be living in council housing and are likely to be in poor quality council housing (Gallie and Vogler, 1993), may be in arrears with their fuel bills and rents or mortgages (Hakim, 1982) and are likely to be more dissatisfied with their family income, standard of living and position relative to others in the community than any other group in work (Daniel, 1990, p. 88).

Feminist research, like studies of unemployment during the depression of the 1930s, shows that women bear the brunt not only of managing household expenditure on reduced incomes but also of the sacrifices made (The Pilgrim Trust, 1938; Komarovsky, 1940; McKee and Bell, 1985, 1986; Morris, 1985, 1990). Much of this research literature suggests that women's skill, resourcefulness and effort in 'stretching' the available money is a critical factor in the family's ability to survive men's unemployment. Further, women may protect both their children and their husbands or partners from the worst effects of 'life on the dole' by concealing their own worries, or prioritising their children's and their husband's or partner's needs. The overall effect is two-fold and in a sense contradictory. On the one hand, women may fare less well than other members of the household in the distribution of household resources. On the other hand, men's status in the household may be weakened and the intensity and importance of women's sphere of activity strengthened (Morris, 1990, pp. 28–9).

(ii)   The psychological and relationship costs

Whereas most early accounts of the psychological consequences of unemployment assumed that its effects are *sui generis* and more or less uniform, recent studies emphasise that its consequences vary over time, between social class and ethnic groups, with the circumstances of unemployment and from individual to individual (Madge, 1983; Morris, 1990). Duration of unemployment, age and stage in the life course, the availability of supportive social networks and ideologies and the modest independence provided by casual earnings in the 'black' economy are among the variables commonly identified as mediating factors. Moreover, the positive nature of employment – and the negative nature of unemployment – are no longer taken for granted: it has been shown that employment may take place in polluted and health-injuring conditions, may be psychologically stressful, may be poorly paid and of low status and may leave little time for family life. Unemployment may therefore bring improvements in health (Allan, 1985), relief from stress (Fineman, 1983, 1987) and time for involvement in childrearing (Coyle, 1984, p. 113; Salfield and Durward, 1985, p. 14).

Nevertheless, from the 1930s onwards psychological research has consistently documented clear statistical correlations between unemployment and various indicators of stress and sociological research has provided vivid accounts of its disruptive effects (see, in particular, Komarovsky, 1940; Jahoda *et al.* 1972, Marsden, 1982; Warr and Jackson, 1985; Warr, 1987; Gershuny, 1993).

Recently, a marked relationship between insecure employment and stress has also been demonstrated (Burchell, 1993). This research literature points to the erosion of personal, social and working skills, to high levels of anxiety, depression and irritability, to loss of self-esteem and self-respect and to demoralisation, isolation and stigmatisation. Further, accounts of the Depression Years as well as contemporary feminist research highlight the centrality of breadwinning in the social construction of masculinity and the effect of unemployment in eroding men's identity as men (Bakke, 1933; Komarovsky, 1940; Marsden, 1982; Coyle, 1984; McKee and Bell, 1985, 1986; Morris, 1985, 1987). These studies show that without employment men feel disorientated, reduced in status and wounded in self-respect. For men, Coyle (1984, pp. 114–15) argues, being at home during the day is 'a daily confrontation with the fact that they are not doing what men are supposed to do; not simply to work, but to be the breadwinners.' She writes:

> Work and masculinity are so entangled that in unemployment men are not only workless, they are seemingly unsexed. They have lost the very point of their existence as men, to work to support a family. (Coyle, 1984, p. 94).

The impact of the economic and psychological stresses of men's unemployment on their wives or partners and on the marriage relationship is touched on in some of the early studies (Bakke, 1933; Komarovsky, 1940) and is a major concern of recent feminist research (McKee and Bell, 1985, 1986; Morris, 1985, 1987). These studies point to women's empathy with the wounded pride and punctured self-respect of their men but they also show that anxiety, resentment and marital conflict are pervasive. It seems that men's unemployment stigmatises the wives of unemployed men, as well as the men themselves, and undermines their status and identity (Komarovsky, 1940; Jackson and Walsh, 1987). Further, women's participation in social networks and leisure activities outside the home seems to be constrained by the financial stringencies of unemployment while their informal socialising with other women in the home may be inhibited by the husband's presence or even actively discouraged by husbands (Morris, 1985; McKee and Bell, 1986; Jackson and Walsh, 1987). Isolation and loneliness may therefore be experienced. In addition, the struggle to 'make ends meet' on reduced incomes may lead to conflict over spending priorities and may be a major source of anxiety (McKee and Bell, 1985, 1986; Morris, 1985). Finally, it seems that the unemployed husband about the home, though sometimes a source of companionship and support in childrearing, disrupts domestic routines, unsettles customary divisions of household labour and generates tension and conflict (Komarovsky, 1940; Marsden, 1982; McKee and Bell, 1985, 1986; Morris, 1985). All these studies point to the exasperation women feel when husbands or partners sit about the house doing nothing, demand frequent cups of tea, disrupt domestic routines by being underfoot and criticise or interfere with their childrearing routines.

The end result of the tensions and stress associated with men's unemployment may be marital breakdown and dissolution – as evidenced by the apparently increased vulnerability of the marriages of unemployed or irregularly employed men to divorce (Lampard, 1993). However, unemployment may be the catalyst rather than the cause of marital break-up. Kelvin and Jarrett (1985) suggest that it brings to breaking point relationships that are already stressed but reinforces those that are strong: it polarises rather than transforms marital relationships.

Most of the available literature on the impact of male unemployment on children dates from earlier periods and is probably of limited relevance to the present situation. For what it is worth, this literature shows that the children of unemployed men feel the stigma and stress of their father's unemployment. Madge's (1983) review of the psychological literature points to disturbed feeding and sleep patterns, vulnerability to accidents, undue dependence, inappropriate sexual behaviour and play patterns involving irritable fathers, overworked mothers and financial hardship. Further, children perform relatively badly at school. Truancy, absence from school because of poor health, reading difficulties and referrals to education psychologists seem to be recurring problems where fathers experience long-term unemployment (Hakim, 1982). Finally, children appear to be at increased risk of physical abuse (see p. 155) and of being taken into care (Madge, 1983).

Most researchers hesitate to assert a direct and unambiguous causal link between male unemployment and the difficulties children experience. Madge (1983, pp. 316–17) argues that, while it is probable that economic hardship, parental stress, changes of routine and insecurity about the future affect children, the effects are complex and are mediated by a number of factors. She emphasises that the unemployed are disproportionately drawn from groups who are already disadvantaged so that the difficulties children experience may be determined by their class status rather than by unemployment itself. She further argues that unemployment may bring some gains, including the opportunity for fathers to spend more time with their children, that children differ in their resilience and that the effects of unemployment are mediated by the pre-existing quality of family relationships and are more likely to be severe where relationships were already poor.

(iii) Male unemployment and the sexual division of labour

Contracting labour markets provide an opportunity for reworking the sexual division of labour through role-sharing strategies (whereby women and men share available jobs by working part-time and assume joint responsibility for the work of the household) or negotiated role reversals (whereby women assume responsibility for breadwinning and men for the work of the household). Feminist studies of male unemployment focus on this issue – and have unambiguously concluded that high levels of male unemployment are not effecting any significant change in conventional definitions of masculinity and femininity.

Role sharing seems to have received little support from trade unions, employers and the government, and labour force statistics suggest that it is not widespread. Where it is found, it seems to have been adopted as a means of enabling women to combine a work role with motherhood through job sharing between women rather than as a solution to unemployment. There is also little evidence of extensive role reversal. Evidence from a variety of sources shows conclusively that the wives of unemployed men are in fact more likely to be economically inactive than the wives of employed men (Martin and Roberts, 1984; Moylan *et al.*, 1984; *GHS*, 1992, Table 7.11; Davies *et al.*, 1993). In Martin and Roberts' (1984) survey of women and employment, for example, only 33 per cent of the wives of unemployed men, compared with 62 per cent of the wives of employed men, were in employment.

Three main explanations for the absence of any significant trend to role reversal have been advanced. First, Joshi (1984) points out that where male unemployment levels are high, employment opportunities for women may also be limited. Secondly, McKee and Bell (1985) argue that the opportunity for primary breadwinning by the partners of unemployed men is bound up with, and limited by, women's location in a specifically female and disadvantaged labour market. They point out that the jobs available to married women with young children are not the equivalent in status and pay of the jobs available to men and, when reductions in benefits and job-related expenses such as travelling and childcare are taken into account, may not result in a significant improvement in the family's living standards. McKee and Bell find that few women opt for employment in these circumstances. Moylan *et al.* (1984), Kell and Wright (1990) and Davies *et al.* (1993) provide further, and quantitative, evidence of the disincentive impact of the benefit system on the labour force participation of the wives of unemployed men. Third, a number of studies suggest that both women and men are convinced of the impropriety of women taking on the male breadwinning role and resist role reversal even where it would make economic sense (Marsden, 1982; Cragg and Dawson, 1984; Coyle, 1984; McKee and Bell, 1985, 1986; Morris, 1985, 1987). It seems that women perceive masculine authority, identity and pride, as well as marital stability as depending on a man's right to provide for his family, and regard the jobs available in a recession as a male prerogative. Thus, although women's part-time or temporary employment may be accepted, there are few families for whom women's primary breadwinning is an appropriate or easy solution. McKee and Bell (1985) say that this model of male breadwinning is not obviously related to social class and is espoused by men who are actively involved in the work of the household as well as by men who are not. Men's control of the right to provide is thus far from disintegrating despite the recession.

When we turn to accounts of the division of domestic labour during periods of male unemployment, we find evidence of a shift in, but not of a fundamental reworking of, traditional patterns. The work of Laite and Halfpenny (1987), Wheelock (1990), Gallie *et al.* (1993) and others shows that unemployed men are more involved in the work of the household than employed men.

However, the level of their participation varies depending on whether or not their wives or partners are in full-time employment (where there may be a distinct shift to a more or less equal sharing of the work of the household), in part-time employment (where men's household labour tends to vary according to the number of hours their wives work) or are not in employment (where change may be modest). Moreover, the in-depth studies of feminist scholars suggest that men's domestic labour is privately negotiated and executed, is perceived by their wives or partners as incompetent, does not intensify and may even decline as unemployment lengthens, and is dropped on re-employment (Morris, 1985; McKee and Bell, 1986, p. 144; Shamir, 1986). On the other hand, activities which are continuous with the traditional male role – DIY repairs, car maintenance, odd jobs for others and, above all, the search for employment – may increase and tend to occupy much of the unemployed man's time (Morris, 1985, 1987; McKee and Bell, 1986).

In interpreting these data, it should be borne in mind that they are for the most part based on studies of workers in traditional heavy industry and that gender roles tend to be sharply defined in this socio-economic group. Further, caution is needed in making judgements about the extent of change given the wide range of activities involved in the work of the household, the disjunctions that may exist between attitudes and behaviour and the likelihood of class, regional, ethnic and cohort variation. Nevertheless, the available data – including the fragmentary data on middle class patterns (such as Hartley, 1987) – are remarkably consistent in pointing to some increase in men's domestic activity, but to women's continuing overall responsibility for the work of the household.

The limited participation of unemployed men in the work of the household seems to reflect, on the one hand, men's resistance to domestic incorporation and, on the other, women's defence of their traditional terrain. Morris (1985), for example, finds that while many of the men in her sample see domestic labour as a means of dealing with the boredom and disorientation of unemployment, they also perceive it to be unmanly, take exaggerated precautions not to be seen doing it and, in some cases, react strongly against it. Resistance, she suggests, is particularly intense where men are involved in a predominantly male social network. Conversely, women may value men's moral support and increased involvement in childcare, but may nevertheless feel that they perform domestic tasks more quickly and thoroughly than men, may re-do tasks done by men to their own standards and may actively discourage male domestication (Coyle, 1984, p. 114; McKee and Bell, 1985, 1986; Morris, 1985, 1987).

Confronted with these data, some researchers have argued that male breadwinning and female domesticity are so deeply embedded in masculine and feminine identities by a lifetime of conditioning that recession and unemployment cannot readily effect change. McKee and Bell (1986) maintain that men feel that they have a public profile and purpose, despite their severance from the labour market. This legitimates their preoccupations outside the home and provides a justification for a limited contribution within the home. Women, for their part, relate the level and standard of male participation in the work of the home to men's incompetence and women's skill and expertise, and experience male domesticity as a disruption of their routines and a threat to their identity. Again, Coyle (1984, pp. 114–15) argues that male unemployment is defined as a temporary phenomenon and one that cannot be, and ought not to be, adjusted to. It cannot therefore have any lasting effect on the division of labour between women and men within the home. Long-term unemployment, says Coyle, may mean that unemployment in fact assumes a sort of permanence, but it is a 'permanent state of suspension'. It cannot therefore be the basis for new initiatives or long–term change.

Women, Unemployment and Family Life

Until quite recently, unemployed women usually 'appeared only as fleeting shadows in the literature on unemployment' (Marshall, 1984, p. 237). Their shadowy presence reflected the everyday assumption that women are primarily wives, mothers and carers and only secondarily workers. The public image of women's unemployment was thus one of its relative unimportance.

Feminist writers challenge this construction of women's employment and unemployment. They seek to demonstrate the importance of employment in the lives of partnered and unpartnered women and to show that unemployment has economic and psychological costs for women and for their families.

The economic costs

Feminist accounts of women's employment depict women's earnings not as 'pin money', but as a significant element in family budgets and as integral to their role as mothers. They have shown that financial necessity is an important element in married women's participation in the labour force, that women's earnings may lift families out of poverty where men's wages are low and that, at all income levels, desired living standards are now commonly built around two incomes (McNay and Pond, 1980; Martin and Roberts, 1984; Wallace, 1987). Further, they (like some critical social policy analysts) have emphasised that lone mothers constitute a growing proportion of women, receive little support from their former partners, experience considerable hardship where they are dependent on state benefits (Bradshaw and Millar, 1991; Millar, 1992) and are less likely to be in poverty where they are in full-time employment than where they are not (Layard *et al.*, 1978; Mitchell and Bradshaw 1991).

Conversely, feminist accounts of women's unemployment are concerned to show that family living standards are significantly affected when women are unemployed. This body of literature shows that women's unemployment has particularly severe consequences for women on their own and – because their wages play a critical part in keeping families out of poverty where men's earnings are low – for poor families (Coyle, 1984; Morris, 1990, p. 137; Callender, 1992). However, there is general agreement that women's unemployment spells financial difficulty for all families. Martin and Roberts (1984, pp. 89–91) say that one-third of all unemployed women, compared with less than 10 per cent of employed women, find it 'very difficult to manage' or 'are not managing at all'. Callender (1992, pp. 142–4) finds that women's redundancy leads to economies that begin with cutbacks on their own personal needs and then range from cutbacks on savings to cutbacks on essentials like food. About half of the women in this study were struggling to meet basic financial commitments. Yet, Callender reports, many husbands realised the importance of their wives' wages to the family economy only with its loss. Similarly, Coyle (1984) finds that redundancy confronts women with what they had always known: that a man's wage is not enough to live on.

The psychological costs

Feminist accounts of the housewife role suggest that it is charac-terised by monotonous and meaningless work, economic depend-ence, low status and social isolation (Oakley, 1974, 1976). Full-time housewifery would thus seem to present women with a structural condition that has much in common with that of the unemployed. At the same time, feminist researchers have consist-ently argued that employment provides women with a way out of the dependence and isolation of full-time housewifery. This research literature suggests that marriage and motherhood remain the primary focus of women's lives but that women never-theless value employment as a means to economic autonomy and incorporation into the public world (Coyle, 1984; Cragg and Dawson, 1984; Martin and Roberts, 1984).

Women's experience of unemployment seems to be the mirror image of the value they place on both family life and employment. Studies of women's unemployment, such as Coyle (1984), Cragg and Dawson (1984), Martin and Wallace (1984) and Callender (1992), show that unemployment cuts women off from the social relationships of the workplace and leaves them without the resources to finance social activity. It thus radically curtails their social contacts and horizons, accentuates the privatised nature of their lives, gives rise to loneliness and boredom and may lead to depression and poor health. In addition, these studies show that unemployment deprives women of the modicum of autonomy, freedom and economic independence that employ-ment had given them. Coyle, for example, reports that, without 'a bit of money' they can call their own, married women feel that they 'are being kept', seek advice where once they would have acted on their own, are obliged to ask for 'pin money' and have to account for its expenditure. Loss of an independent income thus places women in a dependent and supplicatory role and, Coyle suggests, can prompt a personal crisis commensurate with that which men experience over the loss of their breadwinner status.

However, married women's experience of unemployment seems to differ from that of unmarried women and of men. Data on the experiences of unmarried women are slender but those that are available suggest that unmarried women, like men, feel redundant and displaced, tend to be particularly isolated and are subject to a high level of demoralisation (Morris, 1990). In contrast, married women seem to elaborate their domestic roles to fill the vacuums left by unemployment, may even be glad of some relief from the double burden of employment and domesticity and do not in general experience the sense of social redundancy and crisis of identity that men and unmarried women experience.

Martin and Wallace (1984) and Coyle (1984) vividly depict the ambiguities and ambivalences of married women's responses to unemployment. Martin and Wallace find that unemployed women fill their time with a range of domestic activities, perceive their families as appreciating them being at home and believe that their return to full-time domesticity brings some advantages to family life – tea can be on the table when husbands come home from work, children can be exempted from housework, evenings and weekends can be free for relaxation. Very few of the women in this survey felt stigmatised by unemployment, only 24 per cent felt that their unemployment led to tensions in family life and 29 per cent reported improved physical health. At the same time, few women believed that the quality of their housekeeping was improved by full-time domesticity, many felt that housework was intrinsically less interesting than paid employment, most would have preferred to be in employment and significant proportions reported stress, periods of depression, loneliness and missing their workmates.

Coyle also shows that married women elaborate their domestic role to fill the vacuum left by unemployment. She finds that redundancy may be used as an opportunity to catch up on household chores, may serve as a welcome break from the 'bone-grinding' schedule of 'the double shift' and may be the catalyst to pregnancy. Like Martin and Wallace, she suggests that motherhood may be perceived by women as a legitimate alternative to employment and men may be glad to have their partners 'stopping at home'. However, Coyle emphasises that women miss the social contacts of work, are distressed by their loss of autonomy and, once they have caught up with postponed tasks, begin to experience all the problems of surplus unstructured time. The family, says Coyle, may soften the blow, but in the end cannot in any real sense compensate for the loss of employment.

Nevertheless, these and other studies show that unemployed married women perceive their own situation as radically different from that of unemployed men. They may want to return to work and may affirm women's right to employment, but they also perceive the work of the household as work in its own right and tend not to define themselves as unemployed though they may be looking for work. Commenting on such findings, Morris (1990, p. 133) suggests that, despite the dissatisfactions of the housewife-mother role, women do not see employment as an alternative to domesticity but as a source of relief from domesticity and as another dimension to life. Femininity is thus not threatened by unemployment in the way that masculinity is.

Coming of Age Unemployed

Young people are at greater risk of unemployment and sub-employment than older workers (see p. 80). Moreover, the government-sponsored youth training schemes into which they may be propelled provide a respite from the dole queue, but do not appear to provide either effective training for employment or a permanent structural solution to the collapse of youth labour markets (Muncie, 1984; Bates and Riseborough, 1993). In addition, young people's entitlements to social security have been eroded (and their parents' responsibility extended) with, *inter alia*, the removal of income support for 16–17-year-olds and its reduction for those under 24. In the view of some commentators, young people are the primary victims of contracting and casualised labour markets. According to Coffield (1987), they have become the most expendable section of the labour force and are marginalised and stigmatised as an unemployed and unemployable 'lumpenproletariat'. He writes:

In little more than ten years the economic crisis in Western societies has transformed the golden age of youth into a massive social problem...In the 1960s young people were celebrated as the embodiment of sexuality, freedom health and progress; before the end of the 1970s they had again become economically marginalised and began to be treated in the same way as other stigmatised groups...(Coffield, 1987, pp. 87–8).

Sociological accounts of the problematisation of youth unemployment rest on the proposition that in Western societies employment is critical to the transition from childhood to independent, responsible and law-abiding adulthood. In a recent exposition of this thesis, Allatt and Yeandle (1992, pp. 60–94) argue that employment brings young people the achieved status and prestige of 'worker', the power of an independent income and social relationships which are beyond the control of parents. It thus provides the basis for renegotiating rights and obligations with parents and for pushing back the boundaries of parental control. Further, Allatt and Yeandle argue that 'being settled' in a 'proper job' – meaning a steady job with a fair wage – is widely perceived as necessary, albeit in gender-specific ways, to marriage and the establishment of an independent family unit. They find that the construction of paid work as (in the words of one of their respondents) men's 'whole purpose in life, what they function for' means that graduation to full adult masculinity is predicated on family breadwinning. For young working class women, on the other hand, graduation to full adult femininity (married motherhood) is dependent on access, through marriage, to a male wage and thus on men's access to employment. Their own employment is an opportunity to 'live a bit' between childhood and marriage and domesticity (Wallace, 1987).

Unemployment jeopardises this orderly progression through the 'normal' stages of the life course. Unemployed young people, say Allatt and Yeandle, are without an occupational status, have only the limited and 'less deserved' income which state benefits provide, and are deprived of those work relationships which would teach them about work identities and work itself. Their position in the family does not mature into the independence of adulthood, and marriage and parenthood may be deemed unwise. In addition, Allatt and Yeandle (pp. 85–110) argue that, because the daily use of time and space is structured and synchronised by the time schedules of paid work, unemployed young people are literally 'matter out of time, out of place'. They have no reason for getting up at the 'normal time', cannot share in the leisure activities of their peer groups, disrupt domestic routines by their presence in the household and are oppressed by an over-abundance of time. They are outside the work-structured patterns and routines of the everyday world – and in the way of those who must conform to these routines.

Young people's reactions to this situation have been charac-terised in two broadly opposing but overlapping ways. They have been depicted as (i) rebellious, lawless and/or nihilistic and as (ii) troubled but resigned and broadly conforming.

(i)   Rebellious, lawless and nihilistic images

Images of a rebellious, lawless and nihilistic journey through an unemployed youth dominate the media and much of the political rhetoric of the Left and Right.

Media and political commentary depict the unemployed young as poorly educated and unskilled, as effectively excluded from the welfare system and as the victims of family breakdown and home-lessness. They document, and attribute to unemployment and sub-employment, trends towards unmarried parenthood among young women, and rising crime, rioting and racial violence, drug and alcohol abuse and suicide among young men. Representations of unemployed young 'black' people (and in particular of unem-ployed young Afro-Caribbean men) as hanging about street corners, at risk of drifting into crime and of becoming alienated from society, occupy a distinctive and salient place in this imagery of unemployed youth and, according to Solomos (1985), sharpen perceptions of ethnic minority groups as threatening dominant cultural values and institutions.

These images of unemployed young people draw on various social science research findings. Research in both Britain and the USA shows that property crimes rise sharply during recessions (Hakim, 1982; Dickinson, 1994), that significant proportions of young people who come before the courts are unemployed or sub-employed (Hakim, 1982) and that neighbourhoods with rela-tively high levels of youth unemployment and sub-employment are characterised by a high incidence of vandalism, property crime, racial violence and generalised lawlessness. Some researchers also point to links between unemployment and suicide in young adulthood. One report suggests that in England and Wales the suicide rate among men aged 14 to 24 increased by 78 per cent between 1980–90 (Hawton, 1992).

In a speculative analysis of this response to unemployment and sub-employment, Willis (1984a, 1984b) argues that whereas older unemployed people are workers without work, wage earners without the wage and consumers without money, young people are in a state of 'suspended animation'. They are without the golden key to the separate households, couple relationships and consumer power of adulthood. Willis maintains that working class young men are confronted with a 'crisis' of masculinity and may react with anger and an aggressive assertion of masculinity, while working class young women may opt for unmarried motherhood. Young women thus escape the parental home and the failure of trying to find work while achieving a clear role, a limited independence and adult status, but young men have only the collective solace of young male peer groups and the boastful and aggressive fantasies of thwarted masculinity.

This imagery of unemployed young people depicts unemployment as leading to unmarried mother families and the marginalisation of young men and is reminiscent of accounts of the development of the Afro-Caribbean and Afro-American woman-headed family (see p. 43). It fuels beliefs in the growth of an underclass, a social category separated from other classes by its poverty and its lifestyle. The idea of the underclass and theories of its genesis are explored in the concluding section of this chapter.

(ii)   Troubled but conforming images

Media images of lawless and nihilistic unemployed young people contrast with the images of a troubled but stoical acceptance of unemployment which are to be found in a number of sociological studies of youth unemployment. These studies include Allatt and Yeandle (1992), McRae (1987), Wallace (1987) and Hutson and Jenkins (1989).

Allatt and Yeandle, like Willis (above), see the unemployed young as 'in danger of being socially dislodged and disconnected' and as troubled and in some measure troubling. However, unlike Willis, they depict a resigned and broadly conforming response to unemployment. They document loss of faith in educational qualifications, youth training schemes and careers services, anger at the exploitative practices of employers and a widespread feeling that the government and society have opted out of their responsibilities and obligations to the young. They show that bewilderment, anxiety, depression, a sense of unfairness and feelings of marginalisation are commonplace. Nevertheless, the young women and men in their sample see dependence on social security as an unsatisfactory state of affairs, regard having a job, however poor, as a good thing and do not appear to be either losing the motivation to work or drifting into criminality.

McRae, in a study of the social and political attitudes of unemployed young people in four English cities, finds that young women and men are fairly evenly divided between those who feel cheated and angry and those who do not. Some express a deep sense of resentment about lost opportunities, most believe that something could and should be done to improve the situation and many are in principle supportive of collective protest. However, the idea that one must work for one's money seemed to be general, the aspirations of the majority differed little from those in work and political activism was minimal. McRae maintains that most young people expect to be in work in the future and see themselves not as 'the unemployed', but as 'unemployed at present'. Unemployment, says McRae, has not created a pool of hostile young people desirous of overthrowing society, but a pool of unhappy young people waiting their turn to join society.

The unemployed young people in Wallace's (1987) Isle of Sheppey study bear some resemblance to the young people described by Willis (see p. 99). However, Wallace points to ultimate conformity with traditional expectations of male breadwinning. She reports that on leaving school young people find personal relationships, status and identity in local youth subcultures and are ambivalent about employment. They are dismissive of jobs they regard as boring or insufficiently rewarded, are prepared to wait for the right job to turn up rather than to take any available job and sometimes deliberately adopt self-images which are antithetical to those required by employers. Seeing unemployment as a fact of life and a period of unemployment after leaving school as a break between school and work, they hardly consider themselves unemployed.

However, Wallace shows that reactions to unemployment vary with gender and status and change during the journey through youth. She finds that unemployed young women are more likely than unemployed young men to pursue home-based pastimes and to participate in the work of the household. They are more isolated from their peers, but they have a more secure sense of belonging somewhere. Further, she finds that young men in the 'respectable' strata of the working class also spend their time in home-based pastimes and parentally approved hobbies. In contrast, young men in the 'rough' strata of the working class assert a masculine identity by exaggerating the symbols of masculinity. They identify with romantic rebels, prize survival skills that embody an independent individualism and clever if shady deals, and tell highly embellished and dramatised stories of confrontations with authority in which humiliating incidents are transformed into personal triumphs. Some take to pill-popping, drinking binges, fighting and other masochistically 'heroic' activities.

Wallace thus sees unemployed young women as drawn into domestic servitude within the parental home and low status young men as seeking to redeem their impoverished masculinity through fantasy and an aggressive but destructive 'macho' male youth sub-culture. However, she finds that most young men reject the scenario of starting families on the dole, that most young women envisage being married to conventionally employed young men and that the adoption of alternative identities is experimental and short-lived. Five years after leaving school, the unemployed young people in her sample were less involved in local youth cultures and feel unemployment severely. Aspirations had been revised downwards, orientations to work had become instrumental and jobs that would have been rejected at sixteen are tolerated. Wallace attributes this change of attitude to recognition of the lack of viable alternatives, acclimatisation to the jobs they are able to get and the assumption of family responsibilities.

Hutson and Jenkins (1989) provide a relatively optimistic picture of the journey to adulthood through an unemployed youth. First, they argue that unemployment affects young people to different degrees and in all probability severely damages only a minority. Second, they point out that adulthood, before it is anything else, is a legal status which is defined by citizenship rights (such as the right to vote and the right to marry without parental consent) which are not dependent on employment status. Third, they argue that social security benefits, though now reduced, give young people some economic independence. Finally, Hutson and Jenkins argue that adulthood has an important moral dimension based on ideas of 'responsible' behaviour which parents seek to sustain and on the basis of which young people claim adult rights whatever their employment status. Hutson and Jenkins thus seek to qualify the emphasis that most writers have placed on employment as the key to adulthood and to show that there are niches within which the unemployed young can make successful claims to some degree of independence. Adulthood, they say, is a robust, multi-dimensional identity and is not destroyed, though it is impoverished, by unemployment.

All these researchers suggest that parental support and surveillance – and in particular maternal support and surveillance – play an important part in sustaining the morality of work and independence, and in protecting young people from the more brutal consequences of recession. According to Allatt and Yeandle, parents fear not so much that the young cannot survive without employment but that they may be content to do so and may drift into a lifetime of dependence on state welfare and criminality. Fearing this, they seek to succour and control the young. Allatt and Yeandle (as well as Wallace and Hutson and Jenkins) show that parents insist on active and continued job hunting, draw on their knowledge of the job market to guide job-seeking, define social security benefits as degrading and provide emotional support in the face of despondency. Further, parents seek to prevent their sons and daughters sliding into 'bad ways' by 'nagging' about long hours spent in bed and personal untidiness, encouraging participation in the work of the household, fostering the pursuit of home-based hobbies and promoting the skilful management of money. At the same time, parental subsidies enable young people to finance job hunting, to continue with their hobbies and to have a lifestyle that may not be very different from that of their employed contemporaries. These studies show that parental reactions are not without their ambivalences and may veer from affection and the desire to ease the child's life to harshness stemming from the belief that young people should be earning. Where conflict is severe, the young may leave home. Nevertheless, these studies suggest that parental support is an important resource in confronting unemployment. They demonstrate the enduring strength of traditional parental relationships.

However, they also point to the erosion of traditional family bonds in that they show that uncertain and declining employment opportunities are an obstacle to marriage and the formation of new conjugal family units. Allatt and Yeandle, Hutson and Jenkins, and Wallace report that most young men feel that they must be breadwinners in order to marry – and most young women and their parents view unemployed young men as unsuitable prospective husbands. In this situation, young men may lose interest in 'girls', may adopt a predatory lifestyle or may move down-market and seek partners among schoolgirls whose own limited resources and expectations are unthreatening (Hutson and Jenkins, 1989). Young women may drift into lone motherhood (Wallace, 1987). Couples may opt for unmarried cohabitation; in Wallace's study, nearly half of the young men in cohabiting relationships were unemployed while nearly all the married young men were employed. It seems that cohabitation, as a relationship based on flexibility and impermanence, may be preferred to marriage where unemployment prevents young men from assuming a breadwinning role.

Two recent studies of cohabitation, McRae (1993, p. 29) and Kiernan and Estaugh (1993, p. 15) also find that the partners of cohabiting mothers are more likely than the partners of married mothers to be unemployed. Significantly, population statistics seem to sustain the suggestion that unemployment depresses marriage rates: they show that unmarried men are somewhat more likely to be unemployed than married men (*GHS*, 1992, Table 7.13).

3.3 THE UNDERCLASS DEBATE

Images of a widening and hardening gap between unemployed and employed people – in terms of their employment prospects, living standards and lifestyles – and of the growth of a poverty-stricken, frustrated, apathetic and/or lawless underclass culture are now appearing with increasing frequency in the media, in political debate and in some sections of academic thought. The notion of the underclass identifies the growth of a social category which is outside or below society at large. In the USA, where it was first coined in the late 1970s, the term denotes the social position of people trapped in inner city ghettoes – and in particular the position of poor African-Americans and Latinos. It signifies a category that is unskilled and unemployed or poorly paid and is characterised by solo parenthood and long-term dependence on state welfare. In Britain and elsewhere in Europe, the term is used in a more general sense to refer to groups of people – 'black' or 'white' and living on run-down council estates or in inner city areas – who are disadvantaged in a number of ways and who have lost touch with the official world. As in the USA, it identifies a hard core of marginalised people who have little stake in society. Estimates of its size range from 1 per cent to 15 per cent or more (Dahrendorf, 1989).

In the academic literature, there is disagreement and confusion as to how 'the underclass' is to be conceptualised. There is disagreement as to whether it is to be seen as the bottom stratum of the working class or as outside the working class. Further, some writers define the underclass as a social category that has no stable relationship to employment – and thus seem to exclude from its ranks groups such as pensioners who, though very poor, have had an historically stable position in the labour market (see, for example, Buck, 1992) – while other writers use it to refer to systematic disadvantage whatever its source and include in its ranks not only the unemployed but groups such as the low paid and pensioners (see, for example, Field, 1989). However, most definitions see the underclass as a social category which is separated from other social groups by its poverty and lifestyle. Further, the unemployed and sub-employed – and in particular the young unemployed – occupy a salient place in most images of the underclass. Phrases such as 'the abandoned generation' (*The Guardian*, 1 June 1994) and 'the legion of the lost' (*The Times*, 6 October 1981) vividly exemplify perceptions of the underclass fate of the unemployed young. In addition, contemporary images of the underclass tend to imply that the divide between the underclass and the majority of the population is an increasingly salient and challenging social division and is eclipsing the older divisions of class (Westergaard, 1992).

However, the emergence and growth of the underclass has been accounted for in very different ways. It has been seen as a structural condition created by the social and political forces of contemporary capitalism, as a cultural condition rooted in the manners, morals and attitudes of its members, and as a condition created by a masculine response to unemployment. Each of these arguments presents us with a different interpretation of the nature and direction of the link between unemployment and the social pathologies said to be associated with an underclass position. Each has different political reasonances. The first reflects Centre-Left, the second Centre-Right and the third feminist political positions.

In its many variants, understandings of the underclass as a structural condition hinge on the notion that economic restructuring has divided the labour force into core and peripheral workers, with the former representing a skilled workforce in secure employment and the latter an unskilled workforce in a casualised labour market (Gallie, 1994). This argument suggests that peripheral workers are hired and fired in accordance with fluctuating labour market demands, consequently have access only to intermittent and insecure low-paid employment, and are increasingly locked into a poverty-stricken class position on the margins of the productive order. Further, some writers have argued that in many Western societies, but particularly in Britain and the USA, the plight of workers on the periphery of the labour market has been exacerbated by the erosion under Right-wing governments of education, health, housing and social security provision (Field, 1989; Rodger, 1992). The result has been cumulative disadvantage and the emergence of an underclass.

In these discourses, the social problems associated with unemployment are seen as predictable responses to unemployment, poverty and exclusion from mainstream society. Thus, Wilson (1987) presents rising rates of solo parenthood, welfare dependency and male criminality among African-Americans in de-industrialising inner city areas as a behavioural response to their worsening economic plight. Dahrendorf (1987) maintains that the underclass have no stake in society and cannot be expected to comply with its norms: crime, he says, becomes one of its modes of life, rioting an expression of its frustration and a culture characterised by hostility to middle-class society, association in changing groups of gangs, drug and alcohol abuse, and a laid-back sloppiness its end result.

This line of analysis defines unemployment and sub-employment as a structural condition created by the social and political processes of contemporary capitalism and sees the pathologies associated with unemployment as the consequence of economic and social marginalisation. In contrast, accounts of the underclass as a cultural condition have at their core the notion that underclass status is rooted in a defective sub-culture. In these discourses, unemployment and poverty are attributed to an unwillingness to work and a willingness to rely on state welfare.

Some versions of this thesis attribute the growth of the underclass to the social and political environment created by Left-wing ideologies and social policies. Thus, Dennis and Erdos (1992) argue that the underclass are victims of a cultural environment created by marxism. They claim that responses to poverty are mediated by values and can be lawful when, as in the earlier part of this century, social values encourage perseverance, discipline and industry. However, Dennis and Erdos maintain, marxist notions of the intrinsic unjustness of existing social structures, together with the growth of a permissive morality, have fostered a new and anarchistic spirit of defiance, self-regarding enjoyment and hostility to rule-bound, other-regarding constraints among young men and, to a lesser extent, among young women. The young people who most thoroughly accept this value system, say Dennis and Erdos, are inevitably the young people most frequently recruited to the ranks of the unemployed.

In another, and perhaps the most often cited version of the cultural condition thesis, Murray (1984, 1990) revives nineteenth and early twentieth century distinctions between the 'deserving poor' (those who have fallen into unemployment and poverty as a result of socio-economic conditions but who remain committed to the work ethic) and the 'undeserving poor', those whose lifestyle and attitudes mark them off from the rest of society, lead to unemployment, poverty and other social ills and have created an underclass phenomenon. Whereas the structural-condition argument sees the erosion of state welfare as reinforcing the marginality of already marginalised workers, Murray argues that the growth of the welfare state has damaged the work ethic. He maintains that the failure of state welfare systems in both Britain and the USA to distinguish between the deserving and undeserving poor has, on the one hand, undermined the position of the deserving poor by failing to reward their efforts and, on the other, reinforced the repugnance to regular labour of the undeserving poor by providing them with a livelihood.

Solo parenthood appears in these images of underclass culture as one of its characteristic features and as a potent force in its reproduction. Both Murray and Dennis and Erdos argue that solo parenthood leaves young men without a model of the 'good father and provider', makes men marginal to family life and is a critical factor in the growing 'unemployability' and lawlessness of young men. Unemployment, say Dennis and Erdos, may indeed be the key to lawlessness among young people, but unemployment not in terms of the absence of opportunities to work but in terms of the absence of the expectation that young men prepare themselves for employment in a lifetime partnership of mutual support between a man and a woman, employment to which a job is merely instrumental. Young men growing up in fatherless families, say Dennis and Erdos, do not have a taken-for-granted project for life of responsibility for a wife and children.

Feminist writers present us with a third interpretation of the relationship between unemployment and underclass status. Campbell (1993) seeks to show that the anarchic and nihilistic hedonism of the unemployed young is a masculine response to economic crisis. She argues that the difference between what women and men do with their troubles and their anger leads to different responses to economic crisis. It produces strategies of self-help, solidarity and survival among women but of criminality and destruction among men. Masculinity, she claims, establishes its identity by enforcing difference through the gendering of family obligations and establishing men as providers rather than as parents. Employment thus legitimates men's absence from the domestic domain. Unemployment removes their licensed means of escape from the home, but they nevertheless refuse to be domesticated. Difference, she maintains, is reasserted in a failure to cooperate with women in the creation of a democratic domesticity. Masculinity comes to be defined by lawlessness rather than work and is sustained by a popular culture that constructs masculinity as brittle, impregnable and volcanic, as about proving yourself by having bottle, looking for fights, being a bit crazier than everybody else, being able to control others. Nothing in male culture, Campbell argues, encourages men to create a domestic domain. Unemployment thus *reveals* a mode of masculinity rather than *causes* a crisis of masculinity.

Each of these theses emphasises a particular aspect of reality. Notions of the underclass as a structurally-created economic condition focus on the political and economic processes of capitalism. The cultural-condition argument emphasises the deviant behaviour and attitudes of the underclass and relate them to the ideologies of the Left. Feminism focusses on the social construction of masculinity as determining men's response to economic crisis.

In focussing on a particular aspect of reality, each of these discourses distorts reality. First, they stereotype the unemployed and, in particular, unemployed young men. The studies of the young unemployed reviewed in Section 3.2 provide considerable evidence of the reproduction by parents of the work ethic and of its resilience among young men and women. Again, Daniel (1990) shows that in general the unemployed attach a high priority to being employed, devote considerable energy to the search for work and tend to take whatever job they can get so as to return to work. Being unemployed, says Daniel, is not a role that people embrace or even become reconciled to. Second, some sociologists question the existence of an unemployed/sub-employed underclass as a clearly defined, cohesive and segregated category. Though there is evidence of the concentration of unemployment and sub-employment in families, of the repetition of unemployment in career histories and of cumulative disadvantage among the unemployed, it has also been argued that the unemployed are not a fixed and homogeneous group of people, neither see themselves as members of a group nor define themselves as permanently unemployed and are not totally segregated from employed people (Daniel, 1990; Morris and Irwin, 1992a, 1992b; Westergaard, 1992). Further, Westergaard (1992) maintains that shifts in income distribution point to widening inequalities across the board but not to a sharp divide between an outcast underclass and an incorporated middle mass. Finally, each of these discourses is partial. The structural-condition argument, by failing to examine the way in which values and ideologies mediate responses to economic situations, frequently slides into a mechanical economic determinism. The cultural-condition argument fails to take account of the scale of structurally produced unemployment and sub-employment and seems to hold the unemployed and the poor responsible for their own exclusion from society. Campbell's feminist account seems to slide into essentialism in its characterisation of masculinity and to ignore economic realities. Moreover, it fails to consider the possibility that the male breadwinning role may be constructed by women *and* men and does not take account of young women's reluctance to establish a domestic domain with unemployed young men.

The partial nature of each of these theses points to the need for an interactive analysis of the 'underclass phenomenon'. Nevertheless, whatever their deficiencies, underclass discourses express the fears and anxieties generated by unemployment and by the range of social problems which sometimes appear in conjunction with unemployment but which may also appear independently of unemployment. They reflect concerns and anxieties about poverty, solo parenthood, poor educational attainment, drug and alcohol abuse, and crime and violence in the public domain. In particular, they connect with perceptions of increasing lawlessness among young men in areas of chronic and enduring unemployment. Like all debates about unemployment, they are informed by the sense that masculinity is in crisis – that the contraction and casualisation of the labour market has left men not only without jobs but also without a role in family life and in society.

4

Population Ageing and the 'Problem' of Care

In almost every country of the Western world, the number and proportion of older people in the population has increased markedly over the past fifty years. As a result, later life has become a long and distinctive phase in the life course and the balance between young and old in family networks and in the population as a whole has shifted significantly. This considerable change in population age structures is a source of mounting public concern and alarm. In much everyday thought, later life is construed as a period of physical and mental decline, as burdensome to the families of 'the old' and as hateful to 'the old' themselves. In the political sphere, analyses of the 'problem' of resourcing the income, housing, health and welfare needs of an ageing population are permeated by phrases such as 'the rising tide of the elderly', 'the growing burden of dependency' and 'the pension time-bomb'.

> 'Old age' is conventionally defined as beginning with retirement and eligibility for a pension. The statutory retirement age varies between societies and may differ as between women and men. In Britain, it is currently being equalised at 65 for women and men.

Debates about the 'problem' of eldercare and the role of 'the family' and the state in its solution revolve around a number of competing ideological positions and values. At one extreme, the New Right and moral conservatism seek to sustain the family as a unit of care. At the other extreme, some feminist writers reject the ideal of family care and urge the expansion of state-provided care while the disability movement urges the development of policies which will enable people with disabilities, old and young, to buy in the services they need and to be independent of both family and state. More conservatively, the political and academic Left and Centre seek to construct a new partnership between state and family in which disabled people have the support of both informal family and neighbourhood networks and institutional services. In the everyday world, values and behaviour are complex, and are often ambiguous and contradictory.

This chapter examines these debates and the research litera- ture on caring values and patterns. Section 4.1 explores the emer- gence of 'old age' as a 'social problem'. Section 4.2 explores debates about, and patterns of, family care.

4.1 THE CONSTRUCTION OF 'OLD AGE' AS A SOCIAL PROBLEM

In Western societies, perceptions of 'old age' as a major social problem are not new, but historically concern has fluctuated and varied in intensity. At the present time, as often in the past, 'old age' has become the source of acute and sustained concern in the context of: (i) population ageing; (ii) ideas and beliefs of later life as a period of physical and mental decline; and (iii) the organisation of productive activity.

The Demographic Ageing of Populations

In Western societies, long-term downward trends in fertility have reduced the proportion of children and young people in the popu- lation to historically low levels. At the same time, falling mortality has resulted in successive increases in the proportion of each birth cohort surviving to 'old age'. Demographic analyses show that these trends have combined to produce significant increases in the number and proportion of older people in the population (Walker and Phillipson, 1986, p. 4). However, women and men have not been equally implicated. As Table 4.1 indicates, women's average life expectancy is greater than men's and, though there has been some narrowing of the gender gap in recent decades, it has lengthened relative to men's over the course of the twentieth century. As a result, women considerably outnumber men, and

Table 4.1   *Life expectancy in the United Kingdom 1901–91*

| Year | Life expectancy | | | |
| | At birth | | At age 60 | |
	Men	Women	Men	Women
1901	45.5	49.0	13.3	14.6
1931	58.4	62.4	14.4	16.4
1961	67.9	73.8	15.0	19.0
1991	73.2	78.6	17.8	21.8

SOURCE   *Social Trends*, 1993, Table 7.4.

widows outnumber widowers, in both the 'young old' (65–74) and 'old old' (75 and over) age groups.

Changes in life expectancy and in the numbers and proportions of older people in the United Kingdom are illustrated in Tables 4.1 to 4.3. Table 4.1 shows that over the course of the twentieth century men's life expectancy at birth increased by nearly twenty-eight years and women's by nearly thirty years. Table 4.2 shows that approximately one in every six persons is now aged 65 and over, compared with approximately one in every twenty persons at the beginning of the century. This Table also demonstrates that, although those aged 75 and over are a relatively small proportion of all older

Table 4.2   *Numbers and proportions of older people in the United Kingdom, 1901–90*

| Year | Numbers[1] Aged | | Numbers | %[2] |
	65–74	75+	Over 65	Over 65
1901	1.3	0.5	1.8	4.7
1931	2.5	1.0	3.5	7.6
1951	3.7	1.8	5.5	10.9
1981	5.2	3.3	8.5	15.0
1990	5.0	4.0	9.0	15.7
Men	2.2	1.4	3.6	
Women	2.8	2.6	5.4	

[1]   In millions.
[2]   Of the total population.
SOURCE   *Social Trends*, 1986, Table 1.1; the United Nations *1992 Demographic Yearbook*, Table 7.

people, their numbers have increased eight-fold since the beginning of the century whereas the numbers of those aged 65–74 have increased four-fold. Women constitute two-thirds of those aged 75 and over. Table 4.3 shows that 63 per cent of women over 75, but only 30 per cent of men over 75, are widowed. As Table 4.4 indicates, the ageing patterns found in the United Kingdom are broadly replicated in other advanced industrial societies.

These demographic trends seem to have had important consequences for the individual, for family structures and for social policy. First, demographers argue that increasing longevity has reshaped the life course: that it has prolonged the post-childrearing stage of the life cycle, lengthened retirement, and made 'old age' a long and distinctive period of life. Laslett (1987) estimates that under current mortality and retirement conditions a newborn baby will spend one-fifth of life if a boy, and one-quarter of life if a girl, in 'old age'. The individual, says Laslett, cannot as in the past discount the possibility of growing old.

Second, population ageing, in conjunction with declining fertility, seems to have changed the shape of family structures. Hagestad (1986) points out that increasing longevity has made four-generation and even five-generation families commonplace – about one-half of all individuals over sixty-five are great-grandparents – while declining fertility has resulted in the contraction of intragenerational kin relationships. This means that family networks are now

Table 4.3 *Marital status of women and men over 65 in Great Britain, 1992*

| | Aged 65–74 | | Aged 75 and over | |
	Women	Men	Women	Men
	%	%	%	%
Never married	6	7	8	5
Married	53	76	26	63
Cohabiting	0	1	0	0
Widowed	35	12	63	30
Divorced/Separated	6	4	3	1
All	100	100	100	100

SOURCE *General Household Survey*, 1992, Table 2.4.

Table 4.4   *Life expectancies and proportions of the population aged 65 and over in selected industrial societies, 1991*

Country	Life expectancy Men	Life expectancy Women	Proportion aged 65 and over All
Belgium	72.8	79.5	13.9
Denmark	72.5	78.0	14.6
France	72.9	81.1	13.1
German Fed. Rep.	72.1	78.7	13.9
Netherlands	74.0	80.1	12.0
United Kingdom	73.2	78.6	15.7
European Union	72.8	79.4	13.6
Sweden	74.9	80.5	17.8
Japan	75.9	81.7	12.0
USA	72.8	79.9	12.0

SOURCE   Eurostat, *Demographic Statistics*, 1993, Tables D.2 and D.3.

largely composed of intragenerational relationships, whereas under earlier demographic conditions they were largely composed of intragenerational relationships. Relatedly, the relative balance between old and young in family networks has changed. Hagestad claims that for the first time in history the average married couple now has more parents than children and families may contain two generations who are past the retirement age.

Third, population ageing is generally interpreted as leading to rising levels of dependency. This understanding of 'old age' is supported by evidence of a progressive, though variable, deterioration of physical and mental health with advancing age and of the vulnerability of older people to poverty. British and American gerontological research shows that, while most older women and men have no or only minor disabilities, the incidence of acute and chronic illness, disability of varying degrees of severity and the use of medical and welfare services increases with age (*GHS*, 1986, 1992; Martin *et al.*, 1988; Age Concern, 1992, ch. 3). In addition, the research literature shows that although some groups of older people are relatively affluent, incomes are in general lower, disposable assets more limited and the risk of poverty greater than at younger ages (Victor, 1987; Walker, 1990a, 1992; Age Concern, 1992, pp. 174–80). Older people may therefore be dependent on state-provided income support, frequently experience considerable material deprivation and may be unable to service disability-related needs. Tables 4.5 and 4.6 provide a brief indication of disability and poverty levels in later life.

Understandings of population ageing as entailing growing dependency have in most Western societies, but particularly in Britain and the USA, been attended by mounting political concern and alarm (Thane, 1987; Walker, 1990b). This has in turn played an important part in placing 'old age' on political and academic agendas and has prompted the development of social policies which seek to shift the 'burden' of income support from the state to occupational and personal pension schemes and the 'burden' of care from state institutions to 'the family'. At the same time, however, there are fears that the family's capacity to care has been eroded by contemporary patterns of family formation and dissolution – that declining family size has left older women

Table 4.5 *Disability level of older women and men by age, Great Britain, 1985*

| | *Disability level*[1] | | | | | |
| | *None/slight*[2] | | *Moderate*[3] | | *Severe/very severe*[4] | |
Age group	*Women*	*Men*	*Women*	*Men*	*Women*	*Men*
	%	%	%	%	%	%
65–9	86	89	9	6	6	5
70–4	78	87	14	8	7	4
75–9	67	80	17	10	15	11
80–4	50	67	25	22	24	11
85+	30	48	27	29	43	24
All	70	83	16	10	14	7

[1] Based on ability to perform six activities: climbing stairs, cutting toenails, walking down the road, washing all over and bathing, getting round the house and getting into and out of bed and scored so as to yield a maximum score of 12.
[2] Score 0/1–2.
[3] Score 3–5.
[4] Score 6–8/9–12.
SOURCE Arber and Ginn, 1992, Table 5.1.

Table 4.6   *Poverty rates among people over 65 in selected industrial
countries*

Country	Poverty Rates[1]		
	At 65–74	At 75 and over	At all ages
Canada	11.2	12.1	12.1
W. Germany	12.7	15.2	7.2
Sweden	0.0	0.0	5.0
United Kingdom	16.2	22.0	8.8
USA	17.8	25.5	16.9

[1]   Poverty rate defined as percentage of persons in families with adjusted disposable income below half of the median for all families in the population.
SOURCE   Derived from Hedström and Ringen, 1987, Table 6.

and men with few potential family carers, that high levels of marriage mean that unmarried daughters, conventionally regarded as
providing a pool of readily available filial carers, have virtually dis-
appeared and that trends towards divorce, remarriage, cohabitation and the participation of married women in the labour
market are fracturing family support systems and decreasing the
likelihood of family care (G. Parker, 1990).

However, the relationship between advancing age and dependence and between population ageing and the alarm it has evoked
is not a straightforward one. Sociological analysis suggests that
responses to ageing, and to a considerable extent the process of
ageing itself, are mediated by ideological, economic and political
processes. Analysis has focussed on the prevalence of stereotyped
images of later life, the institutionalisation of retirement as a
means of manipulating the size and composition of the labour
force and the dominance of political ideologies based on opposition to the expansion of state welfare. These arguments, to which
we now turn, are addressed within a range of sociological perspectives, but most forcefully within a relatively new and radical school
of social gerontology, known as the political economy perspective
or critical social gerontology.

Images of Ageing

In contemporary Angio-Saxon and northwest European cultures,
images of later life as a period of ill-health, economic and social

redundancy, dependence and poverty are pervasive and dominant, though images of later life as 'a third age' of freedom, relative affluence and leisure are also to be found (see, for example, Laslett, 1989). Studies of the way in which older people are portrayed in literature, the media and everyday thought show that ageing is widely equated with increasing illness, disability and senility, with the inability to work or to perform other socially useful roles, and with poverty, isolation and imminent death (Stearns, 1977; Levin and Levin, 1980; Scrutton, 1990). In medicine and the caring professions, ageing is defined in terms of physical and psychological decline and the social problems which older people experience tend to be attributed to the infirmity of ageing (Stearns, 1977; Levin and Levin, 1980; Fennell *et al.* 1988, pp. 38–40; Scrutton, 1990; Estes and Binney, 1991). Further, analyses of social policy-making suggest that it is permeated by the notion that an ageing population constitutes a growing 'burden of dependency' and is a massive drain on national resources (Phillipson and Walker, eds,1986; Walker, 1990b).

Social science analysis is not immune from this 'cultural pessimism' about later life. For example, some strands of sociological thought assert the existence of social roles and divisions based on age-linked competences and present us with the argument that in the modern world the rapidity of technological and social change means that older people lack relevant social skills and are socially redundant. In a distinctive version of this thesis, Cumming and Henry (1961) and Cumming (1963) argue that individual activity and social involvement reach a high point in middle age and then decline, first as children leave home, then because of retirement and widowhood, and ultimately in preparation for death. The disengagement of the older person from social relationships, says Cumming, is paralleled by reduced pressures from others to maintain an active life and involves a triple withdrawal: loss of roles, contraction of contact and decline in the commitment to norms and values. Though they refer to social arrangements which mediate the experiences of later life, Cumming and Henry assume that disengagement is a universal and inevitable process with a biological basis.

This negative imagery of later life is not gender neutral. Feminist analysis shows that older women are confronted with the double jeopardy of ageism and sexism. Sontag (1978), Itzin

(1990) and Arber and Ginn (1991), for example, argue that because the social worth of women is defined in terms of their reproductive potential and sexual attractiveness and because both are associated with youth – whereas masculinity is identified with talents such as competence, autonomy and self-control which may be enhanced by experience and age – there is a double standard about everyday images of ageing that denounces older women with particular severity.

Accounts of 'old age' as a period of infirmity and withdrawal entail a perception of senescence as overriding economic and social constraints (Phillipson, 1982, p. 11), identify 'old age' with a particular chronological age (Neugarten and Neugarten, 1986) and explain the problems commonly associated with later life in terms of the inevitable infirmity of the ageing process and/or failure to adjust to and make adequate provision for that process. They thus contain the implicit assumption that population ageing is inherently problematic.

Critical social gerontology challenges this way of thinking about later life. Scholars writing from this perspective argue that notions of later life as a period of decline stereotype older people, the majority of whom, as Table 4.5 demonstrated, are neither disabled nor dependent, some of whom are relatively affluent and most of whom make an important contribution to social life through their involvement in a range of voluntary activities (Phillipson and Walker eds, 1986; Qureshi and Walker, 1989; Victor, 1987; Thane, 1987). It is further argued that older people are not a homogeneous group but are differentiated by gender, class, ethnicity and the specific historical experiences of their cohort (see p. 121). Later life is thus said to be a variable and changing phenomenon. In addition, the idea that population ageing necessarily results in increased demand for health and welfare care has been contested. Some researchers maintain that, as a result of general improvements in health, levels of illness and disability among older people are declining (Fries, 1980, 1989). However, this thesis runs into contradictory evidence of stability in, and even of increases in, levels of longstanding illness (*GHS*, 1992, Figure 3D). Finally, it has been argued that conceptions of dependence as intrinsic to later life fail to take account of the social processes which create or exacerbate dependence. Scholars such as Minkler and Estes, eds (1984, 1991), Walker and

Phillipson(1986) and Townsend (1981, 1986) maintain that notions of dependence as inherent in the ageing process leave unexamined the relationship between ageing and economic life and exclude from the analysis the primary cause of official alarm at the public sector consequences of an ageing population, namely ideological opposition to increasing state expenditure.

These arguments point to the variable and socially constructed nature of 'old age' and suggest that dependence in later life is not a biological rule. However, the belief that later life is a period of dependence gives it a distinctive shape. Scrutton (1990) maintains that systematic stereotyping provides us with images through which we perceive, categorise and respond to older people. Ageism, Scrutton maintains, is a structured feature of modern Western societies. It constructs older people as a dependent group, separates them from other people, and provides a rationale for discriminating against and disadvantaging them. It would seem to play an important part in the sense of crisis that surrounds population ageing.

These arguments raise questions as to why and how later life in contemporary Western societies has come to be perceived and structured as a state of dependence. We now turn to this issue.

The Relationship of Older People to the Economy

Critical social gerontology rests on the proposition that the status of older people and, to a considerable extent, the ageing process itself are determined by economic and social processes. More specifically, this school of thought argues that dependence in later life is a distinctively modern phenomenon and is located within the complex shifts of the organisation and reorganisation of production and of social welfare under capitalism. This argument is elaborated in a number of ways.

First, scholars writing from this perspective (for example, Townsend, 1981; Phillipson, 1982; Walker, 1983, 1990a) maintain that retirement at a pre-determined age is a critical factor in structuring the experience of later life. According to Walker (1983, 1990a), the institutionalisation of retirement in the twentieth century has ensured that an increasing proportion of older workers are excluded from the labour force, are denied access to earnings, occupational status and the psychological benefits of the workplace, and are drawn into dependence on state welfare. Walker further argues that retirement at a specified age is not determined by ageing but is a key strategy for regulating the size and composition of the labour force. He identifies as critical factors in the institutionalisation of retirement, and more recently of early retirement: capitalism's historical tendency to reduce necessary labour to the minimum, the belief that efficiency depends on the removal of workers with low levels of marginal productivity from the workforce, the presumption that productivity is related to age, technological innovation, and the advent of large-scale unemployment in the 1930s and its return in the 1980s.

> At the beginning of the century, in the USA and in Britain nearly two-thirds of the male population aged 65 and over were economically active. By the late 1980s the proportions were 16 per cent and under 10 per cent respectively (Arber and Ginn, 1991, pp. 23–4.)

Second, critical social gerontology seeks to show that social security policies have not only failed to eradicate poverty among older people but have played an important part in producing and legitimating poverty. Walker (1983, 1990a, 1990b) argues that in Britain and many other Western societies social security policies are informed, on the one hand, by concern about the escalating cost of pension provision and, on the other, by the assumption that income differentials between those who are in employment and those who are not must be maintained if incentives to work are not to be eroded. Consequently, Walker argues, state pensions have from their inception been set at low levels and successive generations of older people have been condemned to poverty. Walker further argues that contemporary concerns over population ageing and escalating pension costs are artificially amplified by ideological opposition to the expansion of public expenditure. Political pessimism about population ageing, he argues, must be set in the context of the growth in Britain, the USA and elsewhere of Right-wing political ideologies and monetarist policies.

Third, critical social gerontology provides a critical analysis of health and welfare services for older people. Accounts of residential care and of community services from this perspective suggest that care tends to be organised in ways that impose age-segregation, inhibit the capacity of older people to care for themselves, leave little scope for choice and reinforce the dependence created by the wider social structure (Walker, 1983; Townsend, 1986).

Fourth, critical social gerontology highlights inequalities among older people. It draws attention to class differences in the income levels and health status of older people and suggests that these represent the continuation and culmination of differentials established during working life (Victor, 1991; Walker, 1990a; Arber and Ginn, 1991, 1993). Further, feminist and other studies show that the social position of older women is significantly different from that of older men. Older women are negatively stereotyped in gender-specific ways (see pp. 117–18), are at each age level more likely than men to experience illness and disability, have limited access to state welfare services and are more often vulnerable to poverty than men (Peace, 1986; Arber and Ginn, 1991; Walker, 1992). Arber and Ginn (1991) relate women's vulnerability to poverty to their role in servicing the domestic and care needs of children, men and older people, their consequent concentration in part-time work and/or in low paid work with limited access to occupational pensions, and their restricted entitlement to state pensions. Finally, differences between ethnic groups in health, income levels, housing and access to welfare services have been demonstrated (Norman, 1985; Cameron *et al.*, 1989; Blakemore and Boneham, 1993).

These arguments suggest that dependence in later life stems in the first place from the exclusion of older people from the labour force, is reinforced by social policies which seek to limit the state's role in the financial and social support of older people and is mediated by the position of the older person in class, ethnic and gender structures prior to retirement. This thesis sees older people as a heterogeneous group, challenges the presumption that 'old age' is itself a cause of poverty and dependence and provides a powerful critique of theories, ideologies and policies that presume that population ageing creates a growing burden of dependence.

Critical social gerontology is now generally viewed as providing the appropriate vantage point from which to view later life and population ageing. However, it is not unproblematic. First, Stearns (1977), Smith (1986) and Thomson (1984) show that forms of retirement and stigmatisation, poverty and dependence in later life are not distinctively modern phenomenon but have a long history. This suggests that they cannot be attributed to capitalism in any straightforward way. Second, Macnicol and Blaikie (1989) question the tendency to explain retirement in terms of labour force requirements only. They argue that the citizen's desire for leisure in later life was an important factor in its institutionalisation. Third, some writers have suggested that an analysis of the economic and political processes that create dependence do not tell us all we need to know about 'old age'. Blakemore (1989) argues that to point out that older people can be viewed as many different groups, each with distinct lifestyles and levels of access to material resources, does not mean that ageing does not exert some influence on everyone. Although membership of privileged social groups and alternative approaches to retirement and state welfare may minimise its effects, the likelihood of experiencing some impairment of physical and mental functioning and a corresponding need for social support do increase with ageing. The ineluctable processes of ageing, Blakemore argues, cannot be ignored. Similarly,Gillian Parker (1990) argues that, although not all older people need special care, the incidence and severity of disability increase with age. Thus an ageing population, by definition, implies a growing population of people with special needs.

4.2   FAMILY LIFE AND ELDERCARE

Debates about the 'problem' of 'old age' have centred on two major concerns: financial support and the physical care needs of older people. In the nineteeth and early twentieth centuries both were defined as the responsibility of 'the family'. However, with the expansion of state welfare after the Second World War, responsibility for the income needs of older people was redefined as being appropriately met through some combination of state pensions, occupational pensions, personal savings and means-tested state benefits. Though the financial support of older people remains a critical issue and though the appropriate role of the state, occupational pension schemes and personal savings in providing for 'old age' continues to be debated and to change, the income needs of older people are not at present regarded as a family responsibility. In contrast, the relative role of the state and of families in providing for the physical and psychological needs of dependent older people is contested.

In the traditional family ideologies of moral conservatism, 'the family' continues to be defined as the appropriate arena of care for dependent older people. This ideological position asserts not only that families have a moral responsibility to care for older people, but that caring in the context of supportive and enduring family relationships provides security, privacy and love and is to be preferred to the impersonal and bureaucratic care of the formal sector. Further, this position construes caring as integral to femininity and as primarily women's responsibility. Care by the family thus becomes care by women. These notions are complemented, on the one hand, by perceptions of state welfare as undermining family autonomy and family responsibility and, on the other, by the deep-rooted belief that contemporary changes in family values and lifestyles are incompatible with eldercare and represent the abandonment of traditional responsibilities.

According to Left-wing and feminist writers, this ideological stance informed the early development of social provision for older people, was reforged in the 1980s by the New Right in the context of persistent fears over the escalating cost of welfare provision, and is now deeply entrenched in community care policies (Moroney, 1976; Walker ed., 1982; Osterbusch *et al.,* 1987; Qureshi and Walker, 1989). Community care, it is repeatedly argued, has come to mean not, as was originally envisaged, care in the community with older people having the support of both informal care networks and institutional services, but care by the community with the emphasis firmly on the role of family carers and of women as primary carers. The state, say Qureshi and Walker (1989), is engaged in constructing or sustaining 'the family' as a unit of care for dependent older people and other disabled adults and seeks to achieve this in part by targeting state support at those without families and in part by the implicit and explicit promotion of an ideology of family caring.

In contrast, the political economy perspective assumes the pervasiveness of family caring but emphasises its burdens and limitations and urges the expansion of state care. It thus challenges traditional conceptions of the state–family relationship. Nevertheless, this position re-casts rather than rejects the ideal of family caring. Writers such as Qureshi and Walker (1989) envisage 'community care' not as care by the family but as a partnership between the state and the family. In this scenario, family care is limited and state care extended, but older people continue to be located in the emotional intimacy of their family networks. It is assumed that such a state–family partnership will, on the one hand, obviate the burdens of family caring and, on the other, curb the power of professionals and state bureaucrats over people's lives.

This argument is complemented and extended by feminist thought. Broadly speaking, the dominant tendency in feminist gerontological research defines caring for older people as another aspect of women's unpaid domestic labour, highlights the burdens and material costs of caring for women and seeks to uncover inequalities in social provision which reinforce women's dependence and subordination. Like the political economy perspective, this feminist argument contains a vigorous critique of state action but it may go further and reject family caring on the grounds that gender inequality is inherent in 'the family'. For example, Finch (1984, 1986) urges the expansion of institutional care while Dalley (1988) advocates the reorganisation of society on the basis of collective living.

These political economy and feminist arguments are marked by considerable conceptual unity. Like the 'traditionalist' ideology they oppose and challenge, they tend to depict older people as the dependent recipients of care, equate caring with women's unpaid labour in the family, and focus on daughters caring for parents. However, whereas 'traditional' ideologies valorise the needs of older people, see caring as a rewarding activity and assume and seek to reinforce the practical and moral desirablity of family care, the political economy argument focusses on the needs of carers as well as older people, and the feminist argument on the needs of carers. Both emphasise the material and emotional costs of caring for women and urge the expansion of state care.

These political economy/feminist arguments dominated academic research in the 1980s. However, new understandings of the realities of family care and new ideological orientations are beginning to emerge. Recent research suggests that, outside the context of marriage, values are in fact contradictory and caring heavily circumscribed. At the same time, it shows that considerable caring takes place within marriage, is as likely to be care by husbands as by wives and is provided by older people themselves. In addition, it reveals the existence of paid domestic labour. These findings suggest that caring cannot be construed simply as women's unpaid labour in the household, that carers are a diverse group of people, and that values are ambiguous and patterns of caring complex. Furthermore, a new and different challenge to family care – and to state-provided care – has emerged. This challenge comes from disabled people of all ages and is based on the proposition that both family care and state care presume and reinforce their dependence on, and subordination to, the able-bodied.

These issues are explored in more detail as we look at different conceptions of the caring task, research accounts of contemporary caring values and patterns and the caring experience. The section concludes with an account of challenges to ageism.

The Caring Task

All the care literature contains the implicit and explicit assumption that the care needs of older people involve two elements: (i) comfort and psychological support and (ii) the provision of a wide array of services: assistance with household tasks, personal and nursing care, mediation between the older person and health and welfare agencies and financial management and help. These two aspects of the 'caring task' are encapsulated in Ungerson's (1983) distinction between 'caring about' (the provision of love and affection) and 'caring for' (the provision of physical and material services).

However, scholars disagree as to whether these aspects of caring are intrinsically interwoven or are in principle separable and deliverable by different categories of people. The former position presumes that 'caring about' necessarily involves 'caring for' and, conversely, that services provided outside the context of a loving relationship are simply services and not 'real care'. The latter position presumes that there are different kinds of care needs which can be met in different ways.

Philip Abrams' (1978) early and influential distinction between formal and informal care invokes the first position. Abrams defines 'informal care' as unpaid care based on personal relationships and 'formal care' as paid care delivered through a bureaucratic structure by specified individuals working within a framework of bureaucratic rules and professional accountability. Formal care, his analysis suggests, is performed on the basis of formal qualifications for a caring job, is in principle available to all disabled people in terms of defined categories of need, and is functionally specific and instrumental. In contrast, informal care is ascribed on the basis of pre-existing personal relationships and is particularistic, diffuse and expressive. In Abrams' view, the personally directed nature of informal care gives it a special quality which formal care can never provide. It provides affection as well as physical care and makes it possible for people to feel cared about as well as cared for.

This equation of 'informal care' with 'real care' underpins 'traditional' ideologies of the family as a unit of care and seems to have common currency in everyday thought. Moreover, informal care tends to be thought of as care by women in the family. In everyday thought, professional ideologies and social welfare policies, as well as in large tracts of feminist thought, 'care', Graham (1983, 1991) maintains, is commonly conceptualised as encompassing concern for others as well as the provision of goods and services. It is perceived as taking place in the private arena of the home, as based on the normative obligations of kinship and friendship rather than the contractual obligations of paid work, and as not only typically provided by women but also as an integral part of women's nature. 'Care', Graham maintains, is widely seen as both 'labour' and 'love', as unwaged, home-based, familial and feminine.

This way of thinking about 'care' has been criticised on the grounds that it excludes not only institutional care but also home-based forms of care, such as paid domestic labour, which are not based on marriage and kinship (Graham, 1991). Further, it seems to set up a dichotomy between public and private care (Ungerson, 1990). It fails to recognise that familial care is not necessarily loving care and, conversely, that in formal caring agencies affectionate relationships can develop between carers and care recipients. In addition, Dalley (1988, pp. 8–15) maintains that it mistakenly gives the menial activities involved in caring for someone affective value and serves to label as deviant and uncaring women who wish to delegate the labour of 'caring for' kin to some other agency. Caring for and caring about, Dalley maintains, are not necessarily inextricably intertwined. Finally, some feminist writers have argued that concepts of caring need to be extended so as to convey the exploitation of women that is embedded in the unequal division of caring between women and men (Ungerson, 1990).

The second approach to conceptualising 'care' is linked with challenges to traditional ideologies. Roy Parker (1981), Ungerson (1990) and, in a reworking of her earlier account of caring as a 'labour of love', Graham (1991) are examples of this approach. These scholars define 'care' as involving both waged and unwaged work and as undertaken by family members, domestic helpers or health and social service personnel. Parker and Ungerson locate 'care' in the public as well as the private domain and see it as taking place in a variety of social settings while Graham, as in her earlier work, locates 'care' in the private world of the home but includes paid domestic labour. Caring is thus broadened to include contractual relationships. While work and love may be seen as combining in different ways in caring relationships, irrespective of their unpaid or paid, familial or non-familial character, 'the labour' and 'love' of caring are seen as analytically separable. Moreover, these scholars are primarily concerned with caring as a work activity and implicitly or explicitly subordinate the emotional labour of caring to its work aspects. In these analyses, the qualities of commitment and affection contained in notions of 'care' as being at one and the same time 'labour' and 'love' no longer appear as intrinsic to caring relationships and the presumption that family care will always be better care is set aside. To the traditionalist, however, they fail to provide an understanding either of deeply rooted resistances to non-familial forms of care or of the qualities of commitment and affection which transform caring-work into a life-work.

The Normative Context of Caring

Moral conservatives tend to believe that family responsibilities have declined over time and are lamentably weak. They cite as both cause and symptom of the erosion of family commitments, the weakening of extended family networks, trends to divorce, unmarried cohabitation and solo parenthood and the increasing participation of women in the labour force. In contrast, scholars writing from political economy and feminist perspectives assert the pervasiveness of a highly gendered obligation to care (Walker, ed., 1982; Dalley, 1988; Lewis and Meredith, 1988; Qureshi and Walker, 1989). Much of this literature suggests that family obligations are sustained through welfare policies that limit state-provided care to those without family resources and through the reproduction by the state of a coercive ideology of gendered family responsibility. However, a third interpretation of the strength and scope of caring values may be drawn from recent research (see especially Finch, 1989; Finch and Mason, 1993). This literature suggests that the obligation to care exists, but is limited, complex and ambiguous and cannot readily be interpreted as demonstrating either the neglectfulness of families or the coercive strength of a gendered injunction to care.

First, there are indications that family obligations are not gendered in a straightforward way. Finch and Mason (1993) find that at least at the level of publicly expressed beliefs, women and men say essentially similar things about the value they place on assistance among kin and the circumstances in which it should operate. Further, it appears that men, like women, are defined as the primary source of assistance for disabled spouses (Qureshi and Walker, 1989), that considerations of equity mean that sons as well as daughters may be defined as sources of assistance for parents (Brody, 1981; Roff and Klemmack, 1986; Finch and Mason, 1990b) and that conventional gender norms may in themselves serve to assign certain caring activities to men rather than to women. Finch and Mason (1990b) report that sons and sons-in-law are rarely chosen for the personal care of older women but are defined as the appropriate providers of financial assistance (which daughters rarely are) and of personal care for older men (from which daughters may be exempted). In addition, Finch and Mason (1990c) argue that societal norms do not, as many early feminist accounts had suggested, unconditionally subordinate women's employment commitments to their caring role. They find that societal norms protect the employment position of women as well as men and that, faced with competing obligations, women search for compromises which enable them to care without abandoning their jobs.

Second, the research literature suggests that the range of liable relatives is narrowly defined. It seems that in contemporary Anglo-Saxon cultures the obligation to care falls first to spouses and then successively to daughters, daughters-in-law and sons (Qureshi and Walker, 1989). It does not typically extend to grand-children or to siblings and other kin (Finch, 1989, pp. 36–56; Finch and Mason, 1990b) and is ambiguous in cohabiting rela-tionships and in in-law relationships which have been disrupted by divorce and remarriage (Finch and Mason, 1990a). Moreover, the evidence suggests that sons and daughters define their obliga-tions to parents as secondary to obligations to their spouses and children (Seelbach, 1984; Aronson, 1990). Finch and Mason (1993) emphasise that, while parent–child relations come closer than any other familial relationship to having fixed responsibili-ties associated with them, filial responsibilities are endorsed less strongly and less predictably than parents' continuing respons-ibility to their adult children.

Third, there is ample evidence of the prevalence in Anglo-Saxon and northwest European cultures of values which empha-sise individual autonomy and independence and set limits to the obligation to care. American and British studies show that older people do not readily give up their independence and are reluc-tant recipients of care (Lee, 1985; Qureshi and Walker, 1989; Arber and Ginn, 1991), that family help is mobilised on the unstated principle of least involvement so as to preserve the inde-pendence of the generations for as long as possible (Matthews and Rosner, 1988; Aronson, 1990), that the expectation of aid usually stops short of financial support (Seelbach, 1984) and that there is widespread reluctance on the part of older people and their children to share a household (Brody *et al.*, 1984; Qureshi and Walker, 1989; Arber and Ginn, 1991, 1993). In some circum-stances the impersonal professional help of bureaucratic agencies may be regarded as less independence-destroying than kin care and may be preferred (Brody *et al.*, 1984; Lee, 1985; Arber and Ginn, 1991, p. 139). Qureshi and Walker (1989) suggest that cul-tural preferences in relations between older people and their adult children are best denoted by the phrase 'intimacy at a dis-tance'. This phrase, first used by Rosenmayr and Kockëis (1963), conveys a desire for contact, closeness and support on the one hand, and for independence and autonomy on the other.

Fourth, the obligation to care appears to be cross-cut not only by cultural emphases on independence but also by reciprocity norms that assert the obligation to give as well as receive. According to Finch and Mason (1993), reciprocity is a key element in all exchanges of kin support and is the mechanism through which family members maintain 'the proper balance of dependence and independence'. However, it is inevitably compromised by the dependence of the caring relationship. Thus, the research evidence suggests that caring, though culturally enjoined, may also be culturally defined as burdensome (Qureshi and Walker, 1989; Aronson, 1990; Arber and Ginn, 1991, pp. 138–46). Further, attempts may be made to structure caring relationships so as to establish a semblance of reciprocity. Older people may struggle to be givers as well as receivers even when they are very frail (Wright, 1983; Qureshi and Walker, 1989, pp. 99–100). Alternatively, filial caring may be conceptualised as part of an intergenerational pattern of care in which carers are repaying their parents for past sacrifices on their behalf and will themselves ultimately benefit from the support of someone in a younger generation (Finch, 1989, pp. 29–30).

Fifth, there is evidence of considerable dissent from filial care norms. In Finch and Mason's study (1990b, 1993, pp. 19–20), 39 per cent of respondents agreed with the bald statement that 'children have no obligation to look after their parents when they are old'. Further, when presented with a choice between state care, privately paid for care, care by relatives and care by friends, between 56 per cent and 70 per cent of respondents opted for some solution other than family care. Again, West *et al.* (1984) report not only that the majority of people see 'family and informal care only' as unacceptable but that people are less likely to advocate 'family care only' for older people than for dependent young people.

Finally, accounts of eldercare in other cultures suggest that the obligation to care is less extensive in Anglo-Saxon cultures than in cultures in which family obligations are rooted in collectivistic values. For example, studies of Asian communities in Britain show that the range of 'liable' relatives is in general widely defined, obligations may be perceived as including financial support and

household-sharing and values tend to emphasise interdependence and solidarity (Barker, 1984; Brah, 1986; Stopes-Roe and
Cochrane, 1990a).

In summary, the evidence under review suggests that in contemporary Anglo-Saxon cultures the injunction to care for older
family members is gendered (though not unambiguously so),
limited to a narrow range of relatives, circumscribed by independence and reciprocity norms and less extensive than in cultures in
which family life is rooted in collectivistic rather than individualistic values. It seems, therefore, that the obligation to care is
complex, ambiguous and often contradictory.

These data and arguments are extended by the proposition
advanced by Finch (1989) and Finch and Mason (1993) that commitments to kin are always the subject of negotiation. These scholars argue that, while a sense of familial responsibility underpins
patterns of assistance between kin and is a central characteristic of
family life, obligations are not absolute and unconditional but are
fluid and negotiable. They show that there is little evidence of the
precise specification of family responsibilities and little consensus
as to what should be done for relatives in any given set of circumstances. Caring commitments, they argue, are in practice established on the basis of a series of normative guidelines which
indicate how to work out the 'proper thing' to do in a given set of
circumstances rather than what should be done by whom.
Familial responsibilities, they maintain, do not flow automatically
from given relationships but are created over time in the context
of the history of particular relationships and the circumstances of
the individuals concerned. Support between relatives may therefore be patchy and idiosyncratic and cannot be predicted simply
on the basis of gender or familial relationships. Finch and Finch
and Mason thus provide us with a theoretical model in which
family obligations are seen, not as clearly defined, imposed and
coercive, but as limited and constructed through the interaction
of family members.

Patterns of Care

A stream of research reports from the 1960s onwards highlighted
the role of family members in eldercare. Researchers emphasised

that older people in institutional care are a small proportion of all older people and are likely to be without close relatives (Wall, 1989, p. 124). Further, they showed that state-provided community care is channelled towards those without family resources and is primarily concerned with crisis intervention and short-term support (Moroney, 1976; Walker, ed., 1982; Qureshi and Walker, 1989). Moreover, studies of informal care revealed that friends and neighbours contribute relatively little to the care of older people and, where they do, provide back up support for a family carer rather than direct care (Charlesworth *et al.*, 1984; Evandrou *et al.*, 1986; Qureshi and Walker, 1989, p. 119). Mark Abrams (1980) estimated that 90 per cent of the help received by older people aged 65–74 and 66 per cent of the help received by those aged 75 and over was provided by kin. In the USA, similar attempts to quantify the role of kin in eldercare suggested that 80 per cent of the constant care needs of older people were provided by kin (Hagestad, 1986).

This research literature also suggested that family care is overwhelmingly care by women. For example, an Equal Opportunities Commission survey (1980, p. 9) found that female carers outnumber male carers by three to one. Again, a small-scale study of couples caring for severely disabled older people found that, on the average weekday, the wives devoted 3 hours 11 minutes and the husbands 13 minutes to caring (Nissel and Bonnerjea, 1982). Further, a range of studies revealed that daughters find it more difficult than sons to resist demands for care, more often than sons give up their jobs or manipulate their work schedules to care, and get more support from sisters than from brothers (Wright, 1983; Lewis and Meredith, 1988, pp. 24–6; Matthews and Rosner, 1988). Studies of caring in ethnic minority groups also suggested that women are the mainstay of hands-on care even where, as in Asian communities, patrilineal bonds are stressed and older people live with a son rather than a daughter (Cameron *et al.*, 1989).

These research findings constructed the typical carer as a middle-aged married woman, produced an image of intensive and extensive family care, and were hailed as invalidating images of the decline of family responsibility (Allan, 1985; Qureshi and Walker, 1989). However, most were based on small samples and/or on samples of particular groups of older people – often of

older people with very severe disabilities – and could not legitimately be, though they frequently were, generalised to the population as a whole (Matthews, 1988; Arber and Gilbert, 1989).
Moreover, they conceptualised caring as women's unpaid care
within the family and focussed on daughters caring for parents.
Consequently, they could not take account of caring within marriage and by older people themselves.

Recent British research by Sara Arber, Jay Ginn and their associates reveals the partial nature of the early empirical generalisations. These researchers base their work on national General
Household Survey data and use a conceptual framework that dis-
aggregates the category of carer. They show that a significant proportion of eldercare takes place in the context of the marriage
relationship. Arber and Ginn (1991, pp. 132–6) report that the
time spent in caring for a spouse constitutes 48 per cent of all in-
house caring and 30 per cent of the total volume of eldercare.
Further, they emphasise that older people are themselves
significant providers of care. They show that older people provide
47 per cent of co-resident care, 17 per cent of extra-resident care
and 35 per cent of all informal care.

Like earlier researchers, Arber and Ginn find that, in the
absence of a spouse, children are the major providers of care and,
overall, are the main providers of care. They report that just over
one half of the informal care of older people – whether measured
in terms of numbers of carers or amount of time spent in caring –
is care for a parent or parent-in-law. However, these and other
studies also suggest that filial caring takes place within limited
parameters. Importantly, the proportion of older people living
with their relatives has declined rapidly over the past fifty years
(Lee, 1985; Dale *et al.*, 1987), caring is concentrated within households and is relatively limited as between households (Evandrou *et
al.*, 1986; Arber and Ginn, 1991, p. 134) and responsibility for
caring is typically assumed by a particular relative, with other
family members providing back-up support (Nissel and
Bonnerjea, 1982; Lewis and Meredith, 1988, pp. 30–1; Qureshi
and Walker, 1989, p. 87). Most older people are thus dependent
on one main carer and do not have a caring network.

Arber and Ginn's analyses, like earlier studies, point to gender
differences in filial care. They show that women spend considerably more time caring for parents and parents-in-law as well as for

other relatives, friends and neighbours than men do (Figure 4.1). However, their data suggest that gender differences in the proportions of women and men caring for parents, parents-in-law, other relatives and friends and neighbours are not as great as

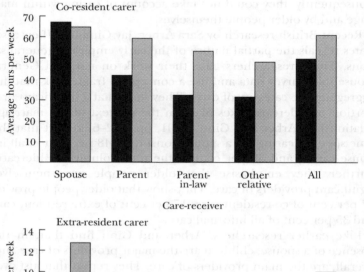

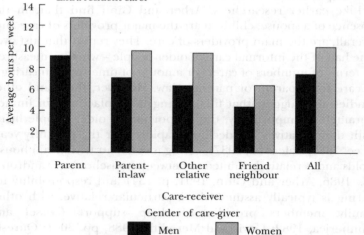

SOURCE   Arber and Ginn, 1991, Figure 8.1.

FIGURE 4.1   *Average hours of informal care provided by (a) co-resident carers and (b) carers in a separate household, by relationship between carer and cared for and by gender of carer.*

earlier studies had asserted. Further, they find that men and women are equally likely to be looking after a spouse and that men spend about the same amount of time (65 hours a week) in spouse-care as women. Overall, their data show that 12 per cent of women, compared with 9 per cent of men, are at any one time caring for an older person (Arber and Ginn, 1991, Table 8.1). Further, there are indications that differences in the proportions of women and men caring for parents and other relatives may in part at least be the outcome of taboos on intimacy between the sexes rather than of conventional identifications of women with caring. Charlesworth *et al.* (1984) report that when carers are relatives, 70 per cent of older men are cared for by male relatives, mostly sons, and 73 per cent of women by female relatives, mostly daughters. These researchers suggest that, since the majority of older people requiring help are women, preferences for same-sex care place a disproportionate responsibility for caring on female relatives.

Evidence of caring patterns among ethnic minority peoples is very patchy. The household composition data cited earlier (p. 51) seem to indicate that older Asians are more likely than older Afro-Caribbeans and 'white' people to be living with relatives. However, this may be a declining tendency given trends towards nuclear family households. Blakemore (1993) points to more general, though patchy, evidence of the erosion of family support among both Afro-Caribbean and Asian populations. Bould (1990) and McCalman (1990) suggest that, as in 'white' populations, eldercare tends to be the major responsibility of one family member.

Finally, it is becoming clear that earlier research emphases on the prevalence of familial caring had obscured the fact that evidence of familial care is not in itself evidence of its adequacy. In Britain, Qureshi and Walker (1989, pp. 94–5) estimate that the care needs of one in ten older people requiring substantial care and of seven in ten older people requiring moderate amounts of care are not being adequately met by either formal or informal carers. Further, though rates of elder abuse appear to be lower than for other forms of abuse, it seems that at all class levels and in all ethnic groups older people may be neglected, financially exploited, psychologically abused, violently maltreated, sexually assaulted or literally 'dumped' by their families. Pillemer and Finkelhor's (1988) large-scale American survey points to mistreatment rates of four in every 1000 for neglect, eleven in every 1000 for verbal aggression, twenty in every 1000 for physical aggression and an overall mistreatment rate of thirty-two in every 1000. They find that 52 per cent of the victims of abuse were men and 48 per cent were women. Of the perpetrators, 58 per cent were spouses and 24 per cent were children, a finding which may be the corollary of co-residence with spouses rather than with adult children.

Evidence of limitations to familial caring are paralleled by indications of the beginnings of a shift away from familial care and towards private sector care. The past twenty years has seen the mushroom growth in most Anglo-Saxon and northwest European societies of domestic help and nursing agencies and of hybrid living arrangements such as sheltered housing, retirement complexes and private residential and nursing homes. This rise in private sector care seems to be driven by a number of forces. Ungerson (1987, pp. 150–5) suggests that rising home ownership has provided the opportunity for realising capital in later life and has thus given older people greater access to private sector care than they had had in the past. Allen (1988) sees the boom in private sector care as an indication that carers are rebelling against family care. At the same time, a number of studies have found that older people are, on the one hand, desirous of maintaining their independence and, on the other, sensitive to their marginal and stigmatised status and anxious not to be a burden to their families (see pp. 129–30). They may therefore themselves prefer formal care when they need long-term care (Daatland, 1990) and sheltered housing or residential care to co-residence with a relative (Arber and Ginn, 1991, pp. 139–40, 1993, pp. 155–6).

In summary, the evidence and arguments under review suggest that the role of 'the family' in eldercare is complex, changing and ambiguous. On the one hand, family members provide the bulk of eldercare and are heavily engaged in caring either as spouses or as children. On the other hand, caring does not usually encompass extended households, is concentrated within the household and the married relationship and is in part provided by elders themselves. In addition, there is evidence of shortfalls in care and of the emergence of private sector care as an alternative to both state care and family care.

The research literature under review also suggests that although women are more often carers than men, gender differences in caring commitments are not as significant as had once been supposed. At the same time, the circumstances in which women and men care – and are cared for – appear to differ markedly: the evidence shows that the majority of male carers are husbands caring for a spouse and unmarried men caring for a parent with whom they have lived for most of their lives. Male caring therefore most often takes place in later life and in the context of a shared life whereas women more often care in the context of a filial or sibling relationship, more often provide extra-resident care, and more often engage in caring in middle age. Conversely, most older men are cared for by their wives whereas older women are more often cared for by daughters, daughters-in-law or sisters and are more likely to be in institutional care.

The Caring Experience

The caring professions have conventionally viewed care within the context of enduring family relationships as care which, in contrast with the intrinsically impersonal and bureaucratic care of the formal sector, provides security, privacy and love as well as physical care (see p. 126). At the same time, policy-makers have fostered family care as crucial to keeping state expenditure within affordable limits. From this 'traditional' perspective, family care is in the best interests of older people themselves and of the collectivity. In contrast, feminist gerontology focusses on carers as a social group, highlights the physical, social, emotional and economic costs of caring and argues that these costs fall disproportionately on women. This literature seeks to show that eldercare is one element in a sexual division of labour that is essentially exploitative of women.

Research in this vein suggests that caring may involve heavy and time-consuming physical work, restrict social activity, entail a heavy burden of responsibility, breach age and gender boundaries in disturbing ways, and be beset by the past and present conflicts of relationships which had never been good or which had deteriorated as a result of the stresses of the caring relationship. Ambivalence and conflict, physical ill-health, isolation, anxiety, resentment and guilt are depicted as common results (Nissel and Bonnerjea, 1982; Qureshi and Walker, 1989; Braithwaite, 1990). Tension and conflict between family members is also said to be a common outcome of family care. Some researchers suggest that sibling rivalry and/or resentment and guilt may arise where siblings are perceived as not shouldering their fair share of the burden of caring (Lewis and Meredith, 1988; Matthews and Rosner 1988; Brody *et al.*, 1989), others that the incorporation of an older relative into the family home compromises privacy, reduces the time available for husbands and children and generates increased costs and financial difficulty (Qureshi and Walker, 1989).

In addition, some feminist writers emphasise that women care for older relatives at the expense of their employment opportunities. This argument suggests that women, unlike men, frequently give up paid employment to care for older relatives or, where they continue in employment, lose time at work, opt for part-time rather than full-time employment and forego promotion and training opportunities (see G. Parker, 1990, for a review of this literature). Joshi (1992) estimates that at average 1990 income levels childless women who give up full-time employment during middle age to care for a disabled relative forego earnings of around £12 750 a year. Mothers (whose earning power would have been depressed by absence from the labour market during childbearing) forego earnings of around £10 500 a year. Joshi further points out that when carers return to the labour market their earning power is reduced as a result of loss of seniority.

The 'burdens of caring' thesis draws attention to the previously neglected and virtually invisible needs and problems of carers as a social group. It challenges community care policies as policies that reproduce women's caring and dependency and has been influential in securing some modest improvements in income benefits and support services for carers. However, the data and arguments reviewed in the preceding sections suggest that the distribution of caring tasks between women and men is more complex and not as unambiguously exploitative of women qua women as had been thought. As we have seen, caring obligations frequently fall to men, are structured not only by notions of 'women's role' but also by cultural taboos on intimacy between the sexes and by differences between women and men in morbidity and mortality and are governed by general guidelines rather than fixed and absolute norms. The characterisation of caring and of the cared for as a burden is also now being challenged from within feminism as well as by the disability movement. The 'generally jaundiced' view of caring found in much of the literature, says Wenger (1987), obscures the diversity of caring situations, is based on generalisations from case studies of particularly difficult situations and treats caring relationships as one-way relationships.

Accounts by Arber and her associates (Arber and Gilbert, 1989; Arber and Ginn, 1991, 1992) of caring in marriage, by unmarried sons and daughters and by married daughters clearly demonstrate the diversity of caring situations. Arber and her co-researchers maintain that caring between spouses in later life may present relatively few conflicts since occupational commitments have been relinquished, obligations to other primary kin are few and norms prescribing social activity outside the home limited. They further argue that caring in marriage develops out of a shared life, may therefore be associated with intimacy, companionship and reciprocity rather than obligation and duty, and may give a sense of purpose to later life, even though it may also bring physical stress and isolation. In contrast, married filial carers face a series of conflicts between, on the one hand, their caring obligations and, on the other, the demands of their own families, their career aspirations and their leisure norms. Further, they care not in the context of a shared life but on the basis of gendered kinship obligations and perceive caring as involving dependence rather than reciprocity. Married daughter carers, say Arber and Ginn, epitomise the 'woman in the middle' described by Brody (1981): the woman in middle age, in the middle generation between parents and children, in the middle of competing demands for their time and energy and in the middle of two competing sets of values – traditional values which emphasise family caring and new values which valorise women's search for an occupational identity. Finally, Arber and her associates suggest that unmarried sons and daughters are in a caring situation that is intermediate between that of spouses and that of married-daughters. They argue that for unmarried children conflicting kin obligations are likely to be limited, that conflicts between caring and paid employment and leisure may be tempered by statutory support (which they are more likely to receive than married daughters) and that where caring develops out of a history of household sharing, the potential for parent-child conflict may be tempered by the mutual reciprocities of a shared life.

In sum, Arber and her co-researchers suggest that caring in marriage is qualitatively different from filial caring. Caring between spouses, in their view, is one of the implicit bargains of the marriage contract whereas caring in other relationships tends to be perceived by both carer and cared for as an imposition and a burden. They thus point to the varied nature of caring contexts and experiences but reproduce images of filial caring (the caring relationship on which the 'burdens of care' thesis implicitly rests) as burdensome.

However, this view of filial caring has also been questioned. Wenger (1987) and Matthews (1988) argue that it is based on generalisations from 'hard' cases and one-sided interpretations of research findings. Dalley's (1993) review of caring studies emphasises the complexity and diversity of the range of emotions and attitudes that surround caring: she emphasises that some respondents report resentment, frustration, guilt, anxiety, overwhelming exhaustion and grim compliance with duty, others report affection, reciprocity, trust, friendship and even joy, while yet others report mixed and contradictory feelings. Lewis and Meredith (1988) suggest that filial caring is an essentially contradictory experience. They point out that affection carries an obligation to care that is distinct from obligations based on kinship, that for many daughters love and obligation are opposite sides of the same coin and that it is often difficult to establish where love ends and duty begins. Finally, Wenger (1987) argues that the emphasis in the caring literature on 'the burdens of caring' constructs caring as a one-way relationship whereas it may take place in the context of a long and continuing history of parental giving. A caring relationship, Wenger suggests, is not necessarily, or even usually a relationship of total dependence. This argument brings us to the discourses of the disability movement to which we now turn.

The Challenge to Ageism

In general, traditional ideologies, critical social gerontology and early feminist gerontology neither speak for older people as older people nor challenge ageism. Traditional ideologies recognise the needs of older people but tend to stereotype them as dependent and are frequently hijacked by a Right-wing political position that has as its primary concern limiting state expenditure. The dominant tendency in critical social gerontology has as its primary concern challenging capitalist processes. The dominant tendency in feminist gerontology represents the needs and interests of carers and challenges a patriarchally ordered sexual division of labour. However, the revisionist work of Arber and Ginn (1991) connects with the ideologies of the disability movement, a new political position which seeks to understand structures of care from the perspectives of disabled people of all ages, and to challenge prejudices against disability.

This new and as yet slender literature recognises that care within the family may be coerced and oppressive for women. It is nevertheless critical of the dominant tendencies in feminist gerontology. Morris (1992), for example, argues that in seeking to show how difficult and unrewarding the work of the carer is, most feminist research reproduces images of older and disabled people as dependent and burdensome. Feminist research, she argues, rarely sees either older or disabled people as having valuable lives, fails to recognise that caring is not always burdensome and has arrived at solutions to the dilemmas of caring (such as residential care) which are unacceptable to older people.

This political tendency draws attention to the 'burden' of being dependent and of being cared for within contemporary structures of care. Writers such as Oliver (1990), Morris (1992) and Wood (1991) argue that the dependence which is often associated with disability is socially created by a society which assumes that people with disabilities cannot take control of their lives and refuses to recognise their basic right to equality of recognition and to the resources that would enable them to be independent of family and state. In their view, dependence on either family members or state-provided services places those being cared for in a position of fundamental inequality with those providing care. They therefore advocate placing money directly in the hands of disabled people so that they may buy in the services which they themselves define as necessary and make free choices about the kind of personal assistance they require. That is, they urge an alternative to both family care and bureaucratically allocated state care which would allow people with disabilities to live in the community on their own terms and in control of the support they need. The boom in private sector care may in part reflect this pressure for independence.

This way of thinking about care reveals divisions between women which are based on their different position in the life course and/or their different levels of able-bodiedness. Feminist research on carers, Morris (1992) argues, fails to recognise that the majority of older people are women and does not generally include them in the category 'woman'. Instead it refers to them as 'such people' or 'dependent people'. Disabled and older women are thus separated off from women, treated as genderless and continuously presented as 'the other', 'the non-person'.

However, this political tendency overlaps with feminism. Later life is a woman's issue not only because caring outside marriage is more often undertaken by women but because women outnumber men in the older age groups, are age-stereotyped in gender-specific ways and have an economic position that is determined by gender divisions in domestic and industrial labour. Anti-ageist activism is thus populated by women, speaks on behalf of women and brings to its theory and action feminist models of social change (Reinharz, 1986). At the same time, recognition of the conflicting interests of women of different ages is effecting a rethinking of feminist gerontology – exemplified in the work of Arber, Ginn and their associates – in which the concerns and interests of older women are addressed and the ageist stereotypes that alienate older women from themselves and from younger women are confronted.

Summary

In sum, older people are at the centre of competing and contradictory ideologies, values and practices. The data and arguments under review show that notions of the moral responsibility of families to care for older people are an important element in traditional family ideologies and are embedded in state welfare policies. Traditional ideologies seem to be underpinned by notions of caring as a 'labour of love', as integral to femininity, as achievable only within the context of the personal and particularistic relationships of family life and as a rewarding activity. They recognise the needs of older people but tend to stereotype them as dependent and have been hijacked by Right-wing political concerns. Critical social gerontology and feminist gerontology challenge traditional values. The dominant tendencies in these discourses conceptualise caring as a work role that is carved up for women in an exploitative division of labour and as in principle separable from family relationships and deliverable in a variety of contexts and by different categories of people. They seek to redraw the boundaries between state responsibility and family responsibility and are pressing for the expansion of state-provided welfare services and a contraction of the caring role of family members. In anti-ageist activism, the concept of caring may be rejected altogether as implying dependence and subordination. This political tendency may reject both family care and state-provided care and demand instead the economic resources that would enable them to buy the care they need.

5

Violence and Sexual Abuse in Family Life

'Violence in the family' encompasses a range of phenomena: physical assaults of varying degrees of severity on children, sexual partners and older people, rape and other forms of sexual coercion of women and the sexual abuse of children. It has been a source of social concern and reform in Britain, the USA and other Western societies for over a century. However, in the past 'familial violence' tended to be perceived either as a 'lower-class phenomenon' or as the action of disturbed or drunken men, and public concern was intermittent and fleeting.

In the early 1970s, 'familial violence' began to be perceived as widespread and as taking place in the context of a long patriarchal tradition of male power and sexual privilege. Initially, public concern focussed on the physical abuse of children by their parents and of women by their husbands. More recently, however, wife rape and the incestuous abuse of children have moved centre stage. At the same time, concern has widened to include not only abuse in other intimate relationships but also the abuse of children in institutional care, sexual harassment in the workplace and the debasement of women and children in pornography.

This chapter focusses on the physical and sexual abuse of children and women in intimate relationships. Section 1 examines changing conceptions of violence and sexual abuse, Section 2 reviews the research literature on their prevalence and Section 3 examines psychopathological, structural and feminist perspectives on, and explanations of, their occurrence.

5.1 CONCEPTUALISING 'VIOLENCE' IN FAMILY LIFE

In most early accounts of violence and sexual exploitation in family life, 'the family' was construed in conventional terms as a married couple and their children, physical and sexual abuse were treated as distinct phenomena and studied separately, and each tended to be conceptualised in terms of a narrowly defined set of acts. For example, violence against a child was defined in Kempe *et al.*'s pioneering study (1962) of 'the battered child' as a clinical condition (a diagnosable physical injury) occasioned by deliberate physical assault. Similarly, Dobash and Dobash (1980, p. 11) restricted their account of violence in intimate relationships to 'wife-battering', which they defined as the systematic, frequent and brutal use of physical force against a marital or cohabiting partner. 'Child sexual abuse' and 'rape' were also conservatively defined, with the former being limited either to sexual intercourse or, less restrictively, to bodily contact and the latter to forced sexual intercourse.

Recently, however, definitional boundaries have been widened.

In the first place, definitions of physical violence have been expanded to include attempted and threatened violence and/or all acts of physical force from 'minor' incidents such as a slap or a push to brutal assaults involving deadly weapons (see, for example, Straus *et al.*, 1980; Saunders, 1988). Similarly, 'rape' has been conceptualised as encompassing not only all forms of sexual assault but also, as Bourque (1989) shows, all pressurised and unwanted sexual experiences whether or not physical force is involved. 'Child sexual abuse' has been similarly broadened. It is comprehensively defined by the Standing Committee on Sexually Abused Children as including any sexual activity involving an adult and a child that is intended to gratify the adult, whether or not physical or genital contact had taken place, whether or not coercion was used and whether or not harmful effects were discernible (Glaser and Frosh, 1988).

In the second place, the range of relationships defined as marking 'family violence' off from violence in other relationships and settings has been widened to include divorced and separated couples and cohabiting, dating and lesbian and gay relationships. In feminist discourse, the widening of definitional boundaries has been accompanied by the delineation of violence and sexual abuse in intimate relationships as typically perpetrated by men and directed against women and girls, and by the coining of terms that reflect its gendered character. For example, 'wife-battering' may be preferred to 'marital violence' (Dobash and Dobash,

1980) or 'father–daughter rape' to incest (Ward, 1984). Violence against wives and children is thus construed as a gender issue rather than a family issue.

In the third place, feminist analysis has moved towards merging violence (the use of physical force) with abuse (maltreatment) and the conceptualisation of male violence as a unitary phenomenon which includes all forms of sexual trespassing and of physical, verbal and emotional abuse against women and children. Thus domestic violence may be construed as including physical violence, pressurised sex and verbal and psychological abuse and the sexual abuse of children may be seen as violent even where force is not involved. Ramazanoglu (1987) presents as violence any action, use of words or structure that diminishes another human being whether or not force is involved. More circumspectly, Kelly (1988a, 1988b) proposes that abusive behaviours directed by men against women be conceptualised as a continuum of sexual violence, that is as a continuous series of elements or events that are connected to one another by the basic common characteristic of the use of physical, verbal and sexual coercion by men against women. Kelly argues that this way of thinking about male violence highlights the connections between 'typical' and 'aberrant' male behaviour and facilitates the documentation of the range of behaviour women experience as abusive. It links together aggressive male behaviours which are directed at women and which often use sex as a means of exercising domination, suggests that different forms of violence/abuse shade into one another and recognises that women respond to similar violent/abusive behaviours in different ways.

Underlying this plethora of definitions lie important difficulties in delimiting 'familial violence'.

The first area of difficulty concerns notions of what constitutes 'violence'. 'Conservative' definitions identify relatively easily measured phenomena, but leave out of the picture much that is malevolent, much that violates a family member's personal space and much that is psychologically injurious. More importantly, many scholars have argued that defining violence/abuse involves making judgements about what is 'normal' or 'acceptable' behaviour and that such judgements vary between social groups and change over time. A violent or abusive act, this argument suggests, is socially constructed as such and is not an objective phenomenon. In addition, conservative definitions of violence are criticised by feminist researchers on two grounds: for failing to recognise that criminal violence against women differs in degree but not in kind from everyday sexism and for failing to examine what women themselves define as violent (Kelly, 1988a, 1988b).

However, the broadening of definitional boundaries is also problematic. In the first place, as in all research, precise definitional categories are needed if researchers, their respondents and their reading public are to have a shared frame of reference. Further, it has been argued that 'catch all' definitions label as abusive and/or violent behaviours that many people would consider acceptable or at any rate not injurious (such as spanking to discipline a child), do not differentiate between behaviours which differ sharply in their motivation, severity and consequences, and trivialise severe acts of violence. Some researchers have attempted to resolve this problem by making distinctions between 'normal' and 'abusive' violence (as in Straus *et al.*, 1980) or between 'least hurtful', 'moderate' and 'most hurtful' violence (Leidig, 1981) or 'very serious' and 'serious' sexual abuse (Russell, 1983). This however raises further questions as to the criteria by which 'violence' is to be defined as 'normal' or 'abusive', 'serious' or 'less serious'. In addition, there are arguments which suggest that physical violence, verbal and psychological abuse and sexual exploitation are different phenomena and cannot be treated as a single entity. Gelles and Cornell (1990, pp. 23–4) argue that the physical pain and suffering which physical violence causes is unique. Physical violence and psychological violence, they maintain, are qualitatively different phenomena and require different explanations. Again, Bograd (1988) argues that physical violence threatens physical safety and bodily integrity in a way that other forms of abuse do not, and intensifies and changes the meanings of threats and humiliation. We must, it seems, think in terms of 'violences' and, in addition, distinguish between violence and abuse.

A second area of difficulty revolves around the question of whether the physical and sexual abuse of girls should be seen as distinct from that of women. Glaser and Frosh (1988, pp. 6–8) argue that it should. Childhood, say Glaser and Frosh, is defined by dependence. Therefore, sexual activity between an adult and a child always represents exploitation of power and can never, by definition, be anything other than abuse. Further, Glaser and Frosh maintain that there is no other relationship in which the power-dependence relationship is so clear and so universal, in which trust is so integral to dependence, and in which there is so marked a difference in physical and emotional maturity. Consequently, Glaser and Frosh argue, the sexual abuse of children is at least quantitatively different from other abusive situations and warrants study in its own right. La Fontaine (1990), pointing out that parents (mothers as well as fathers) stand in a power relationship to children (boys as well as girls), that mothers physically (though so far as is known relatively rarely sexually) abuse children and that boys as well as girls are abused, argues that child abuse is an abuse of *parental power*. Child abuse, La Fontaine implies, has its own specificities and is not co-terminous with men's abuse of women.

A further and related definitional problem stems from variability in the delineation of the boundaries of childhood. In Britain, legal norms define the age of consent as 16 for girls, and as 18 for boys in homosexual relations. In the United States, many states currently define the age of legal consent as 18 while the upper age of childhood is variously defined by researchers as 15, 16 and 17 (Bolton *et al.*, 1989, p. 33). However, Glaser and Frosh (1988) observe that chronological age is an inadequate indicator of the capacity to give informed consent. In addition, it has been argued that many definitions of child sexual abuse assume an adult perpetrator and in so doing exclude abuse by peers. Some researchers are therefore seeking to redefine sexual abuse in order to include coercion by peers. For example, Finkelhor (1984) defines as abusive relationships in which there is a five-year difference in the ages of victim and perpetrator up to a 'victim' age of 12 and a ten-year differential for older 'victims'.

Summary

The foregoing discussion suggests that boundaries between violence and non-violence are drawn in different ways at different points in time and by different social groups. Violence and abuse are not, it seems, objective phenomena waiting to be discovered but are defined by the values and concerns of a particular group at a particular time. They are political terms rather than diagnostic categories (N. Parton, 1985; Dingwall, 1989).

More specifically, the changes in the conceptualisation of familial violence which have taken place over the past two decades owe much to feminism's attempt to challenge men's behaviour and construct a new moral order. This feminist project has broadened our understandings of violence, depicted femicide, rape, child sexual abuse, sexual harassment, pornography and the physical abuse of women and children as interconnected rather than discrete issues, and valorised women's perceptions of violence. However, as we have seen, the widening of definitional boundaries seems to be analytically problematic. It appears to be essential to develop a terminology that, while drawing attention to the range of experiences that women find pressurising and unacceptable, makes distinctions between violent and non-violent abuse and between different kinds of violent/abusive behaviours. Some researchers are now seeking to do this by investigating not the prevalence of abuse or violence as a general category but the prevalence of a wide range of very specific behaviours.

In this text, 'violence' will be used to refer to all behaviours involving physical force. 'Sexual abuse' will be used to refer to all self-gratifying and pressurised sexual behaviours between adults or between adults and children whether or not the use of force is involved. 'Sexual exploitation' and 'sexual coercion' will be used to specify non-violent and violent sexual behaviours, respectively. The definitional convention adopted by the Standing Committee on Sexually Abused Children (see p. 145) will be followed in using the term 'child sexual abuse'. The sexual abuse of children by nuclear and extended family members will be specifically referred to as incestuous child abuse.

5.2 LEVELS OF VIOLENCE

Evidence of the extent and nature of violence and sexual abuse in family life comes from three major sources: (i) official statistics on reported and officially labelled violence/abuse, (ii) small-scale 'clinical' studies of the victims and perpetrators of reported violence/abuse and (iii) population surveys. However, each of these data sources has been shown to be flawed.

The research literature suggests that the stigma of exploitation and victimisation, feelings of helplessness and fear of the consequences keep women, children and men from revealing their plight to formal and informal agencies. Consequently, studies based on reported violence/sexual abuse provide us with data on only a small proportion of all abuse. For example, Dobash and Dobash's study of violence against women in sexual partnerships found that only 2 per cent of abusive experiences were reported to the police (Dobash and Dobash, 1980). Further, it seems that disclosure of an abusive experience does not necessarily mean its registration as abuse. Edwards (1989) shows that police reluctance to intervene in 'domestic disputes' translates into defining and recording procedures which in some police areas almost totally erase domestic violence from official crime statistics. In addition, it has been found that recording and categorisation procedures vary with the type of abuse, from agency to agency and area to area, and over time (Birchall, 1989; Gelles and Cornell, 1990; NCPCA, 1992). Consequently, the reliability of official data is suspect. Moreover, some groups and categories of offence seem to be systematically over-represented in official data and victim and offender studies. It has been found that violence and sexual exploitation in low income families more often come to the attention of formal and informal agencies than abuse in middle-class families (Taylor, 1989; Gelles and Cornell, 1990, pp. 53–4; La Fontaine, 1990, p. 59), that violence against men and the sexual exploitation of boys is under-reported relative to that of women and girls (Steinmetz, 1978; Bolton *et al.*, 1989; La Fontaine, 1990, pp. 84–8), that 'severe' forms of abuse – such as the severe physical injury of a young child, sexual abuse of children within the family and brutal wife assaults – more often come to public attention than less severe or less readily identifiable forms of abuse (Taylor, 1989; La Fontaine, 1990) and that wife rape and date rape are less often reported than rape by strangers (Lundberg-Love and Geffner, 1989). All these considerations suggest that official statistics and victim/offender studies are useful only as indicators of the number and categories of cases that come to

professional attention. Our analysis of prevalence levels will therefore rely on the third data source, population surveys.

Surveys in which the general population, or particular groups
in the population, are questioned about their experiences of
violence/sexual exploitation seek to record a representative set of
'facts'. However, they are also subject to a variety of problems.
The sensitivity and complexity of the issues being studied, the
necessary brevity of survey questionnaires and the fact that
respondents are often asked to recall past events mean that the
validity of respondent answers is suspect (Taylor, 1989; La
Fontaine, 1990; Dobash and Dobash, 1992, p. 276). Moreover,
surveys have covered different populations, used varying
definitions of physical and sexual abuse, encompassed different
categories of relationships and employed different kinds of data
gathering techniques. Unsurprisingly, therefore, population
surveys have produced a bewilderingly wide range of prevalence
levels. In a review and analysis of their findings, Peters *et al.*
(1986) show that higher levels of abuse are elicited by wide rather
than narrow definitions of abuse, face-to-face interviews rather
than self-administered questionnaires and specific rather than
general questions.

Peters *et al.* urge the development of a more careful methodology that will reveal the 'correct' definition of violence and
sexual abuse and the proper methods of discovering their prevalence. This plea for the development of correct procedures
seems to suggest that there are 'true' rates of violence/sexual
abuse which are waiting to be discovered. Many social scientists
doubt this. Taylor (1989) argues that because value structures
intervene between what is in the world and how it is perceived,
the prevalence of familial violence and sexual abuse is not an
objective reality waiting to be discovered. Further, he points out
that researchers themselves impose certain conceptions of abuse
on the data-gathering process by the way in which they define it
and by asking some questions and not others. The levels of
abuse revealed by any particular study are thus always determined by, and relate only to, the definitions used and populations studied.

These problems are not specific to research on violence/sexual
abuse in family life but they show that in this as in all areas of
research the available data must be cautiously interpreted. Not

only must data collection strategies be carefully scrutinised but, because theories of the social construction of abuse cast doubt on the very idea of a 'true' rate, the question to be asked when confronted by a particular statistic is not whether it is a 'true' estimate but what is the particular truth that the researcher was trying to discover (Taylor, 1989).

Nevertheless, the cumulative evidence of a variety of population surveys conclusively suggests that violence and sexual abuse in family life are neither rare phenomena nor underclass pathologies. We examine these findings looking at, first, physical violence against children, second, the sexual abuse of children and, third, violence and sexual abuse in sexual partnerships.

Parental Violence

The work of Straus, Gelles and their colleagues on the Family Violence Program at the University of New Hampshire in the USA provides us with the only available large-scale population surveys of child physical abuse. Their surveys – the first conducted in 1975 (Straus *et al.*, 1980) and the second in 1985 (Gelles and Straus, 1988) – suggest that physical force is routinely deployed by parents against children and is a patterned feature of family life. However, they also suggest that very severe violence is declining.

In their first study, Straus and his colleagues found that most parents regard slapping and spanking as necessary, normal and beneficial forms of discipline and had at some time resorted to some form of physical punishment (Straus *et al.*, 1980, p. 55). Sixty-three per cent of the parents in their sample admitted hitting the 'referrent child' (the child selected as the focus of the interview) during the year preceding the survey, 14 per cent admitted using 'severe violence' and 3.6 per cent admitted using 'very severe or abusive violence' (Table 5.1). In addition, Straus and his colleagues found that abusive assaults were not rare incidents but happened on average 4.5 times a year (Gelles and Cornell, 1990, p. 49). Violence, Straus and his colleagues found, was more often directed at younger children than older children and at boys than girls and was more often used by mothers than by fathers (Straus *et al.*, 1980, pp. 65–72). Nearly 18 per cent of the mothers in their sample, compared with just over 10 per cent

Table 5.1 *Parent-to-child violence in 1975 and 1985 in the USA*

	Rate per 1000 children[1]	
	1975	1985
A. Minor acts of violence		
1. Threw something	54	27
2. Pushed, grabbed, shoved	318	307
3. Slapped or spanked	582	549
B. Severe acts of violence		
4. Kicked, bit, hit with fist	32	13
5. Hit, tried to hit with something	134	97
6. Beat up	13	6
7. Threatened with gun or knife	1	2
8. Used gun or knife	1	2
C. Violence indices		
Overall violence (1–8)	630	620
Severe violence (4–8)	140	107
Very severe (abusive) violence (4,6,8)	36	19

[1] Aged 3 to 17.
SOURCE   Straus and Gelles, 1986, Table 1. Reprinted by permission © National Council of Family Relations.

of the fathers, admitted resorting to severe forms of violence (Straus, 1979).

In their second survey, Gelles and Straus (1988) found that, while the rate of overall violence had not changed, the proportion of children experiencing abusive violence had fallen by 47 per cent to just under 2 per cent (Table 5.1). They concede that, given the growing awareness of violence as abusive, parents may have been more reluctant to admit to using severe violence than in 1975, but they believe that changes in cultural attitudes, the development of prevention programmes, rising living standards and smaller families may have led to a 'real' decline in parental violence. Significantly, they found that there were now no differences between mothers and fathers in their use of severe violence (Gelles and Cornell, 1990, p. 57).

Comparable data for Britain are not available. However, a longitudinal study of childrearing by Newson and Newson

(1989) suggests that, as in the USA, physical punishment is believed in and is commonplace. These researchers found that smacking is seen by most mothers as an appropriate disciplinary tactic and for small children as the only really feasible disciplinary tactic. At age one, 62 per cent of the children in their study were smacked. At age four, 75 per cent of children were smacked at least once a week and nearly all were smacked at some time. As children matured, reasoning was perceived as feasible and smacking declined. Even so, Newson and Newson found that 41 per cent of seven-year-old children were smacked at least once a week and that 22 per cent of mothers used, and an additional 53 per cent threatened to use, straps, canes, slippers or other implements. However by age eleven, only 18 per cent of children were being smacked at least once a week and only 15 per cent of mothers used or seriously threatened to use a strap/stick/slipper. At all ages, mothers were the main 'punishment agents'. As in the Straus surveys, physical punishment was more often directed at boys than girls.

These studies show that physical punishment is more likely to be deployed in low income/working-class families than in high income/middle-class families (Straus *et al.*, 1980; Newson and Newson, 1989) and in families in which the father is unemployed than in families in which he is not (Straus *et al.*, 1980). In their first study, Straus and his colleagues found no differences between Anglo/Euro-American families and African-American families in their use of violence, but in their second study the proportion of African-American parents reporting the use of severe violence had risen (though not significantly), while the proportion of Anglo/Euro-American parents reporting severe violence had fallen. As a result the rate of severe violence toward 'black' children was twice that for 'white' children (Hampton *et al.*, 1989). Newson and Newson's only data (1980) on ethnic differences suggest that Afro-Caribbean parents more often, and Punjabi parents less often, use physical punishment than Anglo-Saxon parents.

These slender survey data are complemented by a voluminous body of data on *reported* child physical abuse. In most Anglo-Saxon countries, the growth of public concern has been accompanied by dramatic increases in the incidence of reported abuse. In the USA, where the reporting of suspected abuse is now mandatory, reported abuse increased by 58 per cent between 1980 and 1986 (Gelles and Cornell, 1990, p. 51) and is continuing to rise, though at a lower rate (NCPCA, 1992). In 1990–91, an estimated eleven in 1000 children were reported to child protection agencies as having been physically abused (NCPCA, 1992). In Britain, reported physical abuse increased by 30 per cent between 1978 and 1986 (Birchall, 1989, Table 1.4) and since then has fluctuated within relatively narrow limits (Creighton, 1992, Table 1). Creighton (1992, Figure 1) suggests that in 1990 just under one in 1000 children under 16 were officially diagnosed as having been physically abused.

Most studies of reported child physical abuse find that children are as often or more often abused by their mothers than by their fathers. However, Creighton's meticulous analyses (1992) of NSPCC child abuse registers casts doubt on this finding. She shows that when differences in the proportion of children living with their mothers/mother substitutes and fathers/father substitutes are taken into account, children are more likely to be abused by their fathers and father substitutes than by their mothers and mother substitutes.

Data on the family circumstances of children who have been identified as abused have been exhaustively analysed in attempts to identify 'risk' factors. Creighton's analysis of NSPCC data (1992) shows that in England and Wales:

— children under five constitute the majority of reported cases of abuse and, overall, registered children are younger than children in general;

— boys more often than girls appear on child physical abuse registers;

— just over one-third of registered children live with both their natural parents whereas nationally 73 per cent of children of comparable socio-economic backgrounds and over 90 per cent of all children live with both their natural parents;

— 43 per cent of fathers are in employment compared with 95 per cent of all fathers with dependent children;

— Social Classes 1 and 2 are significantly under-represented, and Social Classes 4 and 5 significantly over-represented amongst the employed fathers of abused children;

— the families of abused children are more often in receipt of income support than families in general.

Creighton's findings are replicated by other studies of reported abuse and receive broad support from the population surveys cited earlier.

The Sexual Abuse of Children

Surveys which seek to establish the prevalence of child sexual abuse have used widely varying definitions of abuse, differed as to whether they included incidents involving peers, and asked questions of varying degrees of specificity. Consequently, they have produced widely ranging results. In Britain, the prevalence levels reported have ranged from a 'low' of 3 per cent where a narrow definition of abuse was used (BBC, 1987) to a 'high' of 46 per cent where the definition of abuse was broadened to include non-contact offences such as flashing, erotic talk or obscene telephone calls (Nash and West, 1985). Similarly, North American surveys report prevalence rates ranging from 6 per cent to 62 per cent for women and from 3 per cent to 31 per cent for men (Peters *et al.*, 1986, p. 19). However, these surveys demonstrate conclusively that when the whole range of experiences that may be considered abusive are taken into account – from obscene telephone calls to forced intercourse, from once-only experiences to repeated abuse and from abuse by strangers to abuse by family members – then abusive experiences are commonplace. Unsurprisingly, since, as La Fontaine (1990) points out, strangers rarely have the opportunity to be alone with a child, these surveys show that abuse by known people forms a high proportion of abuse involving physical contact. Tables 5.2 and 5.3 demonstrate the findings of one major British and one major American study.

As these Tables show, incestuous abuse forms a 'relatively' small, but none the less 'sizeable', proportion of contact abuse. It constitutes the overwhelming majority of reported abuse cases, has become the major focus of contemporary moral panics about child sexual abuse and tends, albeit mistakenly, to be equated with child sexual abuse (Kelly, 1988c). It breaches not only social norms about the sexual innocence of childhood but also social taboos on sexual relationships between 'blood' relatives and relatives who substitute for 'blood' relatives (such as stepfathers). Survivor accounts suggest that it represents a breach of trust, constitutes an ever-present and inescapable menace in the home and

Table 5.2   *Experiences of sexually abused children, British data*

	Baker and Duncan[1] Men and women
	%
Abuse by a stranger	51
Abuse by known person	49
Abuse by a family member	14
Non-contact abuse	51
Contact abuse not involving intercourse	44
Abuse involving intercourse	5
One incident involving one person	63
Repeated abuse	23
Multiple abuse	14

[1]   This survey was based on a random national survey of 2019 women and men and used an omnibus definition of abuse that included contact and non-contact experiences.
SOURCE   Baker and Duncan, 1985. Reprinted from *Child Abuse and Neglect*, 9, Anthony W. Baker and Sylvia P. Duncan, 'Child Sexual Abuse: A Study of Prevalence in Great Britain', 457–67, Copyright 1985, with kind permission from Elsevier Science Ltd. The Boulevard, Langford Lane, Kidlington, Oxford.

is a singularly traumatic experience. Compliance may be achieved by the exploitation of the child's affection, by the exercise of parental authority and, in some cases, by the use of force or threatened force (Nelson, 1987, pp. 25–6). Incidents may be repeated over years, may involve one or all of the children in the family and, though the average age for the onset of abuse would appear to be 10–11 years, may begin at any age from infancy onwards and may continue into adulthood (Finkelhor and Baron, 1986).

Russell (1986, ch. 5) suggests that the incidence of child sexual abuse has increased over the course of the twentieth century. She estimates that the incidence of incestuous and extra-familial abuse quadrupled between the early 1900s and the early 1970s. Relatedly, she finds that, with the exception of the youngest cohort, each successive cohort of the women in her sample was more likely than each older cohort to have experienced sexual

Table 5.3   *Experience of sexual abuse in childhood, San Francisco data*[1]

Abuse experience	%
Proportion of women experiencing:	
abuse (intra/extra-familial)	38[2]
intra-famililial abuse	16
extra-familial abuse	31
Relationship of abuser to victim:	
stranger	11
known but unrelated	60
relatives	29
Proportion of incidents classified as:	
very serious[3]	
intra-familial	23
extra-familial	53
serious[3]	
intra-familial	41
extra-familial	27
least serious[3]	
intra-familial	36
extra-familial	20

[1] This study was based on a random sample of 930 San Francisco women aged 18 and older.

[2] Abuse was defined as unwanted sexual contact. Intrafamilial abuse was defined as abuse by a relative, however distant the relationship, and included unwanted sexual contact by an age peer.

[3] Russell defined as 'very serious' attempted and completed, forced and unforced oral, anal and vaginal intercourse as well as cunnilingus and analingus; as 'serious' completed and attempted, forced and unforced, genital fondling, digital penetration and simulated intercourse, and as 'least serious' completed and attempted, forced and unforced sexual touching.

SOURCE   Russell, 1983.

abuse in childhood. This finding is replicated by Baker and Duncan (1985).

All the available evidence shows that girls are significantly more likely to be abused than boys. However, population surveys suggest that the abuse of boys is more common than studies based on reported abuse had indicated. American surveys point to a mean ratio of 2.5 female 'victims' to every male 'victim' (Finkelhor and Baron, 1986). Baker and Duncan's (1985) British survey yields a ratio of 3 female to 2 male 'victims'. The research literature also suggests that the circumstances in which girls and boys are abused differ. It appears that boys are more often than girls abused outside the home – a finding which may reflect differences in the independence which boys and girls are typically allowed – and more often experience contact abuse, repeated abuse and abuse in the context of sex rings and the like (Finkelhor, 1984, ch. 10; Baker and Duncan, 1985; Bolton *et al.*, 1989, p. 45). However, abuse within the family is overwhelmingly experienced by girls, with the abuse of boys typically occurring in the context of multiple abuse situations. According to MacLeod and Saraga (1988), the ratio of female to male victims shifts from 3:2 for all sexual abuse to 5:1 where only sexual abuse within the family is considered.

The available evidence also shows that sexual abuse – whether it occurs within the family or outside the family and whether its 'victims' are boys or girls – is nearly always perpetrated by men. According to Finkelhor (1984, p. 177), population survey findings on the proportion of children abused by women range from 0 to 10 per cent where the 'victims' are girls and from 14 to 27 per cent where the 'victims' are boys. Grandfathers, uncles, brothers, fathers, stepfathers and mothers' boyfriends have all been implicated in incestuous abuse but stepfathers and mothers' boyfriends seem to pose the greatest risk. In Russell's San Francisco study (Russell, 1986, ch. 16), one in six women with a stepfather was abused by her stepfather before the age of 14 whereas 'only' one in forty-three women with a natural father was abused by her father. In addition, she finds that abuse by stepfathers more often involved some form of intercourse and was more often violent. Finkelhor (1984, p. 25) reports not only that stepfathers more often abuse their children than natural fathers but that step-parenthood raises the risk of abuse by others. He finds that stepdaughters are five times as likely to be abused by their stepfather as daughters are likely to be abused by their father. They are also five times as likely to be abused by a friend of one or other parent.

Bolton *et al.* (1989) question the rarity of abuse by women. They suggest, first, that childrearing gives women a measure of physical familiarity with children within which sexual abuse may masquerade as affection and, second, that boys may be more reluctant than girls to report abuse. They cite as evidence of the frequency of abuse by women a study by Fritz *et al.* (1981) in which 60 per cent of the young men reporting abuse claimed to have been abused by women. However, there is limited evidence of abuse by women and La Fontaine (1990) maintains that the effort to uncover it may be a product of men's discomfort with the idea that child sexual abuse is overwhelmingly perpetrated by men.

Both British and American studies of the class distribution of child sexual abuse suggest that sexually abused children are equally likely to be found in all social classes (Baker and Duncan, 1985; Nash and West, 1985; Finkelhor and Baron, 1986; BBC, 1987). However, these findings must be interpreted with caution. They are, with few exceptions, based on the present class position of 'victims' and denote neither their class status as children nor the class position of abusers. Moreover, contradictory evidence of a link between low income/poor education and abuse is reported by Kinsey *et al.* (1953) and Finkelhor (1984).

Russell (1986) finds that incestuous abuse (as distinct from abuse in general) is also evenly distributed across the social class structure. In addition, she shows that 'victimisation' rates are similar for African-American and Anglo-American women but relatively high for Latino women and relatively low for Asian women. These data must again be regarded as tentative since they are based on respondents' assessment of the occupational status of their abusers, are limited to those instances where the abuser's status was known and represent the findings of only one study.

Finally, some researchers have drawn attention to the sexual abuse of children by peers. The prevalence of sexual harassment on the school playground has been highlighted by Mahony (1985), Lees (1986a) and Halson (1991). Kelly (1988c) maintains that abuse by peers ranges from touching assaults to rape and attempted rape and is perpetrated by strangers, boyfriends and siblings. Studies which have identified the ages of abusers who come to the attention of 'the authorities' have, with a remarkable degree of consistency, found that about one in three abusers of both girls and boys are themselves under eighteen (NCH, 1992, pp. 7–8).

Violence and Sexual Coercion in Sexual Partnerships

Accounts of violence in sexual partnerships suggest that it is found in dating, cohabiting, marital and post-marital relationships, tends to begin early in a relationship and to escalate in frequency and intensity over time and, in its more severe forms, is most often directed by men against women (see Smith, 1989, for an overview of the literature). It may be occasioned by disputes over money, sex, or the performance of domestic responsibilities and ranges from a single slap or shove to assaults involving being kicked, punched, choked, bitten, burnt, thrown against walls, down stairs or out of cars, stabbed or shot. The injuries caused range from cuts, bruises and black eyes through broken bones to fractured skulls, stab wounds and internal injuries. Permanent disfigurement, persistent ill health, mental anguish, the miscarriage of a child and death are among its outcomes.

The pervasiveness of violence in sexual partnerships has been asserted on the basis of (i) analyses of reported 'domestic violence' as a proportion of all reported criminal violence and (ii) surveys of its prevalence in the general population.

In a 'classic' study, conducted in Edinburgh and Glasgow in the late 1970s, Dobash and Dobash (1980) show that domestic violence forms a significant proportion of reported criminal violence.They found that assault on wives or cohabitees constituted 26 per cent of all reported violent crime and 76 per cent of all reported family violence. In contrast, assaults on husbands constituted just over 1 per cent and mutual assault 0.6 per cent of reported family violence. Edwards (1989) argues that homicide statistics tell the same story. The most recent homicide figures for England and Wales show that in 1991 41 per cent of all female homicide victims were murdered by their current or former husband, cohabitee or lover whereas only 8 per cent of male homicide victims were murdered by a current or former wife, cohabitee or lover (Home Office, 1992, Table 4.4).

Of the limited number of surveys specifically designed to establish the prevalence in the general population of violence in sexual partnerships, the family violence surveys of Straus and his associates (see p. 152) and Mooney's recent British survey (Mooney, 1993) warrant particular attention, the Straus surveys because they are large-scale national surveys, were the first to demonstrate the prevalence of violence in marriage and have generated a wealth of research on violence in intimate relationships, Mooney's study because it is the only large British population survey. Both Straus and his associates and Mooney show that violence in intimate relationships is neither a rare nor inconsequential occurrence.

In their first survey, Straus *et al.* (1980) found that nearly one in four wives and nearly one in three husbands believed that slapping between marital partners is 'at least somewhat necessary, normal or good'. Further, they found that 28 per cent of couples had experienced violence at some point in their marriages, that 13 per cent had experienced abusive violence and that women were nearly as likely as men to resort to severe and non-severe violence (see pp. 164–5 for a further discussion of this issue). In their follow-up study ten years later, Gelles and Straus (1988) report that the annual incidence of men's violence against their partners had fallen somewhat, that women's violence was much the same as it had been ten years earlier and that overall levels were essentially unchanged (Table 5.4). Straus and his co-researchers found marital violence to be markedly more common in disadvantaged than in advantaged social groups. They found that it was more common in low-income groups than in high-income groups, among couples in working-class occupations than among couples in middle-class occupations, in relationships in which the male partner is unemployed or in part-time employment than in relationships in which he is employed and in African-American households than in Anglo-American households.

Mooney provides broadly similar prevalence data for Britain (Table 5.5). Twenty-seven per cent of the women in her North London sample had experienced physical injury in domestic rows and 19 per cent of the men admitted to having used violence

Table 5.4 *Marital violence in the USA, 1975 and 1985*

		Rate per 1000 couples	
Violence index		1975	1985
A.	Husband-to-wife		
	Overall violence[1]	121	113
	Severe violence[1]	38	30
	(Wife beating)		
B.	Wife-to-husband		
	Overall violence	116	121
	Severe violence	46	44
C.	Couple		
	Overall violence	160	158
	Severe violence	61	58
Number of cases		2143	3520

[1]   The categories of violence are the same as those used by Straus and his associates in studying parental violence (see Table 5.1). Overall violence comprised categories 1 to 6 and severe violence comprised categories 4–8.

SOURCE Straus and Gelles, 1986. Reprinted by permission, © National Council on Family Relations.

Table 5.5 *Prevalence of domestic violence among north London women*

Type of violence	% of women experiencing physical violence
Threats of violence or force	27
Actual violence	
Grabbed, pushed or shaken	32
Punched or slapped	25
Kicked	14
Head butted	6
Attempted strangulation	9
Hit with a weapon/object	8
Composite violence[1]	30

[1]   A general rate excluding threats of violence and being grabbed, pushed or shaken.

SOURCE Mooney, 1993, Table 2.

against their partners. In addition, Mooney found that most men see violence as a legitimate means of resolving conflict: only 37 per cent of her respondents said that they would not resort to violence in any of a variety of hypothetical conflict situations.

Studies of levels of violence in different categories of intimate relationships suggest that violence is more common and more severe in cohabiting relationships than in dating or married relationships. For example, Stets and Straus (1989) find that, over the course of a year, violence occurs in 35 in every 100 cohabiting relationships, in 20 in every 100 dating relationships and in 15 in every 100 married relationships. Further, they find that severe violence by both partners is six times as likely to be found in cohabiting relationships as in dating and married relationships. These relationship differences remain after controlling for age, education and occupational status. Stets and Straus find that in all three types of relationships violence by both partners is the majority pattern, female only violence the intermediate pattern and male only violence the least common pattern.

This study, like the Straus surveys cited earlier, point to high levels of violence by women. On the basis of these data, Straus and his co-researchers have suggested that husband-battering is the most under-reported form of family violence (Steinmetz, 1978) and they and other scholars have labelled violence in sexual partnerships 'mutual combat' or 'family violence'. However, feminist and feminist-influenced researchers have severely criticised the measurement instruments and methodology of Straus and his co-researchers and have argued, on the basis of historical data, various victims of crime surveys and studies of reported violence, that violence in sexual partnerships is largely perpetrated by men (see, for example, Dobash and Dobash, 1992, pp. 264–81). Further, they have argued that women who use violence against men usually do so in self-defence or as retaliation against men's violence, tend to do so only after prolonged victimisation and rarely use violence likely to cause severe injury (Saunders, 1988). Thus, Browne (1987) argues that women who kill their husbands do so as a 'desperate final response' to repeated violence whereas men kill their wives as a logical extension of the abuse they have dispensed for years.

However, there is clear evidence of woman-initiated violence. The American surveys under review show that in a significant minority of relationships only the woman is violent. Further, studies of lesbian relationships suggest that violence is no less likely to occur in lesbian than in heterosexual relationships (Brand and Kidd, 1986). Renzetti (1992) finds that in abusive lesbian, as in abusive heterosexual, relationships violence begins early in a relationship, is recurrent and may involve vindictive, brutal and life-threatening behaviours.

Finally, there is growing evidence of the pervasiveness of rape, sexual assault and pressurised sex in sexual partnerships. Russell's pioneering study (Russell, 1990) shows that wife rape occurs quite frequently. Defining rape as forced (actual or threatened) vaginal, oral and anal sex as well as forced digital penetration, Russell found that 14 per cent of the married or formerly married women in her San Francisco sample had been the victims of rape or attempted rape by their husbands or ex-husbands. In the sample as a whole, 44 per cent of women had experienced rape or attempted rape. Eight per cent were the 'victims' of husbands or ex-husbands, 3 per cent of boyfriends, 12 per cent of dates and 6 per cent of lovers/ex-lovers. The relationships between all victims and their abusers is shown in more detail in Table 5.6. In the only comparable British survey, 23 per cent of women said that they had been subjected to forced sex by their partners (Mooney, 1993).

Studies of date rape and of other forms of sexual aggression on American university campuses provide some insight into the prevalence of sexual coercion in courting relationships. They reveal 'victimisation' rates that in some instances are as high as 77 per cent (Muehlenhard and Linton, 1987), the existence of a fraternity culture of gang rape (Sanday, 1990) and the readiness of many young men to obtain sex by force in a variety of circumstances (Scully, 1990, pp. 51–3). These findings cannot be generalised to all young people as it is probable that the culture of student peer groups, together with their freedom from parental and other controls, produces a particularly rape-prone environment. Nevertheless, they show that there are cultural milieux in which sexual coercion is ever-present.

Table 5.6   *Prevalence of rape/attempted rape by relationship between victim and assailant*

Relationship with victim at time of first rape	% of women in sample	% of assailants in each relationship category[1]
Stranger	11	16
Acquaintance	14	23
Friend of family	2	2
Friend of respondent	6	7
Authority figure	6	8
Relative	3	4
Date	12	16
Boyfriend	3	4
Lover or ex-lover[2]	6	8
Husband or ex-husband[3]	8	10
Total		98

[1]   Some women had been threatened/raped by more than one assailant.
[2]   Lover was defined as a friend, date or boyfriend with whom voluntary sex had previously occurred. The distinction between dates and boyfriends was left to the respondent.
[3]   Presented here as a percentage of the entire sample and not of married/formerly married women only. Excludes cases of forced oral, anal and digital sex.
SOURCE   Russell, 1990, Rape in Marriage, 2nd. ed., Table 5.2. Reprinted by permission © Indiana University Press.

Summary

Although population surveys have used widely differing definitions of violence and abuse and reported widely varying prevalence levels, some broad conclusions may be drawn from the existing research. First, it is clear that the proportion of the population who have experienced some form of physical violence and sexual abuse within family life is higher than is commonly believed and may even be widespread. Second, physical violence and sexual aggression tend to be initiated by men and, at least in their more severe manifestations, are more commonly deployed by men than by women. Nevertheless, it is not the exclusive property of men and is not limited to relations involving men. Third, whereas girls are overwhelmingly the victims of child sexual abuse, boys are more often than girls the victims of child physical abuse. Fourth, physical violence and sexual abuse are found in all social groups but would seem to be more common in socially disadvantaged than in socially advantaged groups. Fifth, physical violence and child sexual abuse seem to be significantly more common in cohabiting and step-relationships, respectively, than in married family relationships. This finding holds even when controls for socio-economic status are introduced.

5.3 PERSPECTIVES ON FAMILIAL VIOLENCE/SEXUAL ABUSE

Psychology and psychiatry, conventional (non-feminist) sociology and feminism provide us with three very different interpretations of violence and sexual abuse in family life. Psychological perspectives locate familial violence/sexual abuse in individual pathologies. Non-feminist sociology locates familial violence/sexual abuse in a range of socio-structural processes, including 'deviant' subcultures, the structure of family life, class inequality and even, on occasion, gender structures. Feminist approaches also locate familial violence and sexual abuse in socio-structural processes. However, they place gender structures at the centre of their analysis, define these structures as patriarchal and conceptualise violence and sexual abuse in intimate relationships as violence against women rather than as family violence. These very different explanations of familial violence and sexual abuse are examined in this section.

Psychopathological Perspectives

Most early research on violence and sexual abuse in family life was conducted by psychologists and mental health therapists. This research tradition presents us with diverse and often complex arguments. Nevertheless, almost all the psychological literature is informed by the presumption that violence and sexual abuse are exceptional and pathological behaviours and are rooted in the defective personalities of the individual concerned.

Reviews of this literature (for example, Adams, 1988; L. Smith, 1989; Dobash and Dobash, 1992) show that it presents men who batter their sexual partners as holding rigid views of men's and women's roles, as insecure in their masculine identity and as using violence as a means of demonstrating power and adequacy; as morbidly jealous, sadistic, passive-aggressive, addiction-prone and pathologically dependent; as having poor communication skills, low frustration tolerance, weak impulse control and a proneness to immature outbursts of anger; and as suffering from low self-esteem, feelings of helplessness, powerlessness and inadequacy, fear of intimacy and fear of abandonment, depression and stress.

The catalogue of psychopathologies ascribed to parents (fathers and mothers) who physically abuse their children and to incestuous fathers is also long and diverse. Nigel Parton (1985, pp. 134–6) observes that parents who abuse their children are described in some studies as low in impulse control, grossly immature and chronically aggressive, in others as rigid, cold and detached, and in yet others as excessively anxious, chronically depressed and guilt-prone; some studies find that they have low intelligence while others find that they display the full range of intelligence. Incestuous fathers have been seen as passive, inadequate and pathetic when faced with authority but as exercising an unusual degree of domination over their families, as socially introverted and over invested in their families, and as suffering from feelings of phallic inadequacy and/or impaired impulse control (Waldby *et al.*, 1989).

In pathological models, the 'victims' of violence and sexual abuse become precipitators of their own victimisation and, like perpetrators, are said to be psychologically flawed. Thus, in studies of violence and sexual coercion in intimate relationships, women may be presented as suffering from psychological inadequacies which provoke men to violence (Snell *et al.*, 1964; Gayford, 1975, 1976), render them incapable of taking effective action in response to violence (Walker, 1984; Shainess, 1984) or make them addicted to the drama, chaos and excitement of violence and danger (Pizzey and Shapiro, 1982; Norwood, 1985, 1988). Women have also been depicted as an important element in men's sexual abuse of children (Kempe and Kempe, 1978; Justice and Justice, 1979; the Secretary of State for Social Services, 1988). They have been portrayed as denying their husbands sex, as unable to maintain a nurturing, affectionate relationship with their husbands and daughters, and as physically absent from the household. Whatever the cause of these circumstances – pregnancy, illness, exhaustion, imputed personality defect, the necessity of taking on a breadwinning role or the sexual boorishness, impotence or drunkenness of the husband – men's sexual desires tend to be privileged and mothers are seen as forsaking their wifely and maternal roles and so producing an incestuous situation.

Abused children do not escape this pathologising. Finkelhor (1979) observes that accounts of children's contribution to their sexual victimisation fall into two categories: the first sees the child as a seductress who actively arouses or seeks the sexual attentions of adults, the second accords the child a less active role but nevertheless interprets a lengthy liaison as indicating the child's collusion. In such accounts children may be depicted as seducing their fathers by their unusual attractiveness and charm, as having an abnormal desire for adult attention or sexual excitement, as experiencing emotional needs which have not been met in conventional ways or as simply frightened, lonely, withdrawn, dependent or compliant.

In some psychopathological theories, the origins of the pathologies imputed to offenders and their victims are located in unruly biological drives and in others in bio-chemical or neurological disorders, but the dominant explanation derives from psychoanalytic and psychological theories of the importance of early childhood experiences in personality development. The earliest versions of this argument focussed on the psychodynamics of the mother – child relationship and had a distinctly Freudian orientation. More recently, a cognitive-behavioural approach in which both violent and sexually abusive behaviour are conceptualised as learned behaviours has been advanced. For example, violent or abusive behaviour has been linked with childhood experiences of violence and/or sexual abuse (Straus *et al.*, 1980) and women's failure to leave an abusive relationship has been conceptualised as learned helplessness (Walker, 1984).

The arguments so far discussed focus on the internal pathology of individual perpetrators and their 'victims'. However, attempts have been made to move the focus of analysis away from the individual and towards the network of family relationships within which violence or sexual abuse occur. This family systems approach conceptualises families as systems which, when functioning normally, maintain a homeostatic state and meet the needs of family members. It then conceptualises violence and sexual abuse as arising out of disturbances in family relationships that impair the ability of the family to meet the needs of its members. Thus, accounts of violence against wives speak of mutual psychic imbalances that create violence-prone systems (Dobash and Dobash, 1992, pp. 238–9). Similarly, Furniss's (1984) account of father – daughter incest speaks of emotio-sexual problems and dependences which lead to a breakdown of 'normal' age and sex family boundaries and thence to sexual liaisons in which the child functions both as parent and partner to the father.

In family systems theory, the entire family is disturbed and violence/sexual abuse are symptoms of this underlying dysfunctionality. This thesis locates violence and sexual abuse within the network of family relationships and implicates *the relationship* between wives and husbands, or between parents and children or even between siblings. However, despite the affiliation to relationship concepts, violence and sexual abuse are constructed as psychological diseases.

In sum, psychopathological explanations locate familial violence within the individuals concerned and explain it in terms of personal pathologies. They treat violence and abuse as not fully social behaviours, may be as much concerned with the pathology of the 'victim' as with the pathology of the offender, and render the social and cultural context invisible. Further, whether the phenomenon being discussed is the battering of wives or children, the sexual coercion of wives or the sexual abuse of children, the failure to conform appropriately to traditional images of masculinity and femininity is a recurring theme. In some accounts, men and women are seen as rigidly adhering to highly traditional sex-role identities, in others men are depicted as unable to live up to images of masculinity while wives are depicted as displaying masculine traits.

This model of violence and sexual abuse in the family has been tremendously influential. It underlies training in the therapeutic professions, is reproduced by the media, informs the policing process and forms the basis of the *modus operandi* of the social services (Pahl, ed., 1985; Edwards, 1989; Dobash and Dobash, 1980, 1992). However, non-feminist and feminist sociologists alike have argued, though from different standpoints, that it is fatally flawed.

First, the methodology of studies in this tradition has been scathingly criticised. It has been argued that they are based on small and unrepresentative samples, have not used control groups, fail to define the imputed personality flaws so that there is no way of knowing precisely what is being referred to, and are informed not by specific hypotheses drawn from past research, but by the excuses and rationalisations of offenders, the subjective values and interpretations of the researchers and the common-sense assumptions of everyday thought (N. Parton, 1985, pp. 134–9; Smith, 1989, p. 24; La Fontaine, 1990 *passim*; Scully, 1990, p. 40).

Second, many of its findings have been challenged. Reviews of this literature show that it has attributed a bewildering and contra-dictory range of personality characteristics to offenders and their victims and has not identified a personality profile that is specific to violent or incestuous men, women or families (N. Parton, 1985, p. 135; Glaser and Frosh, 1988, pp. 21–3; Scully, 1990, pp. 37–41; Dobash and Dobash, 1992, p. 223). Further, it has been suggested that the personality characteristics attributed to abusers may be the consequence of being labelled an abuser rather than the cause of abuse and that the imputed characteristics of victims of abuse may be the consequence rather than the cause of victimisation (Gelles and Cornell, 1990, pp. 55, 73–4; Scully, 1990, pp. 44–5; Dobash and Dobash, 1992). Furthermore, and devastatingly, survey evidence of the frequency of violence and sexual abuse has been used to argue that they are not exceptional and abnormal behaviours but are widespread. The ubiquity of violence in the family, says Freeman (1979), means that it cannot be explained in terms of exceptional and aberrant behaviours.

A third set of criticisms are concerned with the conceptual basis of the psychopathological thesis and its failure to locate familial violence and sexual abuse in social structures. Some writers have argued that links are not made between violent/sexually exploita-tive behaviour and class structures, others that links are not made with the social organisation of masculinity. Because violence and sexual abuse are attributed to personality defects, the psychopatho-logical thesis, it is argued, studies offenders and their victims as though they exist in a social vacuum. It fails to confront the power dynamics of either man – woman or parent – child relations or to explore the class and ethnic structures in which these relationships are located (Adams, 1988; Glaser and Frosh, 1988, pp. 41–2; Scully, 1990, p. 46; Dobash and Dobash, 1992, pp. 214–40).

Fourth, and relatedly, the psychopathological thesis is challenged by feminist scholars as sexist. Feminist writers have argued that the catalogue of personality defects from which offenders, their victims and their families are deemed to suffer is based on traditional stereotypes of masculinity and femininity and the construction of departure from these stereotypes as deviant. Further, the implication of women and children in responsibility for their own victimisation is consistently seen by feminist and feminist-influenced researchers as buying into men's self-serving characterisations of women's behaviour and as defining as understandable if unfortunate men's violence against women and sexual abuse of children (Adams, 1988; Glaser and Frosh, 1988; Scully, 1990; Dobash and Dobash, 1992). Agency, it is argued, is transferred away from the violent husband or sexually abusive father to wives, mothers and daughters. Taken-for-granted assumptions of the urgency of male sexual needs and of men's right to command sexual and domestic services from women is not questioned, while a woman's right to refuse sexual relations or negotiate such issues as how money is spent, the time the husband spends away from the household, the assistance he gives in household tasks or the freedom to pursue her own interests is denied.

Non-feminist Sociological Perspectives

Whereas psychopathological discourses locate violence and sexual abuse in the psychic processes of the individual, sociological discourses focus on socially structured forces. They presume that the causes of violent and abusive behaviour, the way in which they are defined and identified, and the forms of social regulation to which they are subject are to be explained in terms of the material and cultural forces which structure social life. It is not denied that psychological problems may be associated with abusive behaviour, but it is presumed that these have social causes.

Sub-cultural explanations

Early sociological accounts of the various manifestations of violence and sexual abuse in family life posited a close connection between their occurrence and social and economic deprivation. Poverty, bad and overcrowded housing, limited educational

resources, unemployment and poor job opportunities, it was variously suggested, create a sense of frustration and repression which
predispose families to abusive behaviour. The physical and sexual
abuse of children and violence in sexual partnerships were thus
defined as sub-cultural phenomena.

In one version of this thesis, violence is said to be a strategy
through which men who have little education, low job prestige,
low incomes and limited interpersonal skills maintain a position
of dominance in family life (Goode, 1971). A second version of
this thesis suggests that violent/sexually exploitative behaviour
and the moral justifications for such behaviour are accepted elements in lower-class cultures, are learned by young children
growing up in these cultures and are culturally transmitted over
the generations. A third version appears in Garbarino and
Gilliam's account (Garbarino and Gilliam, 1980; Garbarino,
1981) of the relationship between neighbourhood environment
and child physical abuse. Arguing that child maltreatment is to
be explained in terms of the interaction between the family and
its environment within an 'ecological niche', Garbarino and
Gilliam seek to identify the 'socially disrupted environment', that
is the environment which fails to provide adequate support for,
and so conspires to compound the 'deficiencies' of, parents. They
characterise the 'socially disrupted' environment as an environment with low levels of 'neighbourly exchange', restricted interaction amongst children, poor housing, poor relations with
institutions such as schools, and a 'pervasive pattern of social
stress'. Further, they associate these 'social deficits' with low
income levels, the prevalence of woman-headed families, the participation of mothers with young children in the labour force, and
high residential turnover.

These arguments move the debate beyond an individualistic
orientation and focus on deprived sub-cultures and environ-
ments. They were deployed particularly, though not exclusively,
in the analysis of child physical abuse and drew upon empirical
findings based on reported child abuse which seemed to show
that abusive families are heavily concentrated in the poorest
social groups. However, this sub-cultural thesis has been heavily
criticised on a number of counts. It has been argued that it (i)
fails to take account of the prevalence of abusive behaviour in all
social groups and implicitly treats some groups as 'healthy' and

others as 'pathological'; (ii) is unheeding of the selective processess which label poor working-class families but not middle-class families abusive; (iii) does not explain gender differences in the perpetration of abuse and (iv), in locating problems of familial violence and sexual abuse primarily *within* particular sub-cultures or structures, fails to examine the links between these sub-structures and wider political, economic and historical structures.

Structural explanations

Structural explanations shift the debate away from notions of the pathological sub-culture and seek to explain physical and sexual abuse in family relationships in terms of the social, economic and ideological structures of the society as a whole.

Gil's attempt to analyse child abuse from a political economy perspective exemplifies this approach. Gil (1970, 1975) maintains that the physical abuse of children is one element in a larger phenomenon of child maltreatment (which he defines as anything that limits developmental opportunities). Focussing on the concentration of abuse in the poorer socio-economic groups, he argues that the position of families in the social structure is a key determinant of the degree of stress and frustration they experience. Poverty and deprivation, Gil suggests, represent structured obstacles to development and evoke reactive personal violence by individuals against individuals. However, Gil argues that concentrations of poverty, and consequently of child maltreatment, in particular sub-groups of a society are to be explained in terms of class inequalities in the control and distribution of resources, which produce deprived groups in the first place, and of social policies and philosophies which consistently fail to take account of their needs.

Straus, Gelles and their colleagues on the Family Violence Research Program at the University of New Hampshire also locate violence in family life in macro-social processes but they do not, as Gil does, reduce these processes to class inequality. These researchers contend that violence in family life is so pervasive (see pp. 152, 162) that it must be seen as a 'normal' part of family life and explained in terms of 'normal' processes. They then proceed to construct a wide-ranging multi-dimensional theoretical model in which family violence is located in cultural values, the structural organisation of family life, blocked opportunities and social learning. Different researchers within the New Hampshire group emphasise different factors to varying degrees. However, their varying arguments (summarised in Gelles and Cornell, 1990, ch. 6) seem to crystallise into four major sets of propositions.

First, they argue that family life exists within a cultural context in which certain forms of violence are tolerated and even mandated. The widespread acceptance of physical punishment as a means of disciplining children represents, they argue, permission for family members to use forms of violence on each other that would not be allowed elsewhere. Further, they argue that because physical punishment is 'normal' in family life, children are socialised into the acceptability of violence under certain conditions. Children, in their view, learn within the family that it is acceptable to hit people you love, for powerful people to hit less powerful people, to use hitting to achieve some end or goal and to hit as an end in itself.

Second, these researchers maintain that the structures of family life breed stress and conflict. The family, they argue, is a social institution in which interaction is intense and wide ranging. Interaction is high in terms of the time which family members spend together, covers a wide range of their activities, makes all their identities visible, presumes both high levels of commitment and the right to influence values and behaviour and makes the misfortunes of any one family member the misfortune of the family as a whole. At the same time, family life is, they argue, confining: the child's membership of the family is involuntary and rarely terminable, the sexes and generations are in a singularly close relationship but their interests may be widely divergent, and roles are assigned on the basis of sex and age rather than interest or competence. In the view of Straus and his associates, these structural conditions make family life stressful and therefore vulnerable to violence. Further, they argue that in the modern world family life is insulated from the eyes and ears of the wider society so that privacy is high but external control low. The private nature of modern family life, say Gelles and Cornell, reduces the likelihood of intervention by neighbours, the police and the courts and makes it possible for family members to 'get away with' levels of violence not generally considered acceptable.

Third, these researchers suggest that structured inequalities between women and men and parents and children lead to differential vulnerability to violence. They maintain that men, because they are typically stronger than women, have higher-status positions and earn more money, can use violence against their partners without risking physical, economic and social retaliation. Similarly, parents may be able to use violence towards their young children without incurring 'costs'. Women and children, say Gelles and Cornell, may be the most frequent victims of family violence because they do not have the resources either to escape from, or inflict costs on, their attackers.

Fourth, Straus and his associates seek to take account of evidence which shows that abusive violence is more prevalent in low income, low status social groups than in other groups. These researchers (see, in particular, Straus, 1980a, 1980b) identify as a critical factor in the generation of violence a disjunction between cultural values which emphasise material success and structural conditions which limit opportunities for success. They point out that cultural expectations of male success include the expectation that men be family breadwinners, heads of households and masters in their own home but that, in poor socio-economic groups, resources for the achievement of success are limited. The result, they claim, is likely to be frustration and therefore aggression and violence. Gelles and Cornell maintain that in 'lower class' sub-cultures an aggressive sexuality and violent behaviour is considered evidence of being 'a real man'. Where occupational opportunities are blocked, this sub-cultural pattern may substitute for occupational success in defining masculinity.

This wide-ranging, multi-factorial analysis seeks to provide an explanation of all forms of violence in the family. It is an ambitious project. Yet it is ultimately unsatisfactory. First, its approach to explanation is *ad hoc*. Dobash and Dobash (1992, pp. 281–2) point out that Straus and his co-researchers have compiled a seemingly endless array of potentially significant factors and empirical generalisations but fail to specify how they interact and connect to produce violent behaviours. Second, they do not address the question of rape, sexual assault and the sexual abuse of children and thus leave out of the picture an important set of exploitative behaviours. Third, their argument is criticised by feminist scholars because it takes 'the family' rather than gender inequality as its unit of analysis and defines violence in intimate relationships as family violence rather than as men's violence. Bograd (1988, p. 19), for example, argues that it sees violence in intimate relationships as a problem of both sexes and fails to take account of what is in her view, and in the view of most feminist researchers, an empirical reality: men's disproportionate responsibility for violence in family life and women's disproportionate 'victimisation'. It thus addresses gender inequality as simply one factor among many, and minimises the importance of men's power in structuring family relationships and generating violence.

Feminist Perspectives

In contrast with conventional sociological analysis, feminist accounts of violence and sexual abuse in family life place gender relationships at the centre of their analysis, see the problem to be explained as men's violence against women and focus on the way in which women define and experience men's violence. Their analyses are diverse and wide ranging, but have at their core the radical-feminist proposition that men's violence and sexual abuse are both products of, and mechanisms for sustaining, a universal patriarchal social order. This thesis rests on two major and interlinked arguments.

First, it is argued that male domination, though sustained and legitimated in a variety of ways, is ultimately sustained by force. For example, Dobash and Dobash (1980) argue that for centuries the authority which was vested in husbands as heads of households included the legal right to chastise their wives for their 'lawful protection'. Further, they maintain that the chastisement of wives, though no longer formally enshrined in legal norms, is still used by husbands to sustain their 'rights' and has widespread cultural support. They find that violence is typically precipitated by real or perceived challenges to their 'right' to deference, domestic services and sexual exclusivity. Violence, say Dobash and Dobash (1988, p. 57), is used to silence women, to win arguments, to express dissatisfaction, to determine future behaviour and to demonstrate dominance.

Second, sexuality is said to be the primary sphere of male power, the solid base from which men establish control over women. This thesis begins with the argument that in nearly all societies and periods of history male sexual desire is defined in terms of (i) virility, conquest and power and (ii) a biologically-driven urgency and compulsivity. In the early radical-feminist writings of Millett (1970) and Firestone (1970), for example, men's sexuality is portrayed as directed to the conquest of women and as involving possession, control, abuse and domination. Again, Ward (1984) argues that male sexual discourse proclaims 'that male sexuality is innately active, aggressive and insatiable' and that women are 'sexual commodities' whom men have a right to use how and whenever they can. In Ward's view, male sexual discourse constitutes an 'ideology of rape' and creates a social structure in which men set out to conquer, invade and plunder women's bodies. Similarly, but more dispassionately, Glaser and Frosh (1988, pp. 23–6) contend that the social construction of masculinity valorises assertiveness and power, turns its face from emotional intimacy and glories in sexual conquest as a symbol of male prowess.

Feminist discourse suggests that aggression and abuse are inherent in this construction of masculinity and seeks to show that wife-battering and killing, date rape and marital rape and child sexual abuse are extreme forms of the sexual aggression which women and children routinely experience (see, for example, Brownmiller, 1976; Ward, 1984; Kelly, 1988b; Scully, 1990; Radford and Russell, 1992). This argument asserts that a predatory male sexuality places women at constant risk of sexual harassment, assault and rape in the public sphere and, in intimate relationships, gives men the right to sexual servicing on demand, emphasises female but not male fidelity and places children (boys as well as girls) at risk of abuse. Further, feminist researchers have shown that the beliefs which surround men's sexuality – such as the belief that men are driven by urgent sexual desire or the belief that only women who ask for it get raped – place the responsibility for avoiding violence and rape and for protecting children on women, lead to victim-blaming and act as a form of social control. The constant threat of male sexual aggression, it is argued, limits women's movements and encounters with other people, prescribes the way they dress and present themselves to the world and renders them dependent on the goodwill of a male protector. The reality and threat of sexual aggression is thus presented as a mechanism through which male domination is perpetuated and has been described as a 'form of policing' (Radford, 1987), 'a condition of sex colonisation' (Barry, 1979, p. 165) and 'a reign of sexist terror' (Caputi and Russell, 1992).

Furthermore, feminist analysis suggests that male violence has institutional support. Men's violence and sexual abuse, it is argued, are supported by everyday myths and assumptions which minimise sexual violence, remove responsibility from men for their actions and make individual pathologies the explanation of violence (Nelson, 1987; Kelly, 1988b, pp. 34–6; Scully, 1990); by legal norms which in the past sanctioned the chastisement of wives, denied the possibility of marital rape and defined incest in a limited way, and which continue to criminalise only extreme forms of sexual violence (Dobash and Dobash, 1980, 1992; Nelson, 1987; Kelly, 1988b, p. 23; C. Parton, 1990); by policing and prosecuting ideologies and procedures which limit intervention in family violence and then filter out of the criminal justice system all but the most blatant forms of violence (Edwards, 1989; Hanmer *et al.*, 1989; Dobash and Dobash, 1992); by sentencing policies which accept provocation as a mitigating plea and impose limited penalties for most forms of sexual violence (Radford, 1992; Lees, 1992); and by medical and social work ideologies and practices which define men's violence as an individual pathology, collude with their rationalisations and prioritise the maintenance of the family as a social unit (Pahl, ed., 1985; Adams, 1988; Ptacek, 1988; Scully, 1990).

Finally, feminist analysis challenges as a myth cultural beliefs in the security and safety of 'the home'. For example, Dobash and Dobash (1980, 1988) argue that marriage is a social structure that gives husbands the right to the domestic and sexual services of their wives, places wives under the control and direction of their husbands, and subjects women to the use of intimidation, coercion and violence as strategies for maintaining male rights and privileges. Dobash and Dobash further argue that familial values structure women's options once violence becomes a part of the relationship. They maintain that familial values burden women with guilt by ascribing to them responsibility for all family problems, whatever their source, and trap women in a violent relationship by defining the exposure of these problems as a betrayal of family loyalties. Furthermore, Dobash and Dobash argue that the dominance of beliefs in the safety and privacy of the family not only obscures the reality of family violence but limits public surveillance and cuts women off from public protection.

Feminist scholars do not deny that particular circumstances may create an abuser out of particular men and a 'victim' out of a particular woman or child or that women and men can create mutually respectful relationships even in the context of patriarchy. To that extent the personality characteristics of the protagonists are taken into account. However, feminist discourses move discussion of the causes of men's physical and sexual abuse of women and children away from the particular circumstances of individual abusers and towards the delineation of a patriarchal culture which defines masculinity in terms of aggression and sexual predatoriness. It seeks to explain not why a particular man abuses his partner or child but why men as a sex–class category are the primary perpetrators of violence and why so little is done about it. It shows that images of masculinity as aggressive and biologically driven permeate popular and elitist culture (Millett, 1970), sexual liberation ideologies (Segal, 1987b) and psychiatric and psychological theory (Adams, 1988; Dobash and Dobash, 1992), inform the way in which legal and welfare institutions respond to sexual violence (Dobash and Dobash, 1980, 1992; Pahl, ed., 1985; Edwards, 1989) and are reflected in and supported by a pornographic industry in which women are always and immutably demeaned (Dworkin, 1981; Russell, ed., 1993).

However, two decades of debate have pointed to difficulties in early radical-feminist theorising and have led to its modification.

In the first place, though the connections between 'normal' masculinity and wife-battering, rape and child sexual abuse are clear, it is also evident that these behaviours are defined by men themselves as deviant. According to Gordon (1989), they tend to be regarded as seamy and reprehensible even when, as in the nineteenth century, they are apparently sanctioned by legal norms. Our theoretical models must therefore seek to show where the boundaries are drawn between 'normal' and deviant' masculinities and to delineate the circumstances in which these boundaries are transgressed. Feminist theory sometimes does this but does not do so in a systematic way. It explains, says Lorna Smith (1989, p. 29), why the perpetrators of sexual violence are usually men, but fails to explain why not every man abuses and not every woman is abused.

Second, feminism has been reluctant to confront the reality of women's violence (Gordon, 1986; Kelly, 1991). Thus women's violence against men tends to be viewed as rare and/or defensive, an argument that, on the one hand, obscures the extent of women's violence (see pp. 164–5) and, on the other, slides into exonerating it. There is a growing awareness of violence in lesbian relationships but research and theorising remain tentative (Kelly, 1991). Women's physical and sexual abuse of children (and indeed men's physical abuse of children) is not prominent in feminist analysis (Gordon, 1986; C. Parton, 1990). When it is addressed, it tends to be explained in terms of the power relations between women and men.and/or of class disadvantage. Thus women's 'failure' to protect their children from male violence may be attributed to their relative powerlessness (La Fontaine, 1990, pp. 193–4) and their abuse of children to the stress generated by their exclusive, wide-ranging and burdensome responsibility for childcare, isolation from supportive kin and neighbourhood networks or poverty and deprivation (C. Parton, 1990). However, this argument does not take account of the normative acceptance by women as well as men of physical punishment as an appropriate way of disciplining children (see p. 152). Further, Christine Parton (1990) argues that it fails to confront the issue of age domination. Power structures, Parton maintains, are divided along age lines. The abuse of children is thus an abuse of adult/parental power and cannot be reduced to the dynamics of male-female relationships.

Third, the image of a monolithic and unvarying masculinity and femininity that emerges from most early radical-feminist accounts of male violence has been challenged. As some writers have observed, ethnographic evidence of the existence in pre-industrial societies of non-aggressive masculinities and even of rape-free cultures points to cross-cultural variation in the social construction of masculinity (Sanday, 1981; La Fontaine, 1990; Scully, 1990). Further, the history of Anglo-Saxon sexuality points to historically varying and contradictory tendencies in our sexual scripts. The predatory male sexuality which feminist writers depict describes the sexuality of the permissive revolution, but is condemned in the Christian tradition as 'lust'. It stands in opposition to notions of 'married love' as involving commitment, mutual affection, fidelity, trust and respect which were central to the Puritan tradition and which, some writers have argued, underpinned the emergence of the modern Western conjugal family (George, 1973; Hall, 1979). Finally, marxist and 'black' feminists have consistently and convincingly argued that class and ethnic inequality interact with, and cross-cut, patriarchal relations to shape male power, the construction of masculinity/feminity and violence against women in complex and varying ways (Segal, 1987b; Hooks, 1982; C. Parton, 1990). These and similar accounts of the varying and changing construction of sexuality are leading radical feminism to the adoption of a mode of analysis – exemplified in a recent collection of readings on femicide (Radford and Russell, 1992) – which, while retaining the notion that patriarchy is universal and is universally sustained by force, recognises that male violence takes forms that are specific to particular cultural, political and economic contexts.

In Conclusion

Psychology and psychiatry, non-feminist sociology and feminism provide us with distinctive understandings of violence and sexual abuse in family life. These distinctive approaches are not necessarily incompatible with each other. Radical-feminist theory relates violence/sexual abuse in family life to the social construction of masculinity within a patriarchal society and shows why men, as a sex–class category, are the primary perpetrators of violence and abuse and why women and children are their victims. Non-feminist sociological approaches offer the possibility of linking radical-feminist understandings of patriarchal processes to class and other structural processes which mediate, and are mediated by, patriarchy. Psychological approaches help us to understand why, given particular structural arrangements, particular men and women become abusers.

Nevertheless, each of these approaches carries its own ideological baggage and is in ideological conflict with each of the other approaches. Psychopathological approaches are permeated by patriarchal notions of the sexualities of men and women. Conventional sociological approaches reveal and challenge class inequalities and reveal a variety of socially-structured sources of strain but fail to challenge gender inequality. Feminist analysis has changed our understanding of what constitutes violence and abuse, revealed the scale of male violence and shown that dominant strategies for dealing with it pander to men's aggression and privilege men's sexual desire. It challenges dominant ideas of a biologically-driven and not easily controllable male sexual desire as notions that are constructed in the context of a patriarchal order, demean women and can and ought to be changed. It is in effect an attempt to establish values and norms that make men responsible for their aggression, protect the innocence of children and give women the right to sexual adventurousness but with men of their choosing and in circumstances of their choosing.

6

AIDS: Battleground of Competing Moralities

AIDS is a painful and fatal condition for which there is as yet no known medical preventive or cure. It typically involves death at a young age, it is pandemic and it has evoked predictions of a holocaust. Areas of the world in which prevalence levels in the heterosexual population are high, such as sub-Saharan Africa, face severe shortages of labour, the orphaning of large proportions of the child population and declining rates of population growth (Barnett and Blaikie, 1992). In the view of some commentators, AIDS is the most serious health crisis that the world has faced this century.

However, AIDS is more than a painful and devastating medical condition. Because it is predominantly transmitted through sexual activity, because multiple relationships increase the risk of transmission and because, in the Western world, transmission has been largely associated with homosexual relationships, it has become the battleground of conflicting moral values and ways of life.

This chapter examines the AIDS phenomenon. We consider its epidemiological basis, the way in which it is represented in contending moral discourses and its impact on sexual behaviour.

6.1 EPIDEMIOLOGICAL CONSIDERATIONS

AIDS (Acquired Immune Deficiency Syndrome) is a condition in which the body's natural immune system breaks down and is therefore susceptible to invasion by a host of opportunistic infections and cancers. Moreover, because the immune system is compromised, diseases which could otherwise be fought off or treated prove fatal.

Most medical researchers believe that this condition is the result of infection by a virus, or family of viruses, currently known as human immunodeficiency virus (HIV), and that this virus is transmitted through contact with infected body fluids (such as blood, semen and cervical and vaginal secretions). Transmission, it is suggested, occurs in three basic ways: (i) as a result of penetrative sexual activity with an infected partner; (ii) through direct exposure to infected blood as in the sharing of contaminated needles and syringes by intravenous drug users or the use of contaminated blood products, blood transfusions and medical equipment; and (iii) from an infected mother to her child during pregnancy, at birth and, possibly, in breast milk.

In all parts of the world HIV-transmission has occurred primarily as a result of sexual activity. A number of findings as to the circumstances in which transmission occurs and AIDS develops are of particular significance. First, the medical and epidemiological data suggest that transmission occurs more readily during anal intercourse between men or between men and women than during vaginal intercourse (Brandt, 1987, pp. 185–6, 189; Needle *et al.*, 1989, p. 21). Second, in heterosexual relationships women are at greater risk of infection than men (Brandt, 1987, pp. 185–6; Needle *et al.*, 1989, p. 26). Third, woman-to-woman transmission has been reported, but appears to be rare (*The Independent*, 22 July 1994). Fourth, multiple relationships appear to be associated with both an increased risk of infection to the individual and rapid transmission within any given social group. Pinching (1990, pp. 29–30) argues that the importance of multiple relationships in HIV-transmission can be simply demonstrated by reference to a model of two populations representing extremes of sexual behaviour: one in which nearly all people have only one sexual partner and the second in which most people have multiple partners. The virus will spread only very slowly, if at all, in the first population, but rapidly in the second so that even those with 'quiet' lifestyles will be at risk. Finally, most researchers believe that, although the speed of progression from infection to AIDS and death varies depending on whether or not immune systems were already weak, all or nearly all HIV-infected people will ultimately develop AIDS. Current studies show that 15–20 per cent of HIV-carriers develop AIDS within three years, 30 per cent within five years and 50 per cent within ten years (Pinching 1990, p. 31). Hopes of developing either a vaccine against HIV infection, or drugs that will inhibit progression to AIDS or significantly extend the lifespan of people with AIDS have not yet been realised (*The Guardian*, 8 April 1994, 11 April 1994).

The distribution throughout the world of HIV-infection and AIDS is demonstrated in Figure 6.1. In sub-Saharan Africa, the Caribbean, South America and south and southeast Asia, transmission is predominantly associated with heterosexual activity. In the USA and other Anglo-Saxon countries and in Northwest Europe, transmission is primarily associated with homosexual activity and, to a lesser extent, with intravenous drug use. Prevalence levels in eastern Europe, eastern Asia, Australasia and north Africa remain very low.

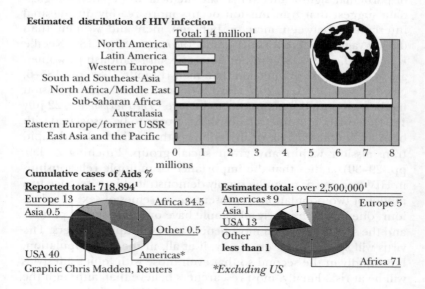

Estimated distribution of HIV infection

Total: 14 million[1]

North America
Latin America
Western Europe
South and Southeast Asia
North Africa/Middle East
Sub-Saharan Africa
Australasia
Eastern Europe/former USSR
East Asia and the Pacific

0   1   2   3   4   5   6   7   8
millions

Cumulative cases of Aids %

Reported total: 718,894[1]

Europe 13
Asia 0.5
Africa 34.5
Other 0.5
USA 40
Americas*

Graphic Chris Madden, Reuters

Estimated total: over 2,500,000[1]

Americas* 9
Asia 1
USA 13
Other less than 1
Europe 5
Africa 71

*Excluding US

[1] Inadequacies in the collection of data on AIDS cases mean that in many parts of the world, and particularly in the Third World, reported AIDS cases usually underestimate actual numbers. Data on estimated levels of HIV-infection are usually based on fairly small samples drawn from high-risk groups, blood donors and pregnant women and are of limited reliability. Estimates of the prevalence of AIDS and HIV-infection are therefore best regarded as guestimates.

SOURCE   The *Guardian Supplement*, 30 November 1993 (based on WHO data).

FIGURE 6.1   *Aids throughout the world, mid–1993*

As Figure 6.1 shows, Africa currently accounts for over 70 per cent of the estimated global total of AIDS cases. World Health Organisation estimates suggest that in the cities of central Africa one in three of the adult population is HIV-positive (*The Guardian*, 11 April 1994). In these areas, all sexually active people appear to be at risk, women and men form roughly equal proportions of the affected population, and mother–child transmission is relatively high.

In the West, AIDS was first identified among homosexual men in the United States in 1981 and escalated rapidly in gay communities with a 'fast lane' lifestyle. It is estimated that, in some American cities, the proportion of the gay population who are HIV-positive reaches 70 per cent (Needle *et al.*, 1989, p. 21). As Table 6.1 shows, gay and bisexual men constitute the overwhelming majority of AIDS cases. However, intravenous drug users constitute a significant minority of all AIDS cases and nearly 50 per cent of cases among women. In Britain, the number of people with AIDS remains quite small (Table 6.2) and the prevalence rate is low relative to that found in most European Union countries (Figure 6.2). As elsewhere in the West, HIV-transmission is predominantly homosexual transmission.

The extent to which the general population in the West is at risk is the subject of considerable debate. Early predictions of exponential escalations in the incidence of AIDS have been scaled down (*The Guardian*, 8 June 1993) and, partly as a result of this, some commentators deny the existence of any general threat (see, for example, Fitzpatrick and Milligan, 1990). Others however, argue that bisexual men and injecting drug users are potential vectors of HIV-infection to the general population, that contemporary sexual mores provide the conditions for its escalation and that the African experience demonstrates the need to act to prevent disaster. Whatever the merits of these rival arguments, AIDS and HIV-infection now appear to be rising faster in the heterosexual population than among other groups and, as heterosexual transmission has increased, the risk to women and children has risen. In Britain, in the first six months of 1992, heterosexual intercourse was responsible for 30 per cent of HIV infections, compared with 9 per cent in 1987 (*The Guardian*, 12 November 1992). In London, rates of infection among pregnant women

Table 6.1   *AIDS cases in the USA by exposure category as at 30 June 1993*

Transmission category	New cases reported July 1992–June 1993 Men		Women		Cumulative total	
	No.	%	No.	%	No.	%
Adult/adolescent cases						
Sexual intercourse between men	41029	57	–	–	172085	55
Injecting drug use	16267	22	5685	46	73610	24
Sexual intercourse between men and injecting drug use	4636	6	–	–	19557	6
Haemophilia/ coagulation/ transfusion	1517	2	480	4	8495	3
Heterosexual	2991	4	4556	37	21873	7
Undetermined	5910	8	1651	13	15060	5
Sub-total	72350	100	12372	100	310680	100
Paediatric cases						
Haemophilia/ coagulation/ transfusion	34	9	9	3	523	11
Mother with/ at risk of HIV infection	362	89	382	96	4121	87
Risk not identified	10	2	6	2	66	1
Paediatric sub-total	406	100	397	100	4710	100
Total	72756		12769		315390	

SOURCE   Centers for Disease Control and Prevention, July 1993.

increased from one in 560 in 1990 to one in 380 in 1993 (*The Guardian*, 5 August 1994). In the USA, in 1993, heterosexual sex accounted for 9 per cent of new cases compared with 1.9 per cent in 1985 (*The Times*, 12 March 1994).

Table 6.2   *AIDS cases by sex and exposure category in the United Kingdom to 30 June 1992*

Exposure category	Men	Women	All	
	%	%	%	Nos
Sexual intercourse				
between men	81	–	76	4681
between women and men	6	55	9	559
Injecting drug use	5	20	6	371
Blood				
blood factor (e.g. haemophilia) and blood/tissue transfer (e.g. transfusion)	6	13	6	389
Mother to child	1	9	1	60
Other/undetermined	1	3	1	80
Total	100	100	99	6140

SOURCE   *Social Trends*, 1993, Table 7.12.

6.2   THE SEXUAL POLITICS OF AIDS

As the preceding section has indicated, AIDS is unique in the amount of suffering and death it causes among young people and is difficult to contain. However, AIDS is not simply a physical condition with a biological cause and physically-determined results. Like all illnesses, AIDS is culturally interpreted, signified and given moral meanings. It is a social phenomenon. In Western societies, interpretations of AIDS embody the fears, anxieties and problems of the post-permissive Western era (Weeks, 1985, 1986, 1988, 1989a; Altman, 1986; Vass 1986; Plummer, 1988). It is the terrain on which battles between 'the old morality' of conventional family life and 'the new morality' of the 'permissive revolution' are being waged.

This Section looks briefly and in very general terms at the conflict between 'the old' and 'new' moralities and then at the way in which the AIDS 'pandemic' is represented in moral conservatism and in gay and feminist discourses.

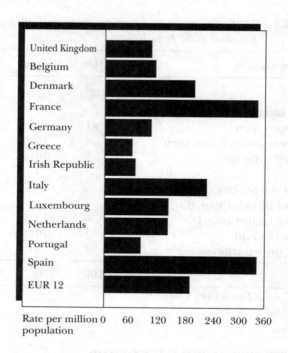

Rate per million 0   60   120 180 240 300 360
population

SOURCE   *Social Trends*, 1993, Figure 7.11.

FIGURE 6.2   *AIDS prevalence rates in the countries of the European Union, March 1992*

The Conflict between the 'Old' and 'New' Moralities

Over the past generation, Anglo-Saxon and northwest European societies have, as Chapter 1 indicated, moved from general conformity with a Christian sexual and family morality based on heterosexuality and lifelong marriage to permissiveness and diversity of sexual lifestyles. In the 'old morality', says Weeks (1985, 1986), sexuality was defined as a powerful and potentially destructive instinctual drive which must be controlled; in 'libertarian morality', on the other hand, sexuality is defined as potentially creative, the pursuit of sensual pleasure as an end in itself is seen as legitimate and new sexual desires have proliferated. However, as Chapter 1 also indicated, the impact of the 'sexual revolution' was uneven and fragmented. The conjugal family remains an ideal for some, various elements of the new order are viewed with considerable ambivalence by many, and vigorous but diverse and frequently mutually antagonistic counter-revolutionary movements have come into being.

Most analyses of this counter-revolutionary tendency suggest that its vanguard consists of the New Right and of a range of 'social purity movements', drawn for the most part from those morally conservative sections of the population for whom the 'new morality' was always an affront to ordinary decencies and established verities. There is disagreement as to the strength of the relationship between moral conservatism and the New Right in Britain: some writers depict a close alliance (Hall *et al.,* 1978; David, 1986; Abbott and Wallace, 1992), others only tenuous links (Durham, 1991). There is, however, general agreement that in the USA the New Right and various social purity movements have joined hands to create a powerful 'moral majority'. According to Weeks (1985, pp. 33–44), this political and moral conservativism embodies a deep hostility to feminism and to gay and lesbian politics, conceives of sexual freedom as the source of all social ills, is implicitly racist in its denigration of all but a narrow social experience and has as its central and unifying theme 'the threatened family'.

Weeks (1985, pp. 18–19; 1986, pp. 91–2; 1988, p.15) suggests that hostility to the moral and social transformations of the 1960s and 1970s is not confined to moral conservatism and the New Right. It is, he argues, also found in the opposition of 'the traditional working classes' to pro-gay policies, in 'disillusioned liberalism' – where the sexual revolution is perceived as having gone astray and as leaving a legacy not only of sexual choice, but also of sexual disease, violence and excess – and in radical feminist critiques of the sexual revolution as a male-oriented revolution.

This analysis suggests that sexuality, gender relations and 'the family' have become battlegrounds of contending political forces, arenas of contradictory tendencies and perceived crises. For radicals, says Weeks (1985, 1986, 1988), the transformations of the past generation are liberating, but modest and constantly under threat; for moral conservatives, on the other hand, the transformations of the past generation are revolutionary and destructive. For moral conservatives, the Victorian era represented a golden age of sexual propriety and the restoration of Victorian values is to be struggled for. For radicals of all tendencies, the 1960s symbolise an egalitarian questioning of an hierarchical and absolutist moral order and the changes that were then effected are progressive and must be protected. The co-existence of 'traditional' and 'permissive' values, Weeks argues, provides fertile ground for a moral panic over AIDS. He suggests that to moral conservatives AIDS epitomises the fearful consequences of all the changes that have occurred over recent decades and symbolises the need for reaffirming 'traditional' values. To liberationists, on the other hand, AIDS threatens the moral transformations of the past generation.

Commentary on AIDS reflects these moral conflicts. In moral conservatism, as articulated by the leaders of fundamentalist religious groups, the tabloid press and the New Right, AIDS is represented as the legacy of the sexual revolution. In gay discourse, moral conservatism is contested and the legitimacy of homosexuality reasserted, but AIDS is interpreted as a challenge to 'liberated' gay ideologies. In a slender but growing feminist commentary, moral conservatism is also eschewed, but AIDS is represented as a challenge to men's construction of sexuality and an opportunity to reconstruct sexual relationships in ways that would valorise women's sexual experience.

Representations of AIDS in the Discourses of Moral Conservativism

Analyses of representations of AIDS in moral conservatism are for the most part the work of gay and feminist researchers. Most are analyses of early responses to AIDS. Most focus on the moral conservatism of fundamentalist religious groups, the New Right and the tabloid press. However, these analyses also implicitly or explicitly suggest that similar sentiments are to be found in large tracts of public opinion. They depict the response to AIDS as informed by a symbolic crusade against the moral 'excesses' of the 1960s and 1970s and as containing four major elements.

First, it is suggested that public opinion in general, but moral conservatism in particular, construes AIDS as the consequence of the violation of traditional sexual mores. Moral conservatism, it is argued, depicts AIDS as 'the wrath of God upon us', the 'wages of sin', 'a self-inflicted scourge', a 'gay plague', and a 'judgement' on promiscuity, homosexuality and fast-lane sex (Altman, 1986; Vass,

1986; Weeks, 1985, 1986, 1988, 1989a). According to Plummer (1988), moral conservatism conceptualises AIDS not in scientific terms but in moral terms and sees, not the AIDS virus, but the lifestyles associated with the transmission of the AIDS virus as the cause of the AIDS crisis.

Second, this construction of AIDS is said to be paralleled by a search for scapegoats. All analyses of the response to AIDS emphasise that it divides people on the AIDS spectrum into two categories. 'the guilty' and 'the innocent' (Vass, 1986; Watney, 1988; Weeks, 1988). Members of groups which are on the margins of acceptability – 'black' people, drug users and those who stand outside the norms of conventional family life (gay men, bisexual men, prostitutes and 'the promiscuous') – are defined as the 'guilty' architects of their own justly deserved fate. In contrast, haemophiliacs, partners of bisexual men and children are seen as their unfortunate and innocent victims.

Third, a holocaust is envisaged. Analyses of early media commentary, for example, show that in its early stages AIDS was typically portrayed as decimating homosexual communities, as putting at risk all those who have sex outside a lifelong, exclusive relationship and as posing the possibility of an uncontrollable and all-destroying pandemic (see, for example, Vass, 1986).

Fourth, conservative moral thought uses AIDS to urge a return to a more circumspect morality. Vass (1986) says that it sees mankind as standing at a crossroads and confronting a choice between chaos and order in which survival means a more conservative and moral, but healthier, sexual lifestyle. It thus presents 'clean' or 'defensive' living as the solution to the dangers posed by AIDS. It may also advocate coercive solutions, ranging from the compulsory testing of those at risk to the segregation of the infected and sick and strict immigration controls.

To most gay writers, this representation of AIDS reflects freefloating fears of permissiveness in general and of homosexuality in particular, and is the response of a profoundly homophobic culture. To moral conservatives, Weeks (1985, 1986, 1988) argues, gay liberation symbolises moral decline and threatens the traditional integration in marriage and 'the family' of sex, domesticity and social order. Given this, AIDS provided a golden opportunity for moral entrepreneurs to raise their profile and to claim that what they had said all along was 'right'.

There are, however, a number of arguments which suggest that responses to AIDS do not reflect only the values of a homophobic and/or anti-permissive culture. In the first place, the danger is real enough.

Second, critiques of moral conservatism run the risk of denying 'fast lane' sexual practices a role in the transmission of AIDS and of constructing condom-use as a talisman against infection. Yet, Brandt's account (1987, pp. 161–76) of the history of sexually-transmitted diseases suggests that it is unlikely that medical remedies will alone combat AIDS. Brandt argues that the rising incidence of sexually transmitted diseases, such as syphilis and gonorrhea, and the appearance of new diseases, such as herpes and AIDS, indicate that medical measures can moderate the effects of sexually transmitted diseases but cannot combat their social and cultural determinants. Evidence of the failure rate of condoms in practice as distinct from their failure rate in the laboratory (*The Guardian*, 7 November 1990), together with analyses of the difficulty of negotiating condom-use (see pp. 210–11), seem to provide some support for this argument. Thus, the possibility that 'fast lane' lifestyles are not without deleterious consequences must be confronted.

Third, there is a tendency to slide into equating religious fundamentalism and the tabloid press not only with moral conservatism as a whole but also with heterosexual responses in general. This has had the effect of characterising all heterosexual responses to AIDS as a moral panic in which gay men are constructed as monsters. However, Watney (1988) points out that AIDS commentary is in fact varied and so cannot readily be characterised as driven by any single and cohesive set of values. Evidence of countervailing tendencies is to be found in British and American public opinion surveys which show that AIDS has not led to increased support for discrimination against homosexual people, that the balance of public opinion is against the curtailment of the legal rights of people with AIDS and that sympathy for people with AIDS coexists with the belief that they have only themselves to blame for their fate (Singer *et al.* 1987; Wellings and Wadsworth, 1990). Moreover, as knowledge of the way in which AIDS is transmitted has grown, as strategies for controlling it have been established, and as the rate of increase has slowed down, the response to AIDS seems to have become less moralistic. Wellings and Wadsworth (1990) find that press reportage has become more temperate, that public opinion has become less censorious and that trends towards an increasing disapproval of homosexuality, which had appeared in the mid-1980s when fears of an impending holocaust were at their height, have been reversed. These data suggest that the anti-gay, anti-permissive backlash was in part at least a feature of early responses to AIDS and that, as understanding of the nature of AIDS and its transmission developed, some of the early fear and loathing diminished (Weeks, 1989a). It therefore seems important to distinguish not only between the responses of religious fundamentalism and the responses of the public in general, but also between responses in different phases of the AIDS pandemic.

Representations of AIDS in Gay Discourses

At one level, gay commentary on AIDS is concerned to counter representations of AIDS as a 'judgement' on homosexuality by denying an intimate connection between AIDS and homosexuality. Thus gay commentary consistently forefronts the viral origins of AIDS, emphasises the vulnerability of groups other than homosexuals to AIDS, insists that AIDS is linked with particular sexual practices (such as anal intercourse) rather than with particular categories of people (homosexuals) and suggests that it could be controlled by modest changes in lifestyle, such as the use of condoms (see, for example, Plummer, 1988; Watney, 1988; Weeks, 1988). Moreover, gay writers may deny that activities such as promiscuity, drug abuse and anal intercourse in themselves constitute danger. Thus Weeks (1988, p. 16) maintains that it is not anal intercourse but unprotected anal intercourse, not promiscuity but what you do with your partner, not drug use but the exchange of dirty needles that is problematic.

At a second level, AIDS has become the starting point for a fundamental re-evaluation of 'liberated' gay culture. Weeks (1985, pp. 47–50) maintains that AIDS has focussed attention on practices and beliefs which were central to the 'liberated' gay ideology of the 1970s but a source of tension within the gay world and between the gay world and the 'straight' world. He shows that in the 1970s the new sexual scripts which gay men sought to construct led to a quantum leap in casual sex and the use of stimulants, the extension of sexual practices to include sado-masochism and the like, and the establishment of gay bath-houses and back-room bars in most of the major cities of the world for the specific purpose of recreational sex. This gay revolution, says Weeks, was in part at least an attempt to break away from the easy assumption that male homosexuality represents the effeminisation of men. It sought to demonstrate that it is possible to be gay and male.

Most gay activists and academics suggest that this macho gay ethos is called into question by AIDS. AIDS, says Altman (1986), forced gay men to confront the life-threatening nature of a sexual lifestyle that had once seemed liberating and is leading them beyond a preoccupation with sex and partying to a new evaluation of community and family. At the same time, Altman maintains, AIDS neither led to a denial of the validity of homo-sexuality nor subverted the attempt to establish a distinctive gay identity. Altman claims that confronted with the dilemma of modifying their lifestyle whilst rebutting the traditional morality that condemns both homosexuality and sex outside committed relationships, gay men either argued for the restriction of sexual partners and, by extension, for monogamy or sought to create a sexual lifestyle in which multiple relationships are combined with risk-free activities. Within the ambit of the first strategy came denunciations of promiscuity and recreational sex and the establishment of therapy groups to deal with 'compulsive' and 'obsessive' sex drives. Within the ambit of the second response came greater selectiveness in the choice of sexual partners and the development of 'safer sex' practices such as 'telephone sex', 'jerk off' clubs, gay pornography and the eroticisation of condoms. This latter response, Altman suggests, is the majority response.

Fitzpatrick and Milligan (1987) demonstrate the existence of a third and reactionary response to AIDS. In the view of Fitzpatrick and Milligan, the safer sex ideological position of gay revisionists endorses the basic message of moral conservatism, namely that homosexual promiscuity is responsible for the spread of AIDS. They claim that the answer to AIDS lies in the long term in a medical cure and in the medium term in targeting advice at HIV-carriers through contact-tracing and, so as to facilitate this, in the de-stigmatisation of homosexuality. The gay movement's adoption of the 'safer sex' position, they maintain, represents acceptance of the official representation of AIDS as a major health hazard, diverts attention away from the struggle to free homosexuality from stigma and transforms the gay movement from a movement that was in the vanguard of sexual experimentation to a movement that supports repression. In their view, the development of a 'safer sex' ideological position has destroyed the gay movement as a progressive force.

However, this reactionary response to AIDS appears to be a minority response. The dominant thrust of post-AIDS gay discourse seeks to promote a circumspect sexual practice whilst retaining a positive image of homosexuality, of sex outside committed relationships and of eroticism for its own sake. 'Liberated' gay ideology is thus being modified but not abandoned.

Representations of AIDS in Feminist Discourses

Initially, feminist spokespersons, like the public in general, tended to perceive AIDS as a gay man's problem and paid it scant attention (Segal, 1987a). However, as it became apparent that AIDS is an issue for heterosexual women and men as well as for homosexual men, feminist writers began to address the different position and interests of women and men in the post-AIDS reconstruction of sexual scripts.

Feminist commentary on AIDS (see especially Coward 1987; Segal 1987a; Richardson, 1990; Holland *et al.*, 1991a) reiterates the argument that dominant sexual ideologies reflect and reinforce the sexual privileges and power of men. It emphasises that contemporary Western sexual scripts equate 'real sex' with penetrative sex, take it for granted that men are 'naturally' less able to control their sexual desires than women, define sexual prowess as a central aspect of masculinity and assign activity and control to men.

Feminist commentators then seek to reveal the dilemmas and difficulties which women face in negotiating 'safer sex' in the context of men's sexual privilege and power. Holland *et al.* (1991b) show that young women are subjected to constant and insistent verbal and physical pressures for penetrative sex and cannot easily avoid, circumvent or resist these pressures or negotiate condom-use. Further, feminist commentary suggests that official responses to AIDS reflect and affirm male sexual scripts.

AIDS education programmes, Richardson (1990) argues, assume that monogamy is difficult for men and assign the major responsibility for the adoption of 'safer sex' practices to women. Women, says Richardson, are thus urged to carry condoms, though to do so presumes a readiness for sex they are supposed to deny and risks their reputation; they are urged to insist on 'safer sex', though to be assertive runs counter to the compliance expected of women; and they are given responsibility for AIDS prevention, though imbalances in the power of women and men mean that they are relatively powerless to negotiate safer sex. Further, feminist commentary shows that the attribution of responsibility for safer sex to women is accompanied by the attribution of blame to women for HIV-transmission and the representation of women in much public discussion as infectors rather than infectees (Campbell, 1990; Richardson, 1990). Scharf and Toole (1992), for example, say that the emphasis is on the consequences for children rather than for women of HIV-infection in mothers, and Campbell (1990) observes that the risk that prostitutes pose for their clients rather than the risk that prostitutes confront from their clients is highlighted.

At the same time, some feminist writers see the AIDS crisis as an opportunity to push for woman-centred sexual scripts. For men, Coward (1987) argues, 'safer sex' represents curtailment and a threat to masculinity. For women, however, 'safer sex' has different resonances. Coward maintains that for women penetrative sex has never been safe, spontaneous or necessarily pleasurable. In her view, the range of activities typically relegated to the category of foreplay not only provides protection against AIDS and pregnancy but in some circumstances may be more satisfying than intercourse. AIDS, in Coward's view, represents an opportunity to explore and expand our ideas of sexual pleasure and to redefine sexuality as 'something other than male discharge into any kind of receptacle'.

Feminist AIDS commentary, like feminist analyses of violence and sexual abuse, provides an important critique of dominant modes of organising sexuality. It asserts that contemporary sexual scripts are the domain of male sexual privilege and irresponsibility, may not meet the sexual pleasure of women through their 'obsession' with penetrative sex, and are now life-threatening. Further, it shows that official policies for preventing HIV-transmission fail to recognise the constraints that limit women's power to control men's behaviour and implicitly privilege and sustain headlong masculine sexual desire.

6.3   THE END OF THE SEXUAL REVOLUTION?

In the absence of either a cure for AIDS or a vaccine against HIV-infection, campaigns aimed at modifying sexual behaviour have become the core strategy for containing AIDS. Guidelines to safer sex have commonly recommended a reduction in sexual partners, avoidance of sex with people known to have had many partners and with members of high risk groups, avoidance of oral, anal and group sex and the regular use of condoms. In addition, drug users are advised not to share needles and may be supplied with clean needles by governmental agencies.

In the mid-1980s, when fears of the rapid escalation of AIDS were at their height, many commentators anticipated a return to a more circumspect morality and the emergence of a new puritanism (Altman, 1986; Vass, 1986; Plummer 1988; Sontag, 1989, pp. 76–8). This section seeks to examine whether or not, and to what degree, the transformations of the 1960s and 1970s have in fact been breached. We examine, first the methodological problems researchers confront in studying change in sexual behaviour; second, the impact of AIDS on relationships among gay men; and, third, the impact of AIDS on heterosexual relations.

Methodological Problems

Research on the impact of AIDS on sexual behaviour confronts a number of methodological problems. In the first place, key concepts such as what is to be regarded as a sexual encounter, the distinction between 'casual' and 'regular' partners, the sexual identity of respondents and 'high risk' sexual activity have a range of meanings in the everyday world, are multi-dimensional and are difficult to define. Hunt and Davies (1991) show that for some people 'having sex' is defined by penetration of some kind with or without orgasm, for others by any genital contact and for yet others by any erotically flavoured physical contact. For some people a 'sexual partner' may be someone with whom 'sex' occurs in the context of love or affection, for others anyone with whom sexual behaviour takes place. Distinctions between 'casual' or 'regular' partners are commonly based on the emotional content and/or length of the relationship, but both categories tend to contain relationships of highly varying and overlapping durations (Fitzpatrick *et al.*, 1990). Furthermore, because people who are neither exclusively homosexual nor exclusively heterosexual in their sexual activities and fantasies variously identify as 'homosexual', 'heterosexual' or 'bisexual', the classification of respondents in terms of their sexual identification is problematic. 'High risk' activity is also a problematic category. For example, the risk involved in unprotected intercourse with casual partners is likely to be high in groups in which seroprevalence levels are high, but low in groups in which seroprevalence levels are low.

A second problem stems from the fact that evidence of behaviour change is necessarily derived from respondents' accounts of their sexual activities. However, respondents may not be truthful and may not accurately recollect their past. Coxon (1988) suggests that respondents' accounts decrease in reliability the more varied their sexual histories, the greater the number of one-off or casual contacts they have and the further back in time an event occurred. Cohort studies avoid the problem of asking respondents to recall the past but present us with the problem that behaviour may be affected by participation in the study and by the ageing of the cohort (Hunt, 1992). These problems are not unique to studies of sexual behaviour and may be alleviated by sensitively-constructed questionnaires, but they are none the less significant.

Third, studies concerned specifically with homosexual and bisexual men are plagued by problems of representativeness. Siegel *et al.* (1989) point out that random samples cannot be used since a complete sampling frame cannot be constructed. Samples have therefore tended to be either clinic-based or based on trawls through gay organisations and, in both cases, are representative only of particular sections of the gay population. Large-scale surveys of the general population, such as the recent Wellcome Trust funded study (Wellings *et al.*, 1994), avoid this problem, but are rare.

Fourth, what counts as 'significant' change depends on the criteria by which significance is evaluated. If our concern is primarily with AIDS-risky behaviour, then systematic condom-use may count as significant change. On the other hand, commentators who are concerned with evaluating moral change are unlikely to see condom-use as 'significant' and may define change in terms of such variables as the prevalence or otherwise of 'open' relationships.

Finally, because change may occur in some aspects of sexual relationships but not in others, may be in contradictory directions, may vary in timing and pace between social groups, and may be associated with a bewildering and diverse array of causal variables – many of which may have nothing to do with AIDS – the pace, direction and sources of change are not easily delineated. Further, Fitzpatrick *et al.* (1989) point out that, as high-risk sexual behaviours decline, we are seeking to explain the behaviour of a decreasing and changing group of people; consequently, the variables that seemed to account for the adoption of 'safer sex' practices at one point in time may not hold at another point in time.

Given the difficulty of researching sexual behaviour, studies of the impact of AIDS must be interpreted with caution.

AIDS and Change in Gay Lifestyles

AIDS is frequently depicted as profoundly affecting gay life. Gay writers argue that it infused gay communities with an awareness of death and dying (Altman 1986; Plummer 1988; Edwards, 1992) and in its early stages prompted, as the preceding section indicated, a fundamental re-evaluation of 'liberated' gay ideology. Moreover, it seems to have brought a new dimension to gay community structures. From a very early stage in the 'epidemic', gay men organised themselves to promote awareness and knowledge of risky behaviours, to encourage 'safer sex' and to provide counselling and welfare services for people with AIDS. AIDS thus produced a new bonding among gay men, which is based on caring rather than on the search for sexual partners or the struggle for gay liberation (Adam, 1992; Cruickshank, 1992, p. 184). Moreover, gay AIDS organisations service heterosexual as well as gay people and have been enlisted by governments in the fight against AIDS. Altman (1986, 1988) suggests that, as a result, the leadership of the gay movement has shifted towards those who claim professional expertise rather than activist credentials and that, despite the homophobia unleashed by AIDS, gay men and women are gaining acceptance as a legitimate minority.

When we turn to accounts of the impact of AIDS on gay sexual behaviour, we find extensive evidence of the rapid and pragmatic adoption of 'safer sex' practices. Researchers report that gay men are avoiding or cutting down on unprotected anal intercourse and oral sex, are having fewer partners, are more selective in their choice of partners and are increasingly adopting a variety of low risk behaviours (Feldman, 1985; McKusick *et al.*, 1985; Joseph *et al.*, 1987; Martin, 1987; Evans, *et al.*, 1989). There is also some evidence of an increased interest in forming relationships (Feldman, 1985; Stulberg and Smith, 1988; Cruickshank, 1992). Further, Stulberg and Smith (1988) suggest that non-sexual relationships are assuming a greater importance in the lives of gay men; they find that almost one third of their sample socialise more often with their friends, more than one quarter report an increased interest in becoming closer to their families and 15 per cent report socialising more with their families.

These findings have been interpreted in two somewhat different ways. They have been interpreted in the media and by some researchers as heralding a movement to more conservative gay lifestyles. Altman (1986), for example, argues that gay life has become calmer, less bound up in a constant round of 'hot' sex places, more focussed on friendship and intimacy. Similarly Cruickshank (1992, p. 185) claims that the party atmosphere of the 1970s has come to an end and is being replaced by a tendency to 'settle down' in couples. Other researchers, however, argue that assumptions of major change in gay behaviour are misconceived. Kotarba and Lang (1986), for example, maintain, first, that the ideological position of the organised gay community must not be confused with everyday sexual behaviour and, second, that systematic studies of gay behaviour point to the variability and complexity of responses to AIDS rather than to a 'wholesale movement towards celibacy and monogamy'. Studies such as Feldman (1985), say Kotarba and Lang, suggest that multiple relationships remain the norm for most gay men. Feldman reports a significant fall in the average number of sexual partners gay men have but finds that they nevertheless average 3.6 partners a month (compared with 6.8 partners a month before the advent of AIDS).

Two recent, large-scale and comprehensive British studies, Fitzpatrick *et al.* (1990) and Project Sigma, a pioneering longitudinal study of the behaviour of homosexual men in the post-AIDS era reported on by Weatherburn *et al.* (1922), provide detailed evidence of the complexity and variability of gay responses to AIDS. Both Fitzpatrick *et al.* and Weatherburn *et al.* find that condoms, though increasingly used in gay relationships, are in general used in 'casual' rather than in 'regular' relationships. At the same time, both studies show that anal intercourse tends to be practised in 'regular' rather than in 'casual' relationships and Weatherburn *et al.* show that, although most gay men engage in anal sex, most gay partnerships do not involve anal sex (Table 6.3). However, Weatherburn *et al.* say that most gay men see 'open' relationships as combining the security of a long-term commitment with the excitement of new encounters, and that 'open' relationships are the preferred relationship pattern. Weatherburn *et al.*, as well as Fitzpatrick *et al.*, find that monogamy is a minority pattern (Table 6.4). Moreover, as Table 6.4 indicates, both these studies show that the average duration of 'regular' relationships is quite short. In addition, Weatherburn *et al.* report that over the four years of their study the average annual number of all sexual partners and, but to a lesser degree, of penetrative sexual partners claimed by gay men rose. Finally, their data suggest that, because gay men are constantly moving between 'casual' and 'regular' but relatively short-lived partnerships, accounts of aggregate change in sexual practices and relationships conceal a considerable amount of individual change

Table 6.3   *Median number of male sexual partnerships of gay men over various time periods*

	All sexual partners	Penetrative sexual partners
Median number of partners over		
The preceding year	4	1
Preceding 5 years	16	3
The life course	38	7

SOURCE Weatherburn *et al.*, 1992, Figure 10.

Table 6.4   *Gay relationship types and durations*

Fitzpatrick et al. study

Relationship category	%
Monogamous relationships	26
Regular, non-exclusive relationships	40
Casual relationships only	19
No current partners	15
Total	100

Median duration of relationships	months
Monogamous relationships	17
Regular but non-exclusive partners	25
Regular and non-regular partners	
regular partners	15
non-regular partners	1
Only non-regular partners	1

Project Sigma

Relationship category	%
Monogamous relationships	26
Open relationships[1]	42
Casual relationships only	32
Total	100

Median duration of regular (monogamous or open) relationships	months
	21

[1]   Relationships in which there are one or more regular partners and/or casual partners. A regular partner was defined in Project Sigma as 'a partner with whom you have sex more than once, where the second and subsequent meetings were not accidental and with whom you intend to have sex in the near future'.

SOURCE   Fitzpatrick *et al.*, 1990; Weatherburn *et al.*, 1992, p. 11.

(Figure 6.3). In short, these studies point to the pragmatic adoption of certain 'safer sex' practices, but not to any significant movement to exclusive and lasting relationships as a gay norm. This conclusion is broadly supported by Wellings *et al.*'s large-scale

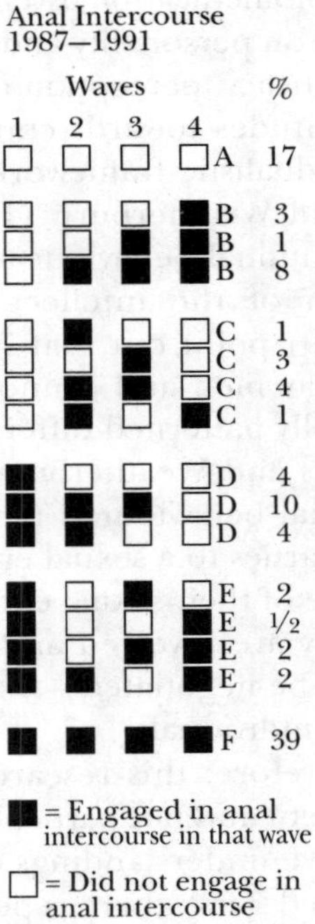

Anal Intercourse
1987–1991

Waves   %

1	2	3	4		
□	□	□	□	A	17
□	□	□	■	B	3
□	□	■	■	B	1
□	□	■	■	B	8
□	■	□	□	C	1
□	□	□	□	C	3
□	□	□	□	C	4
□	■	□	■	C	1
■	□	□	□	D	4
■	■	□	□	D	10
■	■	□	□	D	4
■	□	□	□	E	2
■	□	□	■	E	½
■	□	□	■	E	2
■	■	□	■	E	2
■	■	■	■	F	39

■ = Engaged in anal
    intercourse in that wave

□ = Did not engage in
    anal intercourse

A: Men who never engaged in anal intercourse during the four years of the
      study.
F: Men who engaged in anal intercourse in each year of the study.
B and C: 'Relapsers' – men who were not engaging in intercourse at Wave One
      but who subsequently did so.
D and E: Men who were engaging in anal intercourse at Wave One, but who had
      not done so in at least one of the subsequent Waves.

SOURCE   Weatherburn *et al.*, 1992, p. 32.

FIGURE 6.3   *Proportion of homosexual men engaging in anal intercourse
             with men, 1987–91*

random survey (1994, pp. 365–72) of contemporary sexual
behaviour.
    Considerable research effort has been devoted to discovering
the factors associated with the adoption/non-adoption of 'safer

sex' practices by gay men. Much of this research effort has been undertaken within a biomedical or psychological frame of reference and has focussed on personality and cognitive variables such as anxiety, personal efficacy, perception of risk, knowledge about HIV transmission, attitudes towards condoms and gay network affiliation. This individualistic framework has been heavily criticised. First, Davies and Weatherburn (1991) say that it implies that 'unsafe sex' is irrational behaviour to which men are driven by some malfunction of the intellect or emotions. Second, Fitzpatrick *et al.* (1989) point out that it implicitly assumes the social uniformity of gay men and cannot take account of class, ethnic and other socially patterned differences in their responses to AIDS. Third, Davies and Weatherburn (1991) argue that the 'cause' of unsafe sexual behaviour is more profitably sought in the *interaction* of the parties to a sexual encounter – in the expectations which they have of their sexual encounter, the type of relationship in which they are involved and the processes through which 'safer sex' must be negotiated – than in the personal characteristics of atomised individuals.

Unsurprisingly, therefore, this research effort has produced inconclusive, inconsistent and not particularly meaningful results. Even so, some definitive understandings of change in gay sexual behaviour have emerged. First, there is persistent evidence of the underestimation of personal risk and of the absence of a clear relationship between either knowledge about AIDS or the perception of risk and the adoption of 'safer sex' practices (Fitzpatrick *et al.*, 1989; Cohen, 1991; Weatherburn *et al.*, 1992). Second, Joseph *et al.* (1987) find that, of the range of cognitive and personality variables they examined, beliefs about how gay men in general are changing their behaviour is the only powerful and consistent predictor of the adoption of 'safer sex' practices. This finding seems to point to the importance of peer group norms in influencing change. Third, research findings which show that condom-use is now general in casual relationships but not in regular exclusive relationships (see p. 203) suggest that safe/unsafe sex is relationship-specific and must be examined in terms of the way in which casual/regular relationships are defined.

Finally, Kotarba and Lang (1986) provide us with a useful conceptual model of the direction, variability and determinants of change. These researchers divide gay lifestyles into two categories: 'public' (based on high levels of sexual activity with multiple and/or anonymous partners) and 'private' (based on monogamous or closed group relationships). On the basis of this categorisation, they suggest that change in gay lifestyles may be placed on one of four dimensions: (i) 'public-public' – persistence in a 'fast-lane' lifestyle; (ii) 'private-public' – movement from a 'private' to a 'public' lifestyle; (iii) 'public-private' – movement from a 'public' to a more conservative, 'private' lifestyle and (iv) 'private-private' – a pattern found among men who had practised a private lifestyle before AIDS and who therefore felt no need to modify their lifestyle. Kotarba and Lang locate thirteen of the forty-eight men in their sample on the 'public-public' dimension, five men on the 'private-public' dimension, twenty men on the 'public-private' dimension and ten men on the 'private-private' dimension. In accounting for these divergent lifestyle changes, Kotarba and Lang say: first, that men who remain in the 'fast lane' tend to feel that a 'hot' sexual lifestyle is necessary to them and to be fatalistic about the risk of AIDS; second, that movement into 'fast lane' sex may occur independently of the AIDS phenomenon and in the context of circumstances such as the dissolution of a relationship or a geographical relocation that brings access to 'fast lane' life; third, that a 'private lifestyle' may originate not with AIDS but with other life-cycle circumstances, such as ageing; fourth, that consistently 'private' men are characterised by moralistic attitudes and distinguish sharply between people like themselves whom they perceive to be behaving responsibly in relation to AIDS and others whom they perceive as irresponsible.

Heterosexual Relations in the Shadow of AIDS

Studies of heterosexual relationships in the post-AIDS era show that young people are fairly well-informed about HIV-transmission (Baldwin and Baldwin, 1988; Crawford *et al.*, 1990; Bury, 1991) and are aware of the need for 'caution' in sexual relationships (Waldby *et al.*, 1993; Wellings *et al.* 1994, pp. 361–2). Further, there is evidence of the use of condoms in casual relationships, of greater selectiveness in the choice of partners, of avoidance of one-night stands and sex on a first date and of some modest reductions in numbers of partners (DHSS, 1987, ch. 6; Masters *et al.*, 1988, pp. 130–6; Waldby *et al.*, 1993).

However, the available data provide little support for predictions of a return to a more circumspect morality. Research in Britain, the USA and Australia suggests that intercourse continues to be the norm in 'dating' relationships, that 'sex' with strangers or casual acquaintances is not uncommon, that partnership-turnover remains relatively high among a significant proportion of young people and that young people are likely to average more lifetime partners than their elders will average (DHSS, 1987; Masters *et al.*, 1988, pp. 130–6; Baldwin and Baldwin, 1988; Knox *et al.*, 1993; Wellings *et al.*, 1994, pp. 94–101). In addition, there is little evidence of a reworking of 'permissive' ideologies. In Britain, a public opinion survey, conducted in 1987 when fears of an escalating and uncontrollable epidemic were at their height, yielded some tentative evidence of a modest trend towards more conservative sexual attitudes (Harding, 1988). However, a more recent survey shows a return to the levels of permissiveness prevalent in the early 1980s and an increasing conceptualisation of AIDS as the product, not of homosexuality and promiscuity, but of 'unprotected' penetrative sex (Wellings and Wadsworth, 1990).

In general, 'safer sex' seems to be defined primarily in terms of condom-use, secondarily in terms of either exclusivity or having fewer sexual partners and rarely in terms of non-penetrative sex (Wight, 1992; Wellings *et al.*, 1994, pp. 358–60). At the same time, condom-use appears to be inconsistent and, as in gay relationships, more common in new and casual relationships than in 'steady' relationships (Holland *et al.*, 1991a; Wight, 1992; Wellings *et al.*, 1994, pp. 373–9).

A series of small-scale qualitative studies throws some light on the processes which have shaped this modest response to AIDS. These studies suggest that the impact of AIDS is mediated by the way in which it is culturally interpreted and by an entrenched and not readily changed sexual culture. Four sets of processes seem to be salient.

The first concerns perceptions of risk. All the evidence suggests that in Western societies perceptions of risk have been heavily influenced by the association of AIDS with specific 'high risk' groups – gay men, bisexuals, prostitutes, the 'promiscuous' and injecting drug users who are assumed to be at risk because of their 'deviant' lifestyles – rather than with the general population. Some researchers find that this construction of AIDS leads those who identify themselves as members of 'the general population' to believe that they are not immediately at risk (Holland *et al.*, 1990; Wight, 1993; Schiller *et al.*, 1994), other researchers that it leads to a fatalistic construction of heterosexual infection as the result of 'bad luck' and 'chance' rather than of lifestyle (Warwick *et al.*, 1988). Moreover, this construction of AIDS means that self-identification as heterosexual or gay, 'promiscuous' or not is of considerable significance for perceptions of personal vulnerability. Warwick *et al.* (1988) point out that many men who participate in homosexual acts do not consider themselves to be anything but heterosexual and do not therefore consider themselves to be at risk. Similarly, it has been found that monogamy may be defined in terms of months rather than years, that women are reluctant to define a relationship however tentative as a casual relationship (Holland *et al.*, 1991b) and that unusual multiplicities of relationships may be assumed to be 'the norm' (Leishman, 1987). High risk activities may therefore not be recognised as such. Further, a sense of personal invulnerability appears to be commonplace despite a generalised recognition of the risk of contagion. Abrams *et al.* (1990) find that young people believe it to be unlikely that they will themselves be HIV-positive and are fairly convinced that none of their potential partners could be even though they also believe that one half of their age peers will be HIV-positive in ten years time. Abrams' respondents thus exclude themselves from AIDS vulnerability, despite perceiving young people in general to be at risk.

The selection of 'safe' partners represents a second aspect of the response to AIDS. Wight (1993), in a Scottish study, and Waldby *et al.* (1993), in an Australian study, find that young heterosexual men perceive themselves as possessing an intuitive power to identify 'safe' partners. This intuitive power seems to be rooted in traditional notions of 'loose' and 'respectable' women. Thus, both Wight and Waldby *et al.* find that young men judge young women to be 'safe' or 'unsafe', 'clean' or 'unclean' on the basis of their reputation or, where this is not known, their sexual proclivities as indicated by their pre-emption of masculine sexual initiative, resistance to sex over a period of time, dress, demeanour and putative physical health. Waldby and her co-researchers find that in this categorisation of 'clean' and 'unclean' women, virgins occupy a privileged place. Women who are thought to have entered into an unknown number of relationships with unknown men or with men who belong to 'risk groups' are held at the greatest distance. In effect, Waldby *et al.* find that young men are taking some rudimentary precautions to avoid HIV-infection and that the precautions they take set a new value on virginity and a circumspect sexual career in women. However, they emphasise that young men's construction of a world of 'safe' and 'unsafe' women contains no consciousness of the risk their own sexual careers present for women and no parallel conception of themselves as 'clean' or 'unclean' agents.

There is no similar evidence of the construction by young women of a world of 'clean' and 'unclean' men. However, some researchers have suggested that young women are less confident than young men of their ability intuitively to identify infectious partners and are more cautious (Abrams *et al.*, 1990). They make a sharper distinction between 'regular' and 'casual' partners, are more likely than young men to judge condoms to be necessary and more often see the eliciting of sexual histories as a preventive strategy (Crawford *et al.*, 1990).

A third set of processes concerns the negotiation of condom-use. There is now considerable evidence of the existence of a range of barriers to condom-use, including: embarrassment in buying condoms (Wight, 1992); muteness in the conduct of sexual relations up to, and sometimes beyond, the point at which intercourse first take place, a muteness which makes it difficult to establish sexual histories and to negotiate condom-use (Bury, 1991; Wight 1992); cultural resistances to condom-carrying as incompatible with a romantic code of 'being carried away' by love and to condom-use as diminishing spontaneity and pleasure in sexual relations (Wilton and Aggleton, 1991); perceptions of condom-carrying young men as being 'after one thing' only, and of condom-carrying young women as demonstrating a sexual availability and initiative which marks them out as 'slags' (Holland *et al.*, 1991a; Wight, 1992); and the difficulty of insisting on condom-use without impugning either one's own or one's partner's past and present (Holland *et al.*, 1991a; Mittag, 1991; Kline *et al.*, 1992; Wight 1992, 1993).

These attitudes and beliefs appear to translate into condom-using practices that vary with the nature and stage of relationships. The research evidence (reviewed by Wight, 1992) suggests that condoms are used as a contraceptive strategy rather than as protection against HIV-infection and are associated with one-night stands and sporadic relationships, while 'the pill' is the preferred contraceptive strategy in 'steady' relationships. Further, a number of researchers find that as a relationship endures, partners are distanced from non-safe categories and 'protected' sex comes to be seen not only as unnecessary, but as impugning one's own fidelity or the fidelity of one's partner and as incompatible with the trust believed to be central to a 'steady' relationship (Holland *et al.*, 1991a; Kline *et al.*, 1992; Waldby *et al.*, 1993; Wight, 1993).

The criteria which establish a relationship as a 'steady' relationship have not been investigated in any systematic way. Such insights as there are indicate that relationships may be thought of as 'steady' relationships after the briefest of associations and despite the absence of explicit commitments (Holland *et al.*, 1991a; Wight, 1993; Waldby *et al.*, 1993). Time to first intercourse after becoming a couple was found to be two weeks or less for half, and twenty-four hours or less for one quarter, of the young people in one study (Ingham *et al.*, 1991).

Finally, as the discussion of feminist AIDS commentary in the preceding section indicated, feminist research suggests that sexual relationships take place within the framework of gendered power relations which privilege a headlong male sexual desire and leave little space for women to assert needs and desires which run counter to those of men. Holland *et al.* (1990, 1991a, 1991b) emphasise that male domination is not monolithic and that, in some circumstances, young women successfully resist male demands. Nevertheless, they suggest that young men are in general careless of their own health risks and of the consequences of their health status for their partners. Further, they maintain that women are subject to pressures for sex which range from mild persuasion to rape and may be unable either to say 'no' to penetrative sex or to insist on the use of condoms. Male power, together with the privileging of headlong male sexual desire, Holland *et al.* maintain, acts to sustain AIDS-risky practices and to limit women's freedom to negotiate 'safer sex'. This reality, they argue, is not addressed by public health education programmes which have traditionally made women responsible not only for their own reputations and health but also for policing male sexual drives.

Summary

AIDS, it would seem, epitomises the ambivalences, anxieties and problems of post-permissive Western societies. The data and arguments under review suggest that it has led to the reassertion of traditional values by moral conservatives, the re-evaluation of 'libertarian' gay ideologies by gay leaders, calls from within feminism for the refashioning of sexual scripts in ways that would valorise women's sexual experience and government campaigns for the modification of sexual behaviour as a pragmatic means of controlling HIV-transmission. In the mid-1980s, these pressures for the fashioning of more conservative sexual scripts led some writers to argue that AIDS signalled the end of the sexual revolution.

However,there are contradictory tendencies. Both moral conservatism and gay revisionism are contested. The Left has not sought to refashion 'liberated' sexual scripts. Government campaigns urge circumspection, but presume that it would be unrealistic to urge either celibacy or a return to monogamy. Further and significantly, there is little evidence of any significant behavioural change. Among both gay men and heterosexual men and women, 'safer sex' seems to be defined in terms of condom-use rather than in terms of celibacy or monogamy. Moreover, both homosexual and heterosexual relationships appear to be governed by a range of cultural beliefs which make rational decision-making and the adoption of 'safer sex' practices in the light of knowledge about AIDS highly problematic.

Nevertheless, it would be an oversimplification to say that nothing has changed. Among gay men, a significant shift away from unprotected intercourse, and even from intercourse outside 'regular' relationships, seems to have taken place. In the heterosexual world, a clearly perceived threat and a strong collective identity – factors which were important in effecting some significant changes in gay sexual behaviour – are not present (Wight, 1992) and behaviour change appears to be very modest. Even so, accounts of the construction of a *cordon sanitaire* based on the categorisation of women as 'clean' or 'unclean' revive older distinctions between the 'pure wife' and the 'fallen woman' and may serve to circumscribe the sexual freedom which the sexual revolution seemed to bring women. Again, feminist accounts of contemporary sexual power relationships as inhibiting not only women's negotiation of 'safer sex', but also their sexual pleasure, challenge male sexual privilege and may yet lead to a significant refashioning of sexual scripts.

7

Epilogue

Ethnic differentiation, economic restructuring and the contraction and casualisation of labour markets, population ageing, the pervasiveness of violence and sexual abuse in family relationships and the risk of sexually transmitted disease are not new phenomena. However, they have achieved a heightened and particular salience in the context of the historical, economic, political and ideological conditions of the closing decades of the twentieth century. They are, individually and collectively, changing the face of social life in significant ways and are the source of wide-ranging contradictions, anxieties and conflicts. This text shows that these phenomena interconnect with, and reflect and shape, albeit in different ways, the ordering of gender, sexual and parental relationships. Further, in considering these apparently disparate phenomena together, this text reveals the extent and intensity of the cross-cutting pressures and challenges to which gender, sexual and parental relationships are subject. It shows that contradictions, ambivalences, anxieties and conflicts over the ordering of gender, sexual and parental relationships are central to the concern evoked by ethnic differentiation, labour market dislocation, population ageing, familial violence, sexual exploitation and AIDS.

Debates about inter-ethnic relationships suggest that in Western societies the coexistence of ethnic groups is associated, not with the fusion of different cultural values and norms, but with the continued salience of ethnic allegiances, the growth of cultural pluralism and the emergence of racialised discourses as a central component of everyday life. Our examination of these debates shows that gender and family values are integral to a group's sense of peoplehood and are an important element in racialised discourses. On the one hand, racist/nationalist sentiment constructs the conventional conjugal family as the building block of British national identity, perceives the different family structures of minority groups as epitomising their alienness and as reproducing an alien way of life and defines ethnic minority groups as 'alien wedges' that are destroying 'the British way of life'. On the other hand, anti-racist and 'black' radical movements define relationships between European and non-European peoples as 'black–white' relationships, suggest that they are structured by 'white' racism, contest the ideological hegemony of Anglo/European cultural values and – whereas older generations of people of colour sought integration into 'white' society – seek a social order based on the equal status of different ethnic cultures and groups. In these ideologies, 'the black family' is construed as a symbol of 'black' identity, the site of resistance to racism and an arena within which 'black' ways of life are reproduced and 'black' people equipped with the skills necessary to survive in a 'racist' society. 'Black' feminism extends this discourse: it seeks to make 'black' women visible in both 'black' radicalism and 'white' feminism, argues that racism alters the form and significance of sexism and valorises 'racial', ethnic and national divisions between women. It has been a potent force in the reworking of feminist theory in the 1980s and 1990s to take account of ethnic, 'racial' and national cleavages.

Gender and family relationships are challenged in a different, but far-reaching and corrosive, way by the contracting and unsettled labour market conditions which have accompanied economic restructuring. Accounts of the consequences of unemployment suggest that it leads to family poverty, threatens the traditional organisation of masculinity, jeopardises the transition from dependent childhood to independent and law-abiding adulthood and puts at risk the independence women had achieved through increasing economic activity. It has been linked with psychological and physical ill-health, conflict between family members and family breakdown, cohabitation, unmarried motherhood and depressed marriage rates, vandalism, violence and self-destructive deviancy, and the emergence of an impoverished, marginalised and nihilistic underclass. This perception of the consequences of contracting and casualised labour markets is informed by the belief that high levels of unemployment and sub-employment leave men not only without jobs but also without a role in family life and in society. Moreover, the research literature suggests that, although unemployed men are more involved in the work of the household than employed men, the contraction of male employment opportunities is not leading to a significant reworking either of the conventional division of household labour or of notions of what constitutes appropriate employment for men. Masculinity is thus perceived to be in crisis and young people (young men because they are without secure jobs and young women because their futures are linked with men's breadwinning) are perceived to be without a future.

Yet, although everyday thought and political debate are permeated by images of the wide-ranging and corrosive effects of unemployment and sub-employment, sociological research demonstrates, as we have seen, resilience and stoicism in the face of unemployment, as well as poverty, family breakdown and lawlessness, and suggests that family relationships, though threatened by unemployment, are a resource in confronting unemployment. Thus, men may accept any job in order to sustain their breadwinning role, women's resourcefulness and effort in managing household expenditure on reduced incomes may be a critical factor in a family's ability to survive men's unemployment, and parental support and surveillance may, on the one hand, protect young people from the more brutal consequences of recession and, on the other, sustain the morality of work and independence.

With the emergence of later life as a long and distinctive phase in the life course and the construction, within the context of images of 'old age' as a period of economic and physical dependence, of population ageing as a major social problem, older people have come to occupy a central place in debates about the caring roles of 'the family' and the state and of women and men. Our analysis of these debates shows that traditional family ideologies define caring as a labour of love, construe the conjugal family as a unit of care and caring as integral to femininity, and perceive contemporary changes in family lifestyles as incompatible with traditional eldercare responsibilities. This traditionalist ideology has been hijacked by the New Right, where it is linked with ideological opposition to state welfare activity and underpins the development of community care policies which seek to sustain 'the family' as a unit of care. The political and academic Left and feminist gerontology challenge traditional and New Right ideological positions and seek to redraw the boundaries between state responsibility and family responsibility. The political Left emphasises the 'burden' family care places on family members, is concerned to highlight the capitalistic processes that underpin and limit state provision and urges the development of a new partnership between state and family in which older people have the support of informal care networks and of institutional services. The dominant tendencies in feminist gerontology define caring as a work role and women's caring as one element in an exploitative sexual division of labour, is concerned to uncover gender inequalities in state welfare services, and may reject family caring altogether as inevitably sexist. Each of these ideological positions assumes the dependence of disabled older people. In contrast, anti-ageist activism and/or the disability movement reject both family care and state care as sustaining the dependence and subordination of disabled or older people on the able-bodied, and urges policies which will enable people with disabilities to buy in, and take control of, the services they need and to be independent of both family and state. At the same time, anti-ageist activism seeks to show that the dominant tendencies in feminist gerontology reproduce images of older and/or disabled women as dependent and burdensome and has not generally included them in the category 'woman'. Anti-ageist activism reveals divisions between women based on their different positions in the life course, promotes the interests of older women and confronts ageist stereotypes that alienate older women from themselves and from younger women.

In the everyday world, caring values and patterns are complex and often contradictory. As we have seen, sociological research shows that, whilst gendered caring norms are a central characteristic of family life, obligations are limited to a narrow range of relatives, are circumscribed by independence and reciprocity norms and are ambiguously gendered. Further, it seems that, although the bulk of eldercare is provided by family members and although most people may at some time be involved in caring for an older family member, caring takes place within limited parameters. It does not usually encompass extended households, is concentrated within the household and the married relationship and is in part provided by elders themselves. Moreover, needs may be unmet, caring is sometimes abusive and commercial alternatives are emerging and may in some circumstances be preferred by older people themselves.

Recognition of the ubiquity of men's violence against, and sexual exploitation of, women and children owes much to feminism's challenge to patriarchal power. This feminist project has broadened our understandings of what constitutes violence and sexual exploitation and shown that wife-battering, rape and child sexual abuse are pervasive, and are extreme forms of the aggression and exploitation which women and children routinely experience. It seeks to locate men's violence and sexual exploitation, not in individual psychopathologies or disadvantaged class positions, but in the social construction of masculinity within a patriarchal social order. It reflects and reinforces understandings of family life as oppressive and even violent. However, it also provides a critique of the predatory masculinity which the sexual revolution of the 1960s appears to have unleashed. It challenges men's claim to sexual servicing on demand, the values and beliefs which place the responsibility for avoiding violence and abuse on women, and the welfare and legal ideologies and practices which define men's violence as an individual pathology, prioritise family privacy and privilege a headlong male sexual desire. Feminist discourse is, in effect, an attempt to establish norms and values which make men responsible for their aggression, protect the innocence of children, give women the right to sexual adventurousness, but in circumstances of their choosing, and outlaw a sexuality in which women are usable and disposable sexual commodities and sex an appetite rather than a relationship.

AIDS has also led to the questioning of libertarian values. It has prompted the reassertion of traditional values by moral conservatism, the re-evaluation by gay men of gay 'libertarian' ideologies, feminist demands for the refashioning of sexual scripts in ways that would valorise women's sexual experience and government campaigns for the modification of sexual behaviour as a pragmatic means of controlling its transmission. In the gay world, there seems to have been a significant shift away from intercourse outside 'regular' relationships and a new emphasis on friendship. In the heterosexual world, the construction of a *cordon sanitaire* based on the categorisation of women as 'clean' or 'unclean' revives older distinctions between 'the pure wife' and the 'fallen women'. Nevertheless, it appears that AIDS has not, as some commentators had predicted it would, produced a new puritanism. The dominant thrust of post-AIDS gay discourse seeks to promote a circumspect sexual practice whilst retaining a positive image of homosexuality and of sex outside committed relationships.

Governmental campaigns urge circumspection, but stop short of advocating celibacy and monogamy. In the everyday world, 'safer sex' seems to be defined primarily in terms of condom-use rather than in terms of celibacy and monogamy.

Finally, trends towards the separation of sex, procreation and childrearing from marriage, the reconstruction of marriage as a terminable arrangement and the reworking of gender divisions remain, *in themselves,* sources of ambivalence, confusion and dissension. On the one hand, the freedom to choose between different kinds of sexual, procreational and parental relationships seems to have become a taken-for-granted right in most social groups. Moreover, in many sections of feminism and of the academic Left there is considerable hostility to the very idea of the nuclear family and to attempts to sustain it. On the other hand, as this text has shown, the transformations of the past generation have been partial. Further, a new moral conservatism seems to be gaining ground not only on the New Right but also on the political Left and, albeit somewhat haphazardly, in the media. The concerns and ideological emphases of this new moral conservatism are multi-stranded. However, they seem to be underpinned by common fears of a growing lawlessness and amorality among the young, anxieties over increasing poverty and/or welfare dependency and the belief that the principle of individual responsibility has been abandoned in the quest for individual autonomy and freedom. In these debates, solo parenthood, in particular, but also cohabiting parenthood and serial parenthood, are identified with unwelcome social shifts: they are seen as leading to family poverty, as creating family units that cannot readily care for older people, as leaving young men without appropriate models of the adult masculine role and recruiting them to the ranks of the lawless and unemployed, and as making men irrelevant to family life.

Dissension over the roles of women and men in family life and in the wider society is a critical element in these debates and conflicts. On the one hand, feminism, because of its emphasis on personal autonomy for women and its attack on the conventional conjugal family as a major site of patriarchal domination, is frequently cited as a major cause of change in sexual, marital and parental relationships. Further, solo parenthood, together with the contraction and casualisation of male labour markets, is evoking fears of men's redundancy and a growing sense that masculinity is in crisis. On the other hand, much feminist analysis suggests that the changes of the past few decades have been ambiguous and modest in their impact on women's lives: that gains such as enhanced control over reproduction, the greater freedom to bear and rear children outside marriage or to leave an unhappy marriage and greater access to labour markets are counterbalanced by the poverty associated with solo parenthood, the location of mothers in secondary sectors of the labour market, the modesty of shifts in the conventional sexual division of household labour and the power which men continue to exercise in the public and private world.

Bibliography

Abbott, Pamela and Wallace, Claire (1992) *The Family and the New Right*, London, Pluto Press.

Abrams, Dominic, Abraham, Charles, Spears, Russell and Marks, Deborah (1990) 'AIDS Invulnerability: Relationships, Sexual Behaviour and Attitudes Among 16 to 19 Year Olds', in Aggleton, P., Davies, P. and Hart, G. (eds) *AIDS: Individual, Cultural and Policy Dimensions*, Lewes, Falmer Press.

Abrams, Mark (1980) *Beyond Three Score and Ten: A Second Report on a Survey of the Elderly*, London, Age Concern.

Abrams, Philip (1978) *Neigbourhood Care and Social Policy*, Berkhamsted, Volunteer Centre.

Adam, Barry D. (1992) 'Sex and Caring Among Men: Impacts of AIDS on Gay People', in Plummer, K. (ed.) *Modern Homosexualities: Fragments of Gay and Lesbian Experience*, London, Routledge.

Adams, David (1988) 'Treatment Models of Men Who Batter: A Profeminist Analysis', in Yllö, K. and Bograd, M. (eds) *Feminist Perspectives on Wife Abuse*, Newbury Park, Sage.

Afshar, Haleh (1989) 'Gender Roles and the "Moral Economy of Kin" among Pakistani Women in West Yorkshire', *New Community*, 15, 211–25.

Age Concern (1992) *The Coming of Age in Europe: Older People in the European Community*, London, Age Concern.

Airey, Colin (1984) 'Social and Moral Values', in Jowell, R. and Airey, C. (eds) *British Social Attitudes: The 1984 Report*, Aldershot, Gower.

Allan, Graham (1985) *Family Life*, Oxford, Blackwell.

Allatt, Patricia and Yeandle, Susan (1992) *Youth Unemployment and the Family: Voices of Disordered Times*, London, Routledge.

Allen, Isobel (1988) 'Ageing as a Feminist Issue', *Policy Studies*, 2, 35–46.

Altman, Dennis (1986) *Aids and the New Puritanism*, London, Pluto Press.

Altman, Dennis (1988) 'Legitimation through Disaster: AIDS and the Gay Movement', in Fee, E. and Fox, D. M. (eds) *AIDS: The Burdens of History*, Berkeley, University of California Press.

Amos, Valerie and Parmar, Pratibha (1984) 'Challenging Imperial Feminism', *Feminist Review*, 17, 3–19.

Anthias, Floya (1992) 'Connecting "Race" and Ethnic Phenomena', *Sociology*, 26, 421–38.

Anthias, Floya and Yuval-Davis, Nira (1983) 'Contextualising Feminism – Gender, Ethnic and Class Divisions', *Feminist Review*, 15, 62–75.

Arber, Sara and Gilbert, G. Nigel (1989) 'Transitions in Caring: Gender, Life Course and the Care of the Elderly', in Bytheway, B., Keil, T., Allatt, P. and Bryman, A. (eds) *Becoming and Being Old: Sociological Approaches to Later Life*, London, Sage.

Arber, Sara and Gilbert, Nigel (1992) 'Re-assessing Women's Working Lives: An Introductory Essay', in Arber, S. and Gilbert, N. (eds) *Women and Working Lives: Divisions and Change*, London, Macmillan.

Arber, Sara and Ginn, Jay (1991) *Gender and Later Life: A Sociological Analysis of Resources and Constraints*, London, Sage.

Arber, Sara and Ginn, Jay (1992) '"In Sickness and in Health": Caregiving, Gender and the Independence of Elderly People', in Marsh, C. and Arber, S. (eds) *Families and Households: Divisions and Change*, Basingstoke, Macmillan.

Arber, Sara and Ginn, Jay (1993) 'Class, Caring and the Life Course', in Arber, S. and Evandrou, M. (eds) *Ageing, Independence and the Life Course*, London, Jessica Kingsley.

Ariès, Philippe (1962) *Centuries of Childhood*, London, Jonathan Cape.

Aronson, Jane (1990) 'Women's Perspectives on Informal Care of the Elderly: Public Ideology and Personal Experience of Giving and Receiving Care', *Ageing and Society*, 10, 61–84.

Ashford, Sheena (1987) 'Family Matters', in Jowell, R., Witherspoon, S. and Brook, L. (eds) *British Social Attitudes: The 1987 Report*, Aldershot, Gower.

Baker, Anthony W. and Duncan, Sylvia, P. (1985) 'Child Sexual Abuse: A Study of Prevalence in Great Britain', *Child Abuse and Neglect*, 9, 457–67.

Bakke, E. Wight (1933) *The Unemployed Man: A Social Study*, London, Nisbet.

Baldwin, John D. and Baldwin, Janice I. (1988) 'Factors Affecting AIDS-Related Sexual Risk-Taking Behavior Among College Students', *The Journal of Sex Research*, 25, 181–96.

Ballard, Catherine (1979) 'Conflict, Continuity and Change: Second-generation South Asians', in Saifullah Khan, V. (ed.) *Minority Families in Britain: Support and Stress*, Basingstoke, Macmillan.

Ballard, Roger (1982) 'South Asian Families', in Rapoport, R. N., Fogarty, M. P. and Rapoport , R. (eds) *Families in Britain*, London, Routledge & Kegan Paul.

Ballard, Roger and Ballard, Catherine (1977) 'The Sikhs: The Development of South Asian Settlements in Britain', in Watson, J. L. (ed.) *Between Two Cultures*, Oxford, Blackwell.

Ballard, Roger and Kalra, Virinder, S. (1994) *The Ethnic Dimensions of the 1991 Census: A Preliminary Report*, Manchester, University of Manchester.

Banton, Michael (1979) 'Gender Roles and Ethnic Relations', *New Community*, VII, 323–32.

Barker, Jonathan (1984) *Black and Asian Old People in Britain*, London, Age Concern.

Barker, Martin (1981) *The New Racism*, London, Junction Books.

Barn, Ravinder (1990) 'Black Children in Local Authority Care: Admission Patterns', *New Community*, 16, 229–46.

Barnett, Tony and Blaikie, Piers (1992) *AIDS in Africa: Its Present and Future Impact*, London, Belhaven Press.

Barrett Michèle and McIntosh, Mary (1982) *The Anti-social Family*, London, Verso.

Barry, Kathleen (1979) *Female Sexual Slavery*, New Jersey, Prentice Hall.

Bates, Inge and Riseborough, George (eds) (1993) *Youth and Inequality*, Buckingham, Open University Press.

BBC (1987) *Childwatch – National Survey on Child Abuse*, unpublished manuscript.

Beechey, Veronica and Perkins, Tessa (1987) *A Matter of Hours: Women, Part-time Work and the Labour Market*, Cambridge, Polity.

Bell, Robert R. (1969) 'The Lower-Class Negro Family in the United States and Great Britain: Some Comparisons', *Race* XI, 173–81.

Berger, Brigitte and Berger, Peter L. (1983) *The War Over the Family: Capturing the Middle Ground*, London, Hutchinson.

Bhachu, Parminder (1985) *Twice Migrants: East African Sikh Settlers in Britain*, London, Tavistock.

Bhachu, Parminder (1988) '*Apni Marzi Kardhi* Home and Work: Sikh Women in Britain', in Westwood, S. and Bhachu, P. (eds) *Enterprising Women: Ethnicity, Economy and Gender Relations*, London, Routledge.

Bhachu, Parminder (1991) 'Culture, Ethnicity and Class among Punjabi Sikh Women in 1990s Britain', *New Community*, 17, 401–12.

Bhat, Ashok, Carr-Hill, Roy and Ohri, Sushel (1988) *Britain's Black Population: A New Perspective* (2nd ed.), Aldershot, Gower.

Billingsley, Andrew (1968) *Black Families in White America*, Englewood Cliffs, New Jersey, Prentice-Hall.

Birchall, Elizabeth (1989) 'The Frequency of Child Abuse – What do we Really Know', in Stevenson, O. (ed.) *Child Abuse: Professional Practice and Public Policy*, London, Harvester Wheatsheaf.

Blakemore, Ken (1989) 'Does Age Matter? The Case of Old Age in Minority Ethnic Groups', in Bytheway, B., Keil, T., Allatt, P. and Bryman, A. (eds) *Becoming and Being Old: Sociological Approaches to Later Life*, London, Sage.

Blakemore, Ken (1993) *Minority Families and Community Care: The Case of Older People in Asian and Afro-Caribbean Communities*, paper presented at a conference on *The Family, Minorities and Social Change in Europe*, at the Centre for the Study of Minorities and Social Change, Bristol University, December, 1993.

Blakemore, Ken and Boneham, Margaret (1993) *Age, Race and Ethnicity: A Comparative Approach*, Buckingham, Open University Press.

Blood, Robert O. and Wolfe, Donald M. (1960) *Husbands and Wives: The Dynamics of Married Living*, New York, The Free Press.

Blumstein, Philip and Schwartz, Pepper (1983) *American Couples: Money, Work, Sex*, New York, Morrow.

Bograd, Michele (1988) 'Feminist Perspectives on Wife Abuse: An Introduction', in Yllö, K. and Bograd, M. (eds) *Feminist Perspectives on Wife Abuse*, Newbury Park, Sage.

Bolton, Frank G., Morris, Larry A. and MacEachron, Ann E. (1989) *Males at Risk: The Other Side of Child Sexual Abuse*, Newbury Park, Sage.

Bott, Elizabeth (1957) *Family and Social Network*, London, Tavistock.

Bould, Martin (1990) 'Trapped Within Four Walls', *Community Care*, 19 April, 17–19.

Bourque, Linda B. (1989) *Defining Rape,* Durham, Duke University Press.

Bradshaw, Jonathan, Cooke, Kenneth and Godfrey, Christine (1983) 'The Impact of Unemployment on the Living Standards of Families', *Journal of Social Policy,* 12, 433–52.

Bradshaw, Jonathan and Millar, Jane (1991) *Lone Parent Families in the UK,* Department of Social Security Research Report No. 6, London, HMSO.

Brah, Avtar (1986) 'Unemployment and Racism: Asian Youth on the Dole', in Allen, S., Waton, A., Purcell, K. and Wood, S. (eds) *The Experience of Unemployment,* Basingstoke, Macmillan.

Braithwaite, V. A. (1990) *Bound to Care,* Sydney, Allen & Unwin.

Brand, Pamela A. and Kidd, Aline H. (1986) 'Frequency of Physical Aggression in Heterosexual and Female Homosexual Dyads', *Psychological Reports,* 59, 1307–13.

Brandt, Allan M. (1987) *No Magic Bullet: A Social History of Venereal Disease in the United States Since 1880,* New York, Oxford University Press.

Brewer, Rose M. (1993) 'Theorising Race, Class and Gender: The New Scholarship of Black Feminist Intellectuals and Black Women's Labour', in James, S. M. and Busia, A. P. A. (eds) *Theorizing Black Feminisms,* London, Routledge.

Brody, Elaine M. (1981) '"Women in the Middle" and Family Help to Older People', *The Gerontologist,* 21, 471–80.

Brody, Elaine M., Johnsen, Pauline T. and Fulcomer, Mark C. (1984) 'What Should Adult Children Do For Elderly Parents? Opinions and Preferences of Three Generations of Women', *Journal of Gerontology,* 39, 736–46.

Brody, Elaine M., Hoffman, Christine, Kleban, Morton H. and Schoonover, Claire B. (1989) 'Caregiving Daughters and Their Local Siblings: Perceptions, Strains, and Interactions', *The Gerontologist,* 29, 529–38.

Brown, Audrey (1986) 'Family Circumstances of Young Children', *Population Trends,* 43, 18–23.

Brown, Colin (1984) *Black and White Britain: The Third PSI Survey,* London, Heinemann.

Browne, Angela (1987) *When Battered Women Kill,* New York, The Free Press.

Brownmiller, Susan (1976) *Against our Will: Men, Women and Rape,* Harmondsworth, Penguin.

Bryan, Beverly, Dadzie, Stella and Scafe, Suzanne (1985) *The Heart of the Race: Black Women's Lives in Britain,* London, Virago.

Buck, Nick (1992) 'Labour Market Activity and Polarisation: A Household Perspective on the Idea of the Underclass', in Smith, D. J. (ed.) *Understanding the Underclass,* London, Policy Studies Institute.

Bumpass, Larry L. and Sweet, James, A. (1989) 'Children's Experience in Single-Parent Families: Implications of Cohabitation and Marital Transitions', *Family Planning Perspectives,* 21, 256–60.

Burchell, Brendan (1993) 'The Effects of Labour Market Position, Job Insecurity, and Unemployment on Psychological Health', in Gallie, D., Marsh, C. and Vogler, C. (eds) *Social Change and the Experience of Unemployment,* Oxford, Oxford University Press.

Burgess, Ernest W., Locke, Harvey J. and Thomes, Mary M. (1963) *The Family, from Institution to Companionship*, 3rd ed., Cincinnati, American Book Company.

Burgoyne, Jacqueline and Clark, David (1984) *Making a Go of It: A Study of Stepfamilies in Sheffield*, London, Routledge & Kegan Paul.

Bury, Judith (1991) 'Teenage Sexual Behaviour and the Impact of AIDS', *Health Education Journal*, 50, 43–9.

Buunk, Bram P. and van Driel, Barry (1989) *Variant Lifestyles and Relationships*, Newbury Park, Sage.

Callender, Claire (1992) 'Redundancy, Unemployment and Poverty' in Glendinning, C. and Millar, J. (eds) *Women and Poverty in Britain: the 1990s*, London, Harvester Wheatsheaf.

Cameron, Elaine, Evers, Helen, Badger, Frances and Atkin, Karl (1989) 'Black Old Women, Disability and Health Carers', in Jefferys, M. (ed.) *Growing Old in the Twentieth Century*, London, Routledge.

Campaign Against Racism and Fascism (1983) 'Racism and Children in Care', *Race & Class*, XXV, 80–3.

Campbell, Beatrix (1993) *Goliath: Britain's Dangerous Places*, London, Methuen.

Campbell, Carole A. (1990) 'Women and AIDS', *Social Science & Medicine*, 30, 407–15.

Caputi, Jane and Russell, Diana E. H. (1992) 'Femicide: Sexist Terrorism Against Women', in Radford, J. and Russell, D. E. H. (eds) *Femicide: The Politics of Woman Killing*, Buckingham, Open University Press.

Carby, Hazel V. (1982) 'White Woman Listen! Black Feminism and the Boundaries of Sisterhood', in Centre for Contemporary Cultural Studies, *The Empire Strikes Back: Race and Racism in 70s Britain*, London, Hutchinson.

Cashmore, Ernest(1979) *Rastaman*, London, Allen & Unwin.

Castles, Stephen and Kosack, Godula (1973) *Immigrant Workers and Class Structure in Western Europe*, London. Oxford University Press.

Centers for Disease Control and Prevention (1993) *HIV AIDS Surveillance Report*, Atlanta, United States Centre for Infectious Diseases.

Centre for Contemporary Cultural Studies (1982) *The Empire Strikes Back: Race and Racism in 70s Britain*, London, Hutchinson.

Charlesworth, Ann, Wilkin, David, and Durie, Ann (1984) *Carers and Services: A Comparison of Men and Women Caring for Dependent Elderly People*, Manchester, Equal Opportunities Commission.

Chester, Robert (1985) 'The Rise of the Neo-conventional Family', *New Society*, 9 May, 185–8.

Coffield, Frank (1987) 'From the Celebration to the Marginalisation of Youth', in Cohen, G. (ed.) *Social Change and the Life Course*, London, Tavistock.

Cohen, Mitchell (1991) 'Changing to Safer Sex: Personality, Logic and Habit', in Aggleton, P., Hart, G. and Davies, P. (eds) *AIDS: Responses, Interventions and Care*, London, The Falmer Press.

Cole, Charles L. (1977) 'Cohabitation in Social Context', in Libby, R. and Whitehurst, R. N. (eds) *Marriage and Alternatives*, Illinois, Scott Foresman.

Coleman, D. A. (1989) 'The Contemporary Pattern of Remarriage in England and Wales', in Grebenik, E., Hohn, C. and Mackensen, R. (eds) *Later Phases of the Life Cycle: Demographic Aspects*, Oxford, Clarendon Press.

Coward, Rosalind (1987) 'Sex After AIDS', *New Internationalist*, March, 20–1.

Coward, Rosalind (1992) *Our Treacherous Hearts: Why Women Let Men Get Their Way*, London, Faber and Faber.

Cox, Oliver C. (1948) *Caste, Class and Race*, New York, Doubleday.

Coxon, Tony (1988) 'The Numbers Game – Gay hifestyles, Epidemiology of AIDS and Social Science', in Aggleton, P. and Homans, H. *Social Aspects of AIDS*, hewes, Falmer Press.

Coyle, Angela (1984) *Redundant Women*, London, The Women's Press.

Cragg, Arnold and Dawson, Tim (1984) *Unemployed Women: A Study of Attitudes and Experiences*, Department of Employment Research Paper No. 47, London, HMSO.

Crawford, June, Turtle, Alison and Kippax, Susan (1990) 'Student-Favoured Strategies for AIDS Avoidance', *Australian Journal of Psychology*, 42, 123–37.

Creighton, Susan J. (1992) *Child Abuse Trends in England and Wales: 1988–1990 and an Overview from 1973–1990*, London, NSPCC.

Crow, Graham and Hardey, Michael (1992) 'Diversity and Ambiguity among Lone-Parent Households in Modern Britain', in Marsh, C. and Arber, S. (eds) *Families and Households: Divisions and Change*, Basingstoke, Macmillan.

Cruickshank, Margaret (1992) *The Gay and Lesbian Liberation Movement*, London, Routledge.

Cumming, Elaine (1963) 'Further Thoughts on the Theory of Disengagement', *International Social Science Journal*, XV, 377–93.

Cumming, Elaine and Henry, William E. (1961) *Growing Old*, New York, Basic Books.

Daatland, Svein Olav (1990) '"What Are Families For?"' On Family Solidarity and Preference for Help', *Ageing and Society*, 10, 1–15.

Dahrendorf, Ralf (1987) 'The Erosion of Citizenship and its Consequences for Us All', *New Statesman*, 12 June, 12–15.

Dahrendorf, Ralf (1989) 'The Future of the Underclass: A European Perspective', *Northern Economic Review*, 18, 7–15.

Dale, Angela, Evandrou, Maria, Arber, Sara (1987) 'The Household Structure of the Elderly Population in Britain', *Ageing and Society*, 7, 37–56.

Dalley, Gillian (1988) *Ideologies of Caring: Rethinking Community and Collectivism*, Basingstoke, Macmillan.

Dalley, Gillian (1993) 'Caring: A Legitimate Interest of Older Women', in Bernard, M. and Meade, K. (eds) *Women Come of Age: Perspectives on the Lives of Older Women*, London, Arnold.

Daniel, W. W. (1990) *The Unemployed Flow*, London, Policy Studies Institute.

David, Miriam (1986) 'Morality and Maternity: Towards a Better Union than the Moral Rights Family Policy', *Critical Social Policy*, 16, 40–56.

Davies, Peter and Weatherburn, Peter (1991) 'Towards a General Model of Sexual Negotiation', in Aggleton, P., Hart, G. and Davies, P. (eds) *AIDS: Responses, Interventions and Care*, London, Falmer Press.

Davies, Richard B., Elias, Peter and Penn, Roger (1993) 'The Relationship Between a Husband's Unemployment and His Wife's Participation in the Labour Force', in Gallie, D., Marsh, C. and Vogler, C. (eds) *Social Change and the Experience of Unemployment*, Oxford, Oxford University Press.

Davis, Angela (1982) *Women, Race and Class*, London, Women's Press.

Davison, R. B. (1966) *Black British: Immigrants to England*, Oxford, Oxford University Press.

Dennis, Norman and Erdos, George (1992) *Families Without Fatherhood*, London, Institute of Economic Affairs Health and Welfare Unit.

Dennis, Norman, Henriques, Fernando and Slaughter, Clifford (1956) *Coal Is Our Life* (1st ed.), London, Eyre & Spottiswoode.

Department of Health and Social Security and the Welsh Office (1987) *AIDS: Monitoring Response to the Public Education Campaign, February 1986-February 1987*, London, HMSO.

Dex, Shirley (1983) 'The Second Generation: West Indian Female School Leavers', in Phizacklea, A. (ed.) *One Way Ticket*, London, Routledge & Kegan Paul.

Dhanjal, Beryl (1976) 'Sikh Women in Southall', *New Community*, v, 109–14.

Dickinson, David (1994) *Crime and Unemployment*, mimeo, Department of Applied Economics, Cambridge University.

Dingwall, Robert (1989) 'Some Problems about Predicting Child Abuse and Neglect', in Stevenson, O. (ed.) *Child Abuse: Professional Practice and Public Policy*, London, Harvester Wheatsheaf.

Dobash, R. Emerson and Dobash, Russell (1980) *Violence Against Wives: A Case Against the Patriachy*, London, Open Books.

Dobash, R. Emerson and Dobash, Russell P. (1988) 'Research as Social Action: The Struggle for Battered Women', in Yllö, K. and Bograd, M. (eds) *Feminist Perspectives on Wife Abuse*, Newbury Park, Sage.

Dobash, R. Emerson and Dobash, Russell P. (1992) *Women, Violence and Social Change*, London, Routledge.

Dodson, Jualynne (1988) 'Conceptualisations of Black Families', in McAdoo, H. P. (ed.) *Black Families* (2nd ed.), Newbury Park, Sage.

Dormor, Duncan J. (1992) *The Relationship Revolution*, London, ONE plus ONE.

Driver, Geoffrey (1982) 'West Indian Families: An Anthropological Perspective', in Rapoport, R. N., Fogarty, M. P. and Rapoport, R. (eds) *Families in Britain*, London, Routledge & Kegan Paul.

Drury, Beatrice (1991) 'Sikh Girls and the Maintenance of an Ethnic Culture', *New Community*, 17, 387–99.

Durham, Martin (1991) *Sex and Politics: The Family and Morality in the Thatcher Years*, Basingstoke, Macmillan.

Dworkin, Andrea (1981) *Pornography: Men Possessing Women*, New York, Perigee Press.

Edgell, Stephen (1980) *Middle-Class Couples: A Study of Segregation, Domination and Inequality in Marriage*, London, Allen & Unwin.

Edwards, Susan S. M. (1989) *Policing 'Domestic' Violence: Women, the Law and the State*, London, Sage.

Edwards, Tim (1992) 'The AIDS Dialectics: Awareness, Identity, Death, and Sexual Politics', in Plummer, K. (ed.) *Modern Homosexualities: Fragments of Lesbian and Gay Experience*, London, Routledge.

Eisenstein, Zillah R. (1982) 'The Sexual Politics of the New Right: Understanding the "Crisis of Liberalism" for the 1980s', *Signs*, 7, 567–88.

Elliot, Faith Robertson (1982) *Men's Two Roles: The Dilemmas of the Middle-Class Husband*, mimeo., School of Health and Social Sciences, Coventry University.

Elliot, Faith Robertson (1986) *The Family: Change or Continuity?*, Basingstoke, Macmillan.

Equal Opportunities Commission (1980) *The Experience of Caring for Elderly and Handicapped Dependents*, Manchester, EOC.

Ermisch, John (1989) 'Divorce: Economic Antecedents and Aftermath', in Joshi, H. (ed.) *The Changing Population of Britain*, Oxford, Basil Blackwell.

Estes, Carroll L. and Binney, Elizabeth A. (1991) 'The Biomedicalization of Aging: Dangers and Dilemmas' in Minkler, M. and Estes, C. L. (eds) *Critical Perspectives on Aging: The Political and Moral Economy of Growing Old*, New York, Baywood.

Eurostat (1993) *Demographic Statistics 1993*, Luxembourg, Office for the Official Publications of the European Communities.

Evandrou, Maria, Arber, Sara, Dale Angela and Gilbert, G. Nigel (1986) 'Who Cares for the Elderly? Family Care Provision and Receipt of Statutory Service', in Phillipson, C., Bernard, M. and Strang, P. (eds) *Dependency and Interdependency in Old Age: Theoretical Perspectives and Policy Alternatives*, London, Croom Helm.

Evans, Brian A., McLean, Kenneth A., Dawson, Stephen G., Teece, Steven A., Bond, Robert A., MacRae, Kenneth D. and Thorp, Robert W. (1989) 'Trends in Sexual Behaviour and Risk Factors for HIV Infection Among Homosexual Men, 1984–7', *British Medical Journal*, 298, 215–18.

Faludi, Susan (1991) *Backlash: The Undeclared War Against Women*, London, Chatto & Windus.

Feldman, Douglas A. (1985) 'AIDS and Social Change', *Human Organisation*, 44, 343–7.

Fennell, Graham, Phillipson, Chris and Evers, Helen (1988) *The Sociology of Old Age*, Milton Keynes, Open University Press.

Field, Frank (1989) *Losing Out: The Emergence of Britain's Underclass,* Oxford, Blackwell.

Finch, Janet (1983) *Married to the Job: Wives' Incorporation in Men's Work,* London, Allen & Unwin.

Finch, Janet (1984) 'Community Care: Developing Non-Sexist Alternatives' *Critical Social Policy,* 9, 6–18.

Finch, Janet (1986) 'Community Care and the Invisible Welfare State', *Radical Community Medicine,* Summer, 15–22.

Finch, Janet (1989) *Family Obligations and Social Change,* Cambridge, Polity.

Finch, Janet and Mason, Jennifer (1990a) 'Divorce, Remarriage and Family Obligations', *The Sociological Review,* 38, 219–46.

Finch, Janet and Mason, Jennifer (1990b) 'Filial Obligations and Kin Support for Elderly People', *Ageing and Society,* 10, 151–75.

Finch, Janet and Mason, Jennifer (1990c) 'Gender, Employment and Responsibilities to Kin', *Work, Employment & Society,* 4, 349–67.

Finch, Janet and Mason, Jennifer (1993) *Negotiating Family Responsibilities,* London, Routledge.

Finch, Janet and Morgan, David (1991) 'Marriage in the 1980s: A New Sense of Realism?', in Clark, D. (ed.) *Marriage, Domestic Life and Social Change: Writings for Jacqueline Burgoyne (1944–88),* London, Routledge.

Fineman, Stephen (1983) *White Collar Unemployment: Impact and Stress,* Chichester, Wiley.

Fineman, Stephen (1987) 'Back to Employment: Wounds and Wisdoms', in Fryer, D. and Ullah, P. (eds) *Unemployed People: Social and Psychological Perspectives,* Milton Keynes, Open University Press.

Finkelhor, David (1979) *Sexually Victimised Children,* New York, Free Press.

Finkelhor, David (1984) *Child Sexual Abuse: New Theory and Research,* New York, Free Press.

Finkelhor, David and Baron, Larry (1986) 'High-Risk Children', in Finkelhor, D. (ed.) *A Sourcebook on Child Sexual Abuse,* Beverly Hills, Sage.

Firestone, Shulamith (1970) *The Dialectic of Sex: The Case for Feminist Revolution,* New York, Morrow.

Fitzpatrick, Michael and Milligan, Don (1987) *The Truth About the AIDS Panic,* London, Junius.

Fitzpatrick, Michael and Milligan, Don (1990) 'Reflections on the AIDS Panic', in an interview with Linda Ryan, *Living Marxism,* 15, 14–19.

Fitzpatrick, Ray, Boulton, Mary and Hart, Graham (1989) 'Gay Men's Sexual Behaviour in Response to AIDS – Insights and Problems', in Aggleton, P., Hart, G. and Davies, P. (eds) *AIDS: Social Representations, Social Practices,* Lewes, Falmer Press.

Fitzpatrick, Ray, McLean, John, Boulton, Mary, Hart, Graham and Dawson, Jill (1990) 'Variation in Sexual Behaviour in Gay Men', in Aggleton, P., Davies, P. and Hart, G. (eds) *AIDS: Individual, Cultural and Policy Dimensions,* London, Falmer Press.

Fletcher, Ronald (1962) *Britain in the Sixties: The Family and Marriage* (1st ed.), Harmondsworth, Penguin Books.

Fletcher, Ronald (1988) *The Shaking of the Foundations: Family and Society*, London, Routledge.

Foner, Nancy (1977) 'The Jamaicans: Cultural and Social Change among Migrants in Britain', in Watson, J. L. (ed.) *Between Two Cultures*, Oxford, Blackwell.

Foner, Nancy (1986) 'Sex Roles and Sensibilities: Jamaican Women in New York and London', in Simon, R. J. and Brettell, C. B. (eds) *International Migration: The Female Experience*, New Jersey, Rowman & Allanheld.

Ford, Nicholas and Bowie, Cameron (1988) 'Sexually-related Behaviour and AIDS Education', *Education and Health*, October, 86–91.

Frazier, E. Franklin (1939) *The Negro in the United States*, Chicago, University of Chicago Press.

Freeman, M. D. A. (1979) *Violence in the Home*, Farnborough, Saxon House.

Fries, James F. (1980) 'Ageing, Natural Death, and the Compression of Morbidity', *New England Journal of Medicine*, 303, 130–5.

Fries, James F. (1989) 'Reduction of the National Morbidity', in Lewis, S. (ed.) *Aging and Health: Linking Research and Public Policy*, Michigan, Lewis Publishers.

Fritz, Gregory S., Stoll, Kim, Wagner, Nathaniel (1981) 'A Comparison of Males and Females Who Were Sexually Molested as Children', *Journal of Sex & Marital Therapy*, 7, 54–9.

Fryer, Peter (1984) *Staying Power: The History of Black People in Britain*, London, Pluto.

Furniss, T. (1984) 'Conflict-Avoiding and Conflict-Regulating Patterns in Incest and Child Sexual Abuse', *Acta Paedopsychiat*, 50, 299–313.

Furstenberg, Frank F. and Harris, Kathleen, M. (1992) 'The Disappearing American Father? Divorce and the Waning Significance of Biological Parenthood', in South, S. J. and Tolnay S. E. (eds) *The Changing American Family*, Boulder, Westview Press.

Gallie, Duncan (1994) 'Are the Unemployed an Underclass? Some Evidence from the Social Change and Economic Life Initiative', *Sociology*, 28, 737–57.

Gallie, Duncan and Vogler, Carolyn (1993) 'Labour Market Deprivation, Welfare, and Collectivism' in Gallie, D., Marsh, C. and Vogler, C. (eds) *Social Change and the Experience of Unemployment*, Oxford, Oxford University Press.

Gallie, Duncan, Gershuny, Jonathan and Vogler, Carolyn (1993) 'Unemployment, the Household and Social Networks', in Gallie, D., Marsh, C. and Vogler, C. (eds) *Social Change and the Experience of Unemployment*, Oxford, Oxford University Press.

Garbarino, James (1981) 'An Ecological Approach to Child Maltreatment', in Pelton, L. H. (ed.) *The Social Context of Child Abuse and Neglect*, New York, Human Sciences Press.

Garbarino, James and Gilliam, Gwen (1980) *Understanding Abusive Families*, Lexington, Mass., Lexington Books.

Gayford, Jasper J. (1975) 'Wife Battering: A Preliminary Survey of 100 Cases', *British Medical Journal*, 194–7.

Gayford, Jasper J. (1976) 'Ten Types of Battered Wives' *The Welfare Officer*, 25, 5–9..

Gelles, Richard J. and Cornell, Claire P. (1990) *Intimate Violence in Families* (2nd ed.), Newbury Park, Sage.

Gelles, Richard J. and Straus, Murray A. (1988) *Intimate Violence*, New York, Simon and Schuster.

General Household Survey (1986), Office of Population Censuses and Surveys, London, HMSO.

General Household Survey (1991), Office of Population Censuses and Surveys, London, HMSO.

General Household Survey (1992), Office of Population Censuses and Surveys, London, HMSO.

George, Margaret (1973) 'From "Goodwife" to "Mistress": the Transformation of the Female in Bourgeois Culture', *Science and Society*, 152–77.

Gershuny, Jonathan (1992) 'Change in the Domestic Division of Labour in the UK, 1975–1987: Dependent Labour versus Adaptive Partnership', in Abercrombie, N. and Warde, A. (eds) *Social Change in Contemporary Britain*, Cambridge, Polity.

Gershuny, Jonathan (1993) 'The Psychological Consequences of Unemployment: An Assessment of the Jahoda Thesis', in Gallie, D., Marsh, C. and Vogler, C. (eds) *Social Change and the Experience of Unemployment*, Oxford, Oxford University Press.

Gershuny, Jonathan and Marsh, Catherine (1993) 'Unemployment in Work Histories', in Gallie, D., Marsh, C. and Vogler, C. (eds), *Social Change and the Experience of Unemployment*, Oxford, Oxford University Press.

Gibson, Ashton (1980) *Pregnancy among Unmarried West Indian Teenagers*, London, Centre for Caribbean Studies.

Gil, David (1970) *Violence Against Children: Physical Child Abuse in the United States*, Cambridge, Mass, Harvard University Press.

Gil, David (1975) 'Unravelling Child Abuse', *American Journal of Orthopsychiatry*, 45, 346–56.

Gilroy, Paul (1992) 'The End of Antiracism', in Donald J. and Rattansi, A. (eds) *'Race', Culture and Difference*, London, The Open University/Sage.

Glaser, Danya and Frosh, Stephen (1988) *Child Sexual Abuse*, Basingstoke, Macmillan.

Goode, William J. (1963) *World Revolution and Family Patterns*, New York, The Free Press.

Goode, William J. (1971) 'Force and Violence in the Family', *Journal of Marriage and the Family*, 33, 624–36.

Gordon, Linda (1986) 'Feminism and Social Control: The Case of Child Abuse and Neglect', in Mitchell, J. and Oakley, A. (eds) *What is Feminism?*, Oxford, Blackwell.

Gordon, Linda (1989) *Heroes of Their Own Lives: The Politics and History of Family Violence*, London, Virago.

Graham, Hilary (1983) 'Caring: A Labour of Love', in Finch, J. and Groves, D. (eds) *A Labour of Love: Women, Work and Caring*, London, Routledge & Kegan Paul.

Graham, Hilary (1991) 'The Concept of Caring in Feminist Research: The Case of Domestic Service', *Sociology*, 25, 61–78.

Griffiths, Kathleen (1983) Child-rearing Practices in West Indian, Indian and Pakistani Communities, *New Community*, X, 393–409.

Guy, Catherine (1983) *Asking About Marriage*, Rugby, National Marriage Guidance Council.

Hagestad, Gunhild O. (1986) 'The Ageing Society as a Context for Family Life', *Daedalus*, 115(1), 119–39.

Hakim, Catherine (1979) *Occupational Segregation: A Comparative Study of the Degree and Pattern of the Differentiation between Men and Women's Work in Britain, the United States and Other Countries*, Department of Employment Research Paper no.9, London, HMSO.

Hakim, Catherine (1982) 'The Social Consequences of High Unemployment', *Journal of Social Policy*, 11, 433–67.

Hall, Catherine (1979) 'The Early Formation of Victorian Domestic Ideology', in Burman, S. (ed.) *Fit Work for Women*, London, Croom Helm.

Hall, Stuart, Critcher, Chas, Jefferson, Tony, Clarke, John and Roberts, Brian (1978) *Policing the Crisis: Mugging, the State, and Law and Order*, Basingstoke, Macmillan.

Halson, Jacqui (1991) 'Young Women, Sexual Harassment and Heterosexuality: Violence, Power Relations and Mixed-Sex Schooling', in Abbott, P. and Wallace, C. (eds) *Gender, Power and Sexuality*, Basingstoke, Macmillan.

Hamilton, Roberta (1978) *The Liberation of Women*, London, Allen & Unwin.

Hampton, Robert L., Gelles, Richard J. and Harrop, John W. (1989) 'Is Violence in Black Families Increasing? A Comparison of 1975 and 1985 National Survey Rates', *Journal of Marriage and the Family*, 51, 969–80.

Hanmer, Jalna, Radford, Jill and Stanko, Elizabeth A. (eds) (1989) *Women, Policing, and Male Violence: International Perspectives*, London, Routledge.

Harding, Stephen (1988) 'Trends in Permissiveness', in Jowell, R., Witherspoon, S. and Brook, L. (eds) *British Social Attitudes, the 5th Report*, Aldershot, Gower.

Hartley, Jean (1987) 'Managerial Unemployment: The Wife's Perspective and Role', in Fineman, S. (ed.) *Unemployment: Personal and Social Consequences*, London, Tavistock.

Haskey, John (1989a) 'Current Prospects for the Proportion of Marriages Ending in Divorce', *Population Trends*, 55, 34–7.

Haskey, John (1989b) 'Families and Households of the Ethnic Minority and White Populations of Great Britain', *Population Trends*, 57, 8–19.

Haskey, John (1990) 'Children in Families Broken by Divorce', *Population Trends*, 61, 34–42.

Haskey, John (1991) 'Estimated Numbers and Demographic Characteristics of One-Parent Families in Great Britain', *Population Trends*, 65, 35–48.

Haskey, John (1992) 'Patterns of Marriage, Divorce, and Cohabitation in the Different Countries of Europe', *Population Trends*, 69, 27–36.

Haskey, John and Kiernan, Kathleen (1989) 'Cohabitation in Great Britain – Characteristics and Estimated Numbers of Cohabiting Partners, *Population Trends*, 58, 23–32.

Hawton, Keith (1992) 'By Their Own Hand', *British Medical Journal*, 304, 1000.

Heady, Patrick and Smyth, Malcolm (1989) *Living Standards during Unemployment*, London, OPCS/HMSO.

Hedström, Peter and Ringen, Stein (1987) 'Age and Income in Contemporary Society: A Research Note, *Journal of Social Policy*, 16, Cambridge University Press.

Herskovits, Melville J. (1941) *The Myth of the Negro Past*, New York, Harper.

Hill, Robert (1971) *The Strengths of Black Families*, New York, Emerson Hall.

Hobsbawm, E. J. (1969) *Industry and Empire: From 1750 to the Present Day*, Harmondsworth, Penguin.

Hochschild, Arlie (1990) *The Second Shift: Working Parents and the Revolution at Home*, New York, Viking.

Hoem, Britta and Hoem, Jan M. (1988) 'The Swedish Family: Aspects of Contemporaly Developments', *Journal of Family Issues*, 9, 397–424.

Holland, Janet, Ramazanoglu, Caroline and Scott, Sue (1990) *Sex, Risk, and Danger*, WRAP Paper 1, London, The Tufnell Press.

Holland, Janet, Ramazanoglu, Caroline, Scott, Sue, Sharpe, Sue and Thomson, Rachel (1991a) 'Between Embarrassment and Trust: Young Women and the Diversity of Condom Use', in Aggleton, P., Hart, G. and Davies, P. (eds) *AIDS: Responses, Interventions and Care*, London, The Falmer Press.

Holland, Janet, Ramazanoglu, Caroline, Sharpe, Sue and Thomson, Rachel (1991b) *Pressured Pleasure: Young Women and the Negotiation of Sexual Boundaries*, WRAP Paper 7, London, The Tufnell Press.

Home Office (1992) *Criminal Statistics: England and Wales, 1991*, Cm 2134, London, HMSO.

Hooks, Bell (1982) *'Ain't I a Woman? Black Women and Feminism'*, London, Pluto Press.

Hooks, Bell (1986) 'Sisterhood: Political Solidarity between Women', *Feminist Review*, 23, 125–38.

Hunt, Andrew (1992) *Changes in Gay Men's Sexual Behaviour in England and Wales, 1987–1991*, paper presented to the Sixth Conference on Social Aspects of AIDS, South Bank Polytechnic, 1992.

Hunt, Andrew and Davies, Peter (1991) 'What Is a Sexual Encounter?', in Aggleton, P., Hart, G. and Davies, P. (eds) *AIDS: Responses, Interventions and Care*, London, Falmer Press.

Hutson, Susan and Jenkins, Richard (1989) *Taking the Strain: Families, Unemployment and the Transition to Adulthood*, Milton Keynes, Open University Press.

Ingham, Roger, Woodcock, Alison and Stenner, Karen (1991) 'Getting to Know You... Young People's Knowledge of their Partners at First Intercourse', *Journal of Community and Applied Social Psychology*, 1, 117–32.

Itzin, Catherine (ed.) (1980) *Splitting Up: Single Parent Liberation*, London, Virago.

Itzin, Catherine (1990) *Age and Sexual Divisions: A Study of Opportunity and Identity in Women*, unpublished PhD thesis, University of Kent at Canterbury.

Jackson, Paul R. and Walsh, Susan (1987) 'Unemployment and the Family', in Fryer, D. and Ullah, P. (eds) *Unemployed People: Social and Psychological Perspectives*, Milton Keynes, Open University Press.

Jahoda, Marie (1982) *Employment and Unemployment: A Social-Psychological Analysis*, Cambridge, Cambridge University Press.

Jahoda, Marie, Lazarsfeld, Paul F. and Zeisel, H. (1972) *Marienthal: The Sociography of an Unemployed Community*, London, Tavistock (first published in 1933).

Jeffreys, Sheila (1990) *Anticlimax*, London, The Women's Press.

Jones, Trevor (1993) *Britain's Ethnic Minorities: An Analysis of the Labour Force Survey*, London, Policy Studies Institute.

Joseph, Jill G., Montgomery, Susanne B., Emmons, Carol-Ann, Kessler, Ronald C., Ostrow, David G., Wortman, Camille B., O'Brien, Kerth, Eller, Michael and Eshleman, Suzann (1987) 'Magnitude and Determinants of Behavioral Risk Reduction: Longitudinal Analysis of a Cohort at Risk for AIDS', *Psychology and Health*, 1, 73–96.

Joshi, Heather (1984) *Women's Participation in Paid Work: Further Analysis of the Women and Employment Survey* (Research Paper No. 45, Department of Employment), London, HMSO.

Joshi, Heather (1992) 'The Cost of Caring', in Glendinning, C. and Millar, J., *Women and Poverty in Britain: The 1990s*, London, Harvester Wheatsheaf.

Justice, Blair and Justice, Rita (1979) *The Broken Taboo: Sex in the Family*, New York, Human Sciences Press.

Kell, Michael and Wright, Jane (1990) 'Benefits and the Labour Supply of Women Married to Unemployed Men, *Economic Journal*, 100, Supplement, 119–26.

Kelly, Liz (1988a) 'How Women Define Their Experiences of Violence', in Yllö, K. and Bograd, M. (eds) *Feminist Perspectives on Wife Abuse*, Newbury Park, Sage.

Kelly, Liz (1988b) *Surviving Sexual Violence*, Cambridge, Polity.

Kelly, Liz (1988c) 'What's in a Name?: Defining Child Sexual Abuse', *Feminist Review*, 28, 65–73.

Kelly, Liz (1991) 'Unspeakable Acts', *Trouble and Strife*, 21, 13–20.

Kelvin, Peter and Jarrett, Joanna E. (1985) *Unemployment: Its Social Psychological Effects,* Cambridge, Cambridge University Press.

Kempe, Ruth and Kempe, C. Henry (1978) *Child Abuse,* London, Fontana.

Kempe, C. Henry, Silverman, Frederic N., Steele, Brandt F., Droegemueller, William and Silver, Henry K. (1962) 'The Battered Child Syndrome', *Journal of the American Medical Association,* 181, 17–24.

Kerr, Madeleine (1958) *The People of Ship Street,* London, Routledge & Kegan Paul.

Kiernan, Kathleen (1992a) 'Men and Women at Work and at Home', in Jowell, R., Brook, L., Prior G. and Taylor, B. (eds) *British Social Attitudes: The 9th Report,* Aldershot, Gower.

Kiernan, Kathleen (1992b) 'The Roles of Men and Women in Tomorrow's Europe', *Employment Gazette,* October, 491–9.

Kiernan, Kathleen and Estaugh, Valerie (1993) *Cohabitation: Extra-Marital Childbearing and Social Policy,* London, Family Policy Studies Centre.

Kiernan, Kathleen and Wicks, Malcolm (1990) *Family Change and Future Policy,* York and London, Joseph Rowntree Memorial Trust in association with the Family Policy Studies Centre.

Kinsey, Alfred C., Pomeroy, Wardell B. and Martin, Clyde E. (1948) *Sexual Behaviour in the Human Male,* Philadelphia, Saunders.

Kinsey, Alfred C., Pomeroy, Wardell B., Martin, Clyde E. and Gebhard, Paul H. (1953) *Sexual Behaviour in the Human Female,* Philadelphia, Saunders.

Kline, Anna, Kline, Emily and Oken, Emily (1992) 'Minority Women and Sexual Choice in the Age of AIDS', *Social Science & Medicine,* 34, 447–57.

Knox, E. G., MacArthur, C., Simons, K. J. (1993) *Sexual Behaviour and AIDS in Britain,* London, HMSO.

Komarovsky, Mirra (1940) *The Unemployed Man and His Family,* New York, Octagon Books.

Kotarba, Joseph A. and Lang, Norris, G. (1986) 'Gay Lifestyle Change and AIDS: Preventive Health Care' in Feldman, D. A. and Johnson, T. M. (eds) *The Social Dimensions of AIDS: Method and Theory,* New York, Praeger.

Laczko, Frank, Dale, Angela, Arber, Sara and Gilbert, G. Nigel (1988) 'Early Retirement in a Period of High Unemployment', *Journal of Social Policy,* 17, 313–33.

La Fontaine, Jean (1990) *Child Sexual Abuse,* Cambridge, Polity.

Laite, Julian and Halfpenny, Peter (1987) 'Employment, Unemployment and the Domestic Division of Labour', in Fryer, D. and Ullah, P. (eds) *Unemployed People: Social and Psychological Perspectives,* Milton Keynes, Open University Press.

Lampard, Richard (1993) 'An Examination of the Relationship Between Marital Dissolution and Unemployment', in Gallie, D., Marsh, C. and Vogler, C. (eds) *Social Change and the Experience of Unemployment,* Oxford, Oxford University Press.

Laslett, Peter (1982) 'Foreword' to Rapoport, R. N., Fogarty, M. P. and Rapoport, R., *Families in Britain,* London, Routledge & Kegan Paul.

Laslett, Peter (1987) 'The Emergence of the Third Age', *Ageing and Society,* 7, 133–60.

Laslett, Peter (1989) *A Fresh Map of Life: The Emergence of the Third Age,* London, Weidenfeld and Nicolson.

Lawrence, Errol (1982) 'Just Plain Common Sense: The 'Roots' of Racism', in Centre for Contemporary Cultural Studies (eds) *The Empire Strikes Back: Race and Racism in 70s Britain,* London, Hutchinson.

Lawson, Annette (1988) *Adultery: an Analysis of Love and Betrayal,* New York, Basic Books.

Layard, R., Piachaud, D. and Stewart, M. (1978) *The Causes of Poverty* (Report of the Royal Commission on the Distribution of Income and Wealth, Background Paper No. 5) London, HMSO.

Leach, Edmund, R. (1967) *A Runaway World,* London, BBC Publications.

Lee, Gary L. (1985) 'Kinship and Social Support of the Elderly: The Case of the United States', *Ageing and Society,* 5, 19–38.

Lees, Sue (1986a) *Losing Out: Sexuality and Adolescent Girls,* London, Hutchinson.

Lees, Sue (1986b) 'Sex, Race and Culture: Feminism and the Limits of Cultural Pluralism', *Feminist Review,* 22, 92–102.

Lees, Sue (1992) 'Naggers, Whores and Libbers: Provoking Men to Kill', in Radford J. and Russell D. E. H. (eds) *Femicide: The Politics of Woman Killing,* Buckingham, Open University Press.

Leidig, Marjorie W. (1981) 'Violence Against Women – A Feminist Psychological Analysis', in Cox, S. (ed.) *Female Psychology: The Emerging Self,* New York, St. Martin's Press.

Leishman, Katie (1987) 'Heterosexuals and AIDS', *The Atlantic Monthly,* 259, 39–58.

Leonard, Diana (1980) *Sex and Generation: A Study of Courtship and Weddings,* London, Tavistock.

Levin, Jack and Levin, William C. (1980) *Ageism: Prejudice and Discrimination Against the Elderly,* Belmont, Calif., Wadsworth.

Lewin, Bo (1982) 'Unmarried Cohabitation: A Marriage Form in a Changing Society', *Journal of Marriage and the Family,* 44, 763–73.

Lewis, Jane and Meredith, Barbara (1988) *Daughters Who Care: Daughters Caring for Mothers at Home,* London, Routledge.

Linton, Ralph (1949) 'The Natural History of the Family', in Anshen, R. N. (ed.) *The Family: Its Function and Destiny,* New York, Harper & Bros.

Lonsdale, Susan (1992) 'Patterns of Paid Work', in Glendinning, C. and Millar, J. (eds) *Women and Poverty in Britain: the 1990s,* London, Harvester Wheatsheaf.

Lundberg-Love, Paula and Geffner, Robert (1989) 'Date Rape: Prevalence, Risk Factors and a Proposed Model', in Pirog-Good, M. A. and Stets, J. E. (eds) *Violence in Dating Relationships: Emerging Social Issues,* New York, Praeger.

McCalman, Joy A. (1990) *The Forgotten People: Carers in Three Ethnic Minority Communites in Southwark,* London, Help the Aged.

Macdonald, Petrine and Mars, Gerald (1981) 'Informal Marriage', in Henry, S. (ed.) *Can I Have It in Cash*, London, Astragal Books.

McIntosh, Mary (1978) 'The State and the Oppression of Women', in Kuhn, A. and Wolpe, A. (eds) *Feminism and Materialism: Women and Modes of Production*, London, Routledge & Kegan Paul.

McKee, Lorna and Bell, Colin (1985) 'Marital and Family Relations in Times of Male Unemployment', in Roberts, B., Finnegan, R. and Gallie, D. (eds) *New Approaches to Economic Life*, Manchester, Manchester University Press.

McKee, Lorna and Bell, Colin (1986) 'His Unemployment, Her Problem: The Domestic and Marital Consequences of Male Unemployment', in Allen, S., Waton, A., Purcell, K. and Wood, S. (eds) *The Experience of Unemployment*, Basingstoke, Macmillan.

Macklin, Eleanor D. (1983) 'Nonmarital Heterosexual Cohabitation: an Overview', in Macklin, E. D. and Rubin, R. H. (ed.) *Contemporary Families and Alternative Lifestyles*, Beverly Hills, Sage.

McKusick, Leon, Horstman, William and Coates, Thomas J. (1985) 'AIDS and Sexual Behaviour Reported by Gay Men in San Fransisco', *American Journal of Public Health*, 75, 493–6.

Maclean, M. and Wadsworth, M. E. J. (1988) 'The Interests of Children after Parental Divorce: A Long-term Perspective', *International Journal of Law and the Family*, 2, 155–66.

MacLeod, Mary and Saraga, Esther (1988) 'Challenging the Orthodoxy: Towards a Feminist Theory and Practice', *Feminist Review*, 28, 16–55.

McNay, Marie and Pond, Chris (1980) *Low Pay and Family Poverty*, London, Study Commission on the Family.

Macnicol, John and Blaikie, Andrew (1989) 'The Politics of Retirement 1908–1948', in Jefferys, M. (ed.) *Growing Old in the Twentieth Century*, London, Routledge.

McRae, Susan (1987) 'Social and Political Perspectives Found Among Unemployed Young Men and Women', in White, M. (ed.) *The Social World of the Young Unemployed*, London, Policy Studies Institute.

McRae, Susan (1991) *Maternity Rights in Britain: The Experience of Women and Employers*, London, Policy Studies Institute.

McRae, Susan (1993) *Cohabiting Mothers: Changing Marriage and Motherhood?*, London, Policy Studies Institute.

Madge, Nicola (1983) 'Unemployment and its Effects on Children', *Journal of Child Psychology and Psychiatry*, 24, 311–19.

Mahony, Pat (1985) *Schools for the Boys: Co-education Reassessed*, London Hutchinson.

Malveaux, Julianne (1987) 'The Political Economy of Black Women', in Davis, M., Marable, M., Pfeil, F. and Sprinker, M. (eds) *The Year Left 2*, London, Verso.

Malveaux, Julianne (1988) 'The Economic Statuses of Black Families', in McAdoo H. P. (ed.) *Black Families*, Newbury Park, Sage.

Marsden, Dennis (1982) *Workless: An Exploration of the Social Contract between Society and the Worker* (2nd ed.), London, Croom Helm.

Marshall, Gordon (1984) 'On the Sociology of Women's Unemployment, Its Neglect and Significance', *Sociological Review*, 32, 234–59.

Martin, Jean and Roberts, Ceridwen (1984) *Women and Employment: A Lifetime Perspective*, Report of the 1980 DE/OPCS Women and Employment Survey, London, HMSO.

Martin, Jean, Meltzer, Howard and Elliot, David (1988) *The Prevalence of Disability among Adults*, London, OPCS/HMSO.

Martin, John (1987) 'The Impact of AIDS on Gay Male Sexual Behaviour Patterns in New York City', *American Journal of Public Health*, 77, 578–81.

Martin, Roderick and Wallace, Judith (1984) *Working Women in Recession: Employment, Redundancy and Unemployment*, Oxford, Oxford University Press.

Masters, William H., Johnson, Virginia E. and Kolodny, Robert C. (1988) *Crisis: Heterosexual Behaviour in the Age of AIDS*, London, Weidenfeld and Nicolson.

Matthews, Sarah H. (1988) 'The Burdens of Parent Care: A Critical Evaluation of Recent Findings', *Journal of Aging Studies*, 2, 157–65.

Matthews, Sarah H. and Rosner, Tena Tarler (1988) 'Shared Filial Responsibility: The Family as the Primary Caregiver', *Journal of Marriage and the Family*, 50, 185–95.

Miles, Robert (1982) *Racism and Migrant Labour: A Critical Text*, London, Routledge & Kegan Paul.

Miles, Robert (1989) *Racism*, London, Routledge.

Miles, Robert (1993) *Racism After 'Race Relations'*, London, Routledge.

Millar, Jane (1992) 'Lone Mothers and Poverty', in Glendinning, C. and Millar, J. (eds) *Women and Poverty in Britain: the 1990s*, London, Harvester Wheatsheaf.

Millett, Kate (1970) *Sexual Politics*, New York, Doubleday.

Minkler, Meredith and Estes, Carroll L. (eds) (1984) *Readings in the Political Economy of Aging*, New York, Baywood.

Minkler, Meredith and Estes, Carroll L. (eds) (1991) *Critical Perspectives on Ageing: The Political and Moral Economy of Growing Old*, New York, Baywood.

Mirza, Heidi S. (1992) *Young, Female and Black*, London, Routledge.

Mitchell, Deborah and Bradshaw, Jonathan (1991) *Lone-Parents and Their Incomes: A Comparative Study of Ten Countries*, Unpublished Research Report, University of York.

Mittag, Helga (1991) 'AIDS Prevention and Sexual Liberalization in Great Britain', *Social Science & Medicine*, 32, 783–91.

Modood, Tariq (1988) '"Black", Racial Equality and Asian Identity', *New Community* XIV, 397–404.

Mooney, Jayne (1993) *Researching Domestic Violence: The North London Domestic Violence Survey* (Preliminary Report) London, Centre for Criminology, Middlesex University.

Morokvasic, Mirjana (1983) 'Women in Migration: Beyond the Reductionist Outlook', in Phizacklea, A. (ed.) *One Way Ticket: Migration and Female Labour*, London, Routledge.

Moroney, Robert M. (1976) *The Family and the State*, London, Longman.

Morris, Jenny (1992) '"Us" and "Them"? Feminist Research, Community Care and Disability', *Critical Social Policy*, 33, 22–39.

Morris, Lydia D. (1985) 'Responses to Redundancy: Labour Market Experience, Domestic Organisation and Male Social Networks', *International Journal of Social Economics*, 12, 5–16.

Morris, Lydia D. (1987) 'Domestic Circumstances', in Harris, C. C. (ed.) *Redundancy & Recession*, Oxford, Blackwell.

Morris, Lydia D. (1990) *The Workings of the Household: A US–UK Comparison*, Cambridge, Polity Press.

Morris, Lydia D. and Irwin, Sarah (1992a) 'Employment Histories and the Concept of the Underclass', *Sociology*, 26, 401–20.

Morris, Lydia D. and Irwin, Sarah (1992b) 'Unemployment and Informal Support: Dependency, Exclusion, or Participation', *Work, Employment & Society*, 6, 185–207.

Mount, Ferdinand (1982) *The Subversive Family: An Alternative History of Love and Marriage*, London, Jonathan Cape.

Moylan, S., Millar J. and Davies, R. (1984) *For Richer, For Poorer? DHSS Cohort Study of Unemployed Men*, DHSS Research Report No. 11, London, HMSO.

Moynihan, Daniel P. (1965) *The Negro Family: The Case for National Action*, Washington, D.C., US Department of Labour.

Muehlenhard, Charlene L. and Linton, Melaney A. (1987) 'Date Rape and Sexual Aggression in Dating Situations: Incidence and Risk Factors', *Journal of Counseling Psychology*, 34, 186–96.

Muncie, John (1984) *The Trouble With Kids Today: Youth and Crime in Post-war Britain*, London, Hutchinson.

Murdock, George P. (1949) *Social Structure*, New York, Collier-Macmillan.

Murray, Charles (1984) *Losing Ground: American Social Policy 1950–1980*, New York, Basic Books.

Murray, Charles (1990) *The Emerging British Underclass*, London, Institute of Economic Affairs Health and Welfare Unit.

NCH (1992) *The Report of the Committee of Enquiry into Children and Young People who Sexually Abuse Other Children*, London, National Children's Home.

NCPCA (1992) *Current Trends in Child Abuse Reporting and Fatalities: The Results of the 1991 Annual Fifty State Survey*, Chicago, National Committee for Prevention of Child Abuse.

Nain, Gemma Tang (1991) 'Black Women, Sexism and Racism: Black or Antiracist Feminism?', *Feminist Review*, 37, 1–22.

Nash, C. L. and West, D. J. (1985) 'Sexual Molestation of Young Girls: A Retrospective Survey', in West, D. J. (ed.) *Sexual Victimisation: Two Recent Researches Into Sex Problems and Their Social Effects*, Aldershot, Gower.

Needle, Richard H., Leach, Susan and Graham-Tomasi, Robin P. (1989) 'The Human Immunodeficiency Virus (HIV) Epidemic: Epidemiological Implications for Family Professionals', in Macklin, E. D. (ed.) *AIDS and Families*, New York, Harrington Park Press.

Nelson, Sarah (1987) *Incest: Fact and Myth* (2nd ed.), Edinburgh, Stramullion Co-operative.

Neugarten, Bernice L. and Neugarten, Dail A. (1986) 'Age in the Aging Society', *Daedalus*, 1986, 115(1), 31–49.

Neustatter, Angela (1989) *Hyenas in Petticoats: A Look at Twenty Years of Feminism*, London, Harrap.

Newson, John and Newson, Elizabeth (1980) 'Parental Punishment Strategies with Eleven-Year Old Children', in Frude, N. (ed.) *Psychological Approaches to Child Abuse*, London, Batsford.

Newson, John and Newson, Elizabeth (1989) *The Extent of Parental Physical Punishment in the UK*, London, Association for the Protection of All Children.

Nissel, Muriel and Bonnerjea, Lucy (1982) *Family Care of the Handicapped Elderly: Who Pays*, London, Policy Studies Institute.

Norman, Alison J. (1985) *Triple Jeopardy: Growing Old in a Second Homeland*, London, Centre for Policy on Ageing.

Norwood, Robin (1985) *Women Who Love Too Much*, New York, Pocket Books.

Norwood, Robin (1988) *Letters from Women Who Love Too Much: A Closer Look at Relationship Addiction and Recovery*, London, Arrow Books.

Oakley, Ann (1974) *The Sociology of Housework*, London, Martin Robertson.

Oakley, Ann (1976) *Housewife*, Harmondsworth, Penguin Books.

Office of Population Censuses and Surveys (1993) *1991 Census: Report for Great Britain*, Part 1, vol. 3, London, HMSO.

Oliver, Michael (1990) *The Politics of Disablement*, Basingstoke, Macmillan.

Osterbusch, Suzanne E, Keigher, Sharon M., Miller, Baila and Linsk, Nathan L. (1987) 'Community Care Policies and Gender Justice', *International Journal of Health Services*, 17, 217–32.

Pahl, Jan (ed.) (1985) *Private Violence and Public Policy: The Needs of Battered Women and the Response of the Public Services*, London, Routledge & Kegan Paul.

Pahl, J. M. and Pahl, R. E. (1971) *Managers and Their Wives: A Study of Career and Family Relationships in the Middle Class*, London, Allen Lane/Penguin.

Parekh, Bhikhu (1982) *The Experience of Black Minorities in Britain*, Milton Keynes, Open University Press.

Parker, Gillian (1990) *With Due Care and Attention: A Review of Research on Informal Care* (2nd ed.), London, Family Policy Studies Centre.

Parker, Roy (1981) 'Tending and Social Policy', in Goldberg, E. M. and Hatch, S. (eds) *A New Look at the Personal Social Services*, London, Policy Studies Institute.

Parmar, Pratibha (1982) 'Gender, Race and Class: Asian Women in Resistance', in Centre for Contemporary Cultural Studies, *The Empire Strikes Back: Race and Racism in 70s Britain*, London, Hutchinson.

Parsons, Talcott (1955) 'The American Family: Its Relations to Personality and to the Social Structure', in Parsons, T. and Bales, R. F., *Family, Socialisation and Interaction Process*, New York, The Free Press.

Parsons, Talcott (1949) 'The Social Structure of the Family', in Anshen, R. N. (ed.) *The Family: Its Function and Destiny*, New York, Harper & Bros.

Parton, Christine (1990) 'Women, Gender Oppression and Child Abuse', in The Violence Against Children Study Group (eds) *Taking Child Abuse Seriously: Contemporary Issues in Child Protection Theory and Practice*, London, Unwin Hyman.

Parton, Nigel (1985) *The Politics of Child Abuse*, Basingstoke, Macmillan.

Patterson, Orlando (1982) 'Persistence, Continuity and Change in the Jamaican Working-Class Family', *Journal of Family History*, 7, 135–61.

Patterson, Sheila (1965) *Dark Strangers: A Study of West Indians in London*, Harmondsworth, Penguin.

Payne, Joan and Payne, Clive (1993) 'Unemployment and Peripheral Work', *Work, Employment & Society*, 7, 513–34.

Payne, Joan and Payne, Clive (1994) 'Recession, Restructuring and the Fate of the Unemployed: Evidence in the Underclass Debate', *Sociology*, 28, 1–19.

Peace, Sheila (1986) 'The Forgotten Female: Social Policy and Older Women', in Phillipson, C. and Walker, A. (eds) *Ageing and Social Policy: A Critical Assessment*, London, Gower.

Peters, Stephanie D., Wyatt, Gail E. and Finkelhor, D. (1986) 'Prevalence', in Finkelhor, D. (ed.) *A Sourcebook on Child Sexual Abuse*, Beverly Hills, Sage.

Phillipson, Chris (1982) *Capitalism and the Construction of Old Age*, Basingstoke, Macmillan.

Phillipson, Chris and Walker, Alan (eds) (1986) *Ageing and Social Policy: A Critical Assessment*, London, Gower.

Phizacklea, Annie (1983) 'In the Front Line', in Phizacklea, A. (ed.) *One Way Ticket: Migration and Female Labour*, London, Routledge.

Pilgrim Trust (1938) *Men Without Work*, Cambridge, Cambridge University Press.

Pillemer, Karl. and Finkelhor, David (1988) 'The Prevalence of Elder Abuse: A Random Sample Survey', *The Gerontologist*, 28, 51–7.

Pinching, Anthony (1990) 'AIDS: Clinical and Scientific Background', in Almond, B. (ed.) *AIDS: A Moral Issue: The Ethical, Legal and Social Aspects*, Basingstoke, Macmillan.

Pizzey, Erin and Shapiro, Jeff (1982) *Prone to Violence*, London, Hamlyn.

Plummer, Ken (1988) 'Organising AIDS', in Aggleton, P. and Homans, H. (eds) *Social Aspects of AIDS*, Lewes, The Falmer Press.

Ptacek, James (1988) 'Why do Men Batter Their Wives?', in Yllö, K. and Bograd, M. (eds) *Feminist Perspectives on Wife Abuse*, Newbury Park, Sage.

Qureshi, Hazel and Walker, Alan (1989) *The Caring Relationship: Elderly People and Their Families*, Basingstoke, Macmillan.

Radford, Jill (1987) 'Policing Male Violence – Policing Women', in Hanmer, J. and Maynard, M. (eds) *Women, Violence and Social Control*, Basingstoke, Macmillan.

Radford, Jill (1992) 'Retrospect on a Trial' and 'Womanslaughter: A License to Kill? The Killing of Jane Asher' in Radford, J. and Russell, D. E. H. (eds) *Femicide: The Politics of Woman Killing*, Buckingham, Open University Press.

Radford, Jill and Russell, Diana E. H. (eds) (1992) *Femicide: The Politics of Woman Killing*, Buckingham, Open University Press.

Ramazanoglu, Caroline (1987) 'Set and Violence in Academic Life or You Can Keep a Good Woman Down', in Hanmer, J. and Maynard, M. (eds) *Women, Violence and Social Control*, Basingstoke, Macmillan.

Ramazanoglu, Caroline (1989) *Feminism and the Contradictions of Oppression*, London, Routledge.

Reinharz, Shulamit (1986) 'Friends or Foes: Gerontological and Feminist Theory', *Women's Studies International Forum*, 9, 503–14.

Renzetti, Claire M. (1992) *Violent Betrayal: Partner Abuse in Lesbian Relationships*, Newbury Park, Sage.

Rex, John and Moore, Robert (1967) *Race, Community and Conflict*, Oxford, Oxford University Press.

Richards, Martin P. M. and Elliott, B. Jane (1991) 'Sex and Marriage in the 1960s and 1970s', in Clark, D. (ed.) *Marriage, Domestic Life and Social Change: Writings for Jacqueline Burgoyne (1944–88)*, London, Routledge.

Richardson, Diane (1990) 'AIDS Education and Women: Sexual and Reproductive Issues', in Aggleton, P., Davies P. and Hart, G. (eds) *Individual, Cultural and Policy Dimensions*, London, Falmer Press.

Richardson, John and Lambert, John (1985) *The Sociology of Race*, Ormskirk, Causeway Press.

Rindfuss, Ronald R. and VandenHeuvel, Audrey (1992) 'Cohabitation: A Precursor to Marriage or an Alternative to Being Single?', in South, S. J. and Tolnay S. E. (eds) *The Changing American Family*, Boulder, Westview Press.

Robson-Scott, Markie (1993) 'Back to the Future', *The Guardian*, 31 August.

Rodger, John (1992) 'The Welfare State and Social Closure: Social Division and the "Underclass"', *Critical Social Policy*, 35, 45–63.

Roff, Lucinda L. and Klemmack, David L. (1986) 'Norms for Employed Daughters' and Sons' Behaviour Toward Frail Older Parents', *Sex Roles*, 14, 363–8.

Roll, Jo (1992) *Lone Parent Families in the European Community*, London, European Family and Social Policy Unit and Birmingham, The University of Birmingham.

Rosenmayr, Leopold and Köckeis, Eva (1963) 'Propositions for a Sociological Theory of Ageing and the Family', *International Social Science Journal*, 15, 410–26.

Rossi, Alice S. (1977) 'A Biosocial Perspective on Parenting', *Daedalus*, 106(2) 1–31.

Russell, Diana E. H. (1983) 'The Incidence and Prevalence of Intrafamilial and Extrafamilial Sexual Abuse of Female Children', *Child Abuse and Neglect*, 7, 133–46.

Russell, Diana E. H. (1986) *The Secret Trauma: Incest in the Lives of Girls and Women*, New York, Basic Books.

Russell, Diana E. H. (1990) *Rape in Marriage* (2nd ed.), Bloomington, Indiana University Press.

Russell, Diana E. H. (ed.) (1993) *Making Violence Sexy: Feminist Views on Pornography*, Buckingham Open University Press.

Saifullah Khan, Verity (1979) 'Migration and Social Stress: Mirpuris in Bradford', in Saifullah Khan, V. (ed.) *Minority Families in Britain: Support and Stress*, Basingstoke, Macmillan.

Saifullah Khan, Verity (1981) 'The Role of the Culture of Dominance in Structuring the Experience of Ethnic Minorities', in Husband, C. (ed.) '*Race' in Britain: Continuity and Change*, London, Hutchinson.

Salfield, Angie and Durward, Lyn (1985) '"Coping, But Only Just" – Families' Experiences of Pregnancy and Childrearing on the Dole', in Durward, L. (ed.) *Born Unequal: Perspectives in Pregnancy and Childrearing in Unemployed Families*, London, Maternity Alliance.

Sanday, Peggy Reeves (1981) 'The Socio-cultural Context of Rape: a Cross-Cultural Study', *Journal of Social Issues*, 37, 5–27.

Sanday, Peggy Reeves (1990) *Fraternity Gang Rape: Sex, Brotherhood and Privilege on Campus*, New York, New York University Press.

Saunders, Daniel G. (1988) 'Wife Abuse, Husband Abuse or Mutual Combat? A Feminist Perspective on the Empirical Findings', in Yllö, K. and Bograd, M. (eds) *Feminist Perspectives on Wife Abuse*, Newbury Park, Sage.

Scanzoni, John, Polonko, Karen, Teachman, Jay and Thompson, Linda (1989) *The Sexual Bond: Rethinking Families and Close Relationships*, Newbury Park, Sage.

Scharf, Emily and Toole, Sue (1992) 'HIV and the Invisibility of Women', *Feminist Review*, 41, 64–7.

Schiller, Nina G., Crystal, Stephen and Lewellen, Denver (1994) 'Risky Business: The Cultural Construction of AIDS Risk Groups' *Social Science & Medicine*, 38, 1337–46.

Schoen, Robert and Owens, David (1992) 'A Further Look at First Unions and First Marriages', in South, S. J. and Tolnay S. E. (eds) *The Changing American Family*, Boulder, Westview Press.

Scott, Jacqueline (1990) 'Women and the Family', in Jowell, R., Witherspoon, S. and Brook, H. (eds), *British Social Attitudes: The 7th Report*, Aldershot, Gower.

Scott, Jacqueline, Braun, Michael and Alwin, Duane (1993) 'The Family Way', in Jowell, R., Brook, L. and Dowds, L. (eds), *International Social Attitudes: the 10th BSA Report*, Aldershot, Dartmouth.

Scrutton, Steve (1990) 'The Foundation of Age Discrimination', in McEwen, E. (ed.) *Age: The Unrecognised Discrimination*, London, Age Concern.

Scully, Diana (1990) *Understanding Sexual Violence: A Study of Convicted Rapists*, London, HarperCollinsAcademic.

Secretary of State for Social Services (1988) *Report of the Inquiry into Child Abuse in Cleveland 1987*, Cm 412, London, HMSO.

Seelbach, Wayne C. (1984) 'Filial Responsibility and the Care of Aging Family Members', in Quinn, W. H. and Hughston, G. A. (eds) *Independent Ageing*, Rockville, Maryland, Aspen.

Segal, Lynne (1983) '"Smash the Family?" Recalling the 1960s', in Segal, L. (ed.) *What Is To Be Done About the Family?*, Harmondsworth, Penguin Books.

Segal, Lynne (1987a) 'AIDS Is a Feminist Issue', *New Socialist*, 48, 7–11.

Segal, Lynne (1987b) *Is the Future Female? Troubled Thoughts on Contemporary Feminism*, London, Virago.

Segal, Lynne (1990) *Slow Motion: Changing Masculinities, Changing Men*, London, Virago.

Shainess, Natalie (1984) *Sweet Suffering: Woman as Victim*, New York, Bobbs-Merrill.

Shamir, Boas (1986) 'Unemployment and Household Division of Labour', *Journal of Marriage and the Family*, 48, 195–206.

Shaw, Alison (1988) *A Pakistani Community in Britain*, Oxford, Blackwell.

Siegel, Karolynn, Mesagno, Frances P., Chen Jin-Yi and Christ, Grace (1989) 'Factors Distinguishing Homosexual Males Practising Risky and Safer Sex', *Social Science & Medicine*, 28, 561–9.

Singer, Eleanor, Rogers, Theresa F. and Corcoran, Mary (1987) 'The Polls – a Report: AIDS', *Public Opinion Quarterly*, 51, 580–95.

Smart, Carol (1984) *The Ties that Bind: Law, Marriage and the Reproduction of Patriarchal Relations*, London, Routledge.

Smith, Lorna (1989) *Domestic Violence*, Home Office Research Study 107, London, HMSO.

Smith, Raymond T. (1963) 'Culture and Social Structure in the Caribbean: Some Recent Work on Family and Kinship Studies', *Comparative Studies in Society and History*, 6, 24–46.

Smith, Raymond T. (1988) *Kinship and Class in the West Indies: A Genealogical Study of Jamaica and Guyana*, Cambridge, Cambridge University Press.

Smith, Richard (1984) 'The Structured Dependence of the Elderly as a Recent Development: Some Sceptical Historical Thoughts, *Ageing and Society*, 4, 409–28.

Smith, Tom W. (1990) 'The Polls – a Report: The Sexual Revolution?', *Public Opinion Quarterly*, 54, 415–35.

Snell, John E., Rosenwald, Richard and Robey, Ames (1964) 'The Wifebeater's Wife: A Study of Family Interaction', *Archives of General Psychiatry*, 11, 107–12.

Social Trends (1986) Central Statistical Office, London, HMSO.

Social Trends (1991) Central Statistical Office, London, HMSO.

Social Trends (1993) Central Statistical Office, London, HMSO.

Social Trends (1994) Central Statistical Office, London, HMSO.

Solomos, John (1985) 'Problems, But Whose Problems: The Social Construction of Black Youth Unemployment and State Policies', *Journal of Social Policy*, 14, 527–54.

Solomos, John (1993) *Race and Racism in Britain* (2nd ed.), Basingstoke, Macmillan.

Sondhi, Ranjit (1987) *Divided Families: British Immigration Control in the Indian Subcontinent*, London, Runnymede Trust.

Sontag, Susan (1978) 'The Double Standard of Ageing', in Carver, V. and Liddiard, P. (eds) *An Ageing Population: A Reader and Sourcebook*, Sevenoaks, Hodder and Stoughton and Milton Keynes, The Open University Press.

Sontag, Susan (1989) *Aids and Its Metaphors*, New York, Farrar, Straus and Giroux.

Statistical Abstract of the United States: 1992 (112th edition), Washington, D.C., US Bureau of the Census.

Stearns, Peter (1977) *Old Age in European Society*, London, Croom Helm.

Steinmetz, Suzanne K. (1978) 'The Battered Husband Syndrome', *Victimology* 2, 499–509.

Stets, Jan E. and Straus, Murray A. (1989) 'The Marriage License as a Hitting License: A Comparison of Assaults in Dating, Cohabiting and Married Couples', in Pirog-Good, M. A. and Stets, J. E. (eds) *Violence in Dating Relationships: Emerging Social Issues*, New York, Praeger.

Stone, Karen (1983) 'Motherhood and Waged Work: West Indian, Asian and White Mothers Compared', in Phizacklea, A. (ed.) *One Way Ticket*, London, Routledge & Kegan Paul.

Stopes-Roe, Mary and Cochrane, Raymond (1989) 'Traditionalism in the Family: A Comparison between Asian and British Cultures and between Generations', *Journal of Comparative Family Studies*, XX, 141–58.

Stopes-Roe, Mary and Cochrane, Raymond (1990a) *Citizens of this Country: the Asian-British*, Clevedon, Multilingual Matters.

Stopes-Roe, Mary and Cochrane, Raymond (1990b) 'Support Networks of Asian and British Families: Comparisons between Ethnicities and between Generations', *Social Behaviour*, 5, 71–85.

Straus, Murray A. (1979) 'Family Patterns and Child Abuse in a Nationally Representative American Sample', *Child Abuse and Neglect*, 3, 213–25.

Straus, Murray A. (1980a) 'A Sociological Perspective on the Causes of Family Violence', in Green, M. R. (ed.) *Violence and the Family*, Boulder, Colorado, Westview.

Straus, Murray A. (1980b) 'A Sociological Perspective on the Prevention of Wife-Beating', in Staus M. A. and Hotaling, G. T. (eds) *The Social Causes of Husband-Wife Violence*, Minneapolis, University of Minnesota Press.

Straus, Murray A. and Gelles, Richard J. (1986) 'Societal Change and Change in Family Violence from 1975 to 1985 as Revealed by Two National Surveys', *Journal of Marriage and the Family*, 48, 465–79.

Straus, Murray A., Gelles, Richard J. and Steinmetz, Suzanne K. (1980) *Behind Closed Doors: Violence in the American Family*, Newbury Park, Sage.

Stulberg, Ian and Smith, Margaret (1988) 'Psychosocial Impact of the AIDS Epidemic on the Lives of Gay Men', *Social Work*, 33, 277–81.

Sudarkasa, Niara (1988) 'Interpreting the African Heritage in Afro-American Family Organisation', in McAdoo, H. P. (ed.) *Black Families*, (2nd ed.) Newbury Park, Sage.

Taylor, Steve (1989) 'How Prevalent Is It', in Stainton Rogers, W., Hevey, D. and Ash, E. (eds) *Child Abuse and Neglect: Facing the Challenge*, London, Batsford/Open University.

Thane, Pat (1987) 'The Growing Burden of an Ageing Population?', *Journal of Public Policy*, 7, 373–87.

Thompson, Linda and Walker, Alexis, J. (1989) 'Gender in Families: Women and Men in Marriage, Work and Parenthood' *Journal of Marriage and the Family*, 51, 845–71.

Thomson, David (1986) 'Welfare and the Historians', in Bonfield L., Smith, R. M. and Wrightson, K. (eds) *The World We Have Gained*, Oxford, Blackwell.

Titmuss, Richard M. (1963) 'The Position of Women', in Titmuss, R. M., *Essays on 'The Welfare State'* (2nd ed.), London, Unwin.

Tizard, Barbara and Phoenix, Ann (1989) 'Black Identity and Transracial Adoption', *New Community*, 15, 427–37.

Tizard, Barbara and Phoenix, Ann (1993) *Black, White or Mixed Race: Race and Racism in the Lives of Young People of Mixed Parentage*, London, Routledge.

Townsend, Peter (1981) 'The Structured Dependency of the Elderly: A Creation of Social Policy in the Twentieth Century', *Ageing and Society*, 1, 5–28.

Townsend, Peter (1986) 'Ageism and Social Policy', in Phillipson, C. and Walker, A. (eds) *Ageing and Social Policy: A Critical Assessment*, London, Gower.

Toynbee, Polly (1994) 'Family Fortunes', *The Guardian*, 2 February.

Ungerson, Clare (1983) 'Why Do Women Care?', in Finch, J. and Groves, D. (eds) *A Labour of Love: Women, Work and Caring*, London, Routledge & Kegan Paul.

Ungerson, Clare (1987) *Policy is Personal: Sex, Gender and Informal Care*, London, Tavistock.

Ungerson, Clare (1990) 'The Language of Care', in Ungerson, C. (ed.) *Gender and Caring: Work and Welfare in Britain and Scandinavia*, London, Harvester Wheatsheaf.

United Nations (1994) *1992 Demographic Yearbook*, New York, United Nations.

Vass, Antony A. *(1986) AIDS, A Plague in US: A Social Perspective – the Condition and Its Social Consequences*, Huntingdon, Venus Academica.

Venner, Mary (1985) 'West Indian Families in Britain: A Research Note', *New Comunity*, XII, 504–14.

Victor, Christina R. (1987) *Old Age in Modern Society: A Textbook of Social Gerontology*, London, Croom Helm.

Victor, Christina R. (1991) 'Continuity or Change: Inequalities in Health in Later Life', *Ageing and Society*, 11, 23–39.

Waldby, Catherine, Kippax, Susan and Crawford, June (1993) *'Cordon Sanitaire* – 'Clean' and 'Unclean' Women in the AIDS Discourse of Young Heterosexual Men', in Aggleton, P., Davies, P. and Hart, G. (eds) *AIDS: Facing the Second Decade*, London, The Falmer Press.

Waldby, Cathy, Clancy, Atosha, Emetchi, Jan and Summerfield, Caroline (1989) 'Theoretical Perspectives on Father–Daughter Incest', in Driver, E. and Droisen A. (eds) *Child Sexual Abuse*, Basingstoke, Macmillan.

Walker, Alan (ed.) (1982) *Community Care: The Family, the State and Social Policy*, Oxford, Blackwell and Martin Robertson.

Walker, Alan (1983) 'Social Policy and Elderly People in Great Britain: The Construction of Dependent Social and Economic Status in Old Age', in Guillemard, A. (ed.) *Old Age and the Welfare State*, Beverly Hills, Sage.

Walker, Alan (1990a) 'Poverty and Inequality in Old Age', in Bond J. and Coleman, P. (eds) *Ageing in Society: An Introduction to Social Gerontology*, London, Sage.

Walker, Alan (1990b) 'The Economic 'Burden' of Ageing and the Prospect of Intergenerational Conflict', *Ageing and Society*, 10, 377–96.

Walker, Alan (1992) 'The Poor Relation: Poverty among Older Women', in Glendinning, C. and Millar, J. (eds) *Women and Poverty in Britain: the 1990s*, London, Harvester Wheatsheaf.

Walker, Alan and Phillipson, Chris (1986) 'Introduction' to Phillipson, C. and Walker, A. (eds) *Ageing and Social Policy: A Critical Assessment*, London, Gower.

Walker, Lenore E. (1984) *The Battered Woman Syndrome*, New York, Springer.

Wall, Richard (1989) 'The Living Arrangements of the Elderly in Europe in the 1980s', in Bytheway, B., Keil, T., Allatt, P. and Bryman, A. (eds) *Becoming and Being Old: Sociological Approaches to Later Life*, London, Sage.

Wallace, Claire (1987) *For Richer, For Poorer: Growing Up In and Out of Work*, London, Tavistock.

Wallerstein, Judith, S. and Blakeslee, Sandra (1989) *Second Chances: Men, Women and Children a Decade after Divorce*, New York, Ticknor and Fields.

Wallerstein, Judith, S. and Kelly, Joan B. (1980) *Surviving the Breakup: How Children and Parents Cope with Divorce*, London, Grant McIntyre.

Ward, Elizabeth (1984) *Father–Daughter Rape*, London, The Women's Press.

Warr, Peter (1987) *Work, Unemployment and Mental Health*, Oxford, Clarendon Press.

Warr, Peter and Jackson, Paul (1985) 'Factors Influencing the Psychological Impact of Prolonged Unemployment and of Re-employment', in *Psychological Medicine*, 15, 795–807.

Warwick, Ian, Aggleton, Peter and Homans, Hilary (1988) 'Young People's Health Beliefs and AIDS', in Aggleton, P. and Homans, H. (eds) *Social Aspects of AIDS*, Lewes, Falmer Press.

Watney, Simon (1988) 'AIDS, "Moral Panic" Theory and Homophobia', in Aggleton, P. and Homans, H. (eds) *Social Aspects of AIDS*, Lewes, The Falmer Press.

Weatherburn, Peter, Hunt, Andrew, Hickson, Ford C. I. and Davies, Peter M. (1992) *The Sexual Lifestyles of Gay and Bisexual Men in England and Wales*, Department of Health, London, HMSO.

Weeks, Jeffrey (1985) *Sexuality and Its Discontents*, London, Routledge & Kegan Paul.

Weeks, Jeffrey (1986) *Sexuality*, London, Tavistock.

Weeks, Jeffrey (1988) 'Love in a Cold Climate', in Aggleton, P. and Homans, H. (eds) *Social Aspects of AIDS*, Lewes, The Falmer Press.

Weeks, Jeffrey (1989a) 'AIDS: The Intellectual Agenda', in Aggleton, P., Hart, G. and Davies, P. (eds) *AIDS: Social Representations, Social Practices*, Lewes, The Falmer Press.

Weeks, Jeffrey (1989b) *Sex, Politics & Society: The Regulation of Sexuality Since 1800* (2nd ed.), London, Longman.

Weitzman, Lenore J. (1988) 'Women and Children Last: The Social and Economic Consequences of Divorce Law Reforms', in Dornbusch, S. M. and Strober, M. H. (eds) *Feminism, Children, and the New Families*, New York, The Guilford Press.

Wellings, Kaye and Wadsworth, Jane (1990) 'AIDS and the Moral Climate', in Jowell, R., Witherspoon, S. and Brook, L. (eds) *British Social Attitudes: The 7th Report*, Aldershot, Gower.

Wellings, Kaye, Field, Julia, Johnson, Anne M. and Wadsworth, Jane (1994) *Sexual Behaviour in Britain*, Harmondsworth, Penguin.

Wenger, G. Clare (1987) 'Dependence, Interdependence, and Reciprocity After Eighty', *Journal of Aging Studies*, 1, 355–77.

Werbner, Pnina (1988) 'Taking and Giving: Working Women and Female Bonds in a Pakistani Immigrant Neigbourhood', in Westwood, S. and Bhachu, P. (eds) *Enterprising Women: Ethnicity, Economy and Gender Relations*, London, Routledge.

West, Patrick, Illsley, Raymond and Kelman, Howard (1984) 'Public Preferences for the Care of Dependency Groups', *Social Science & Medicine*, 18, 287–95.

Westergaard, John (1992) 'About and Beyond the "Underclass": Some Notes on Influence of Social Climate on British Sociology Today', *Sociology*, 26, 575–87.

Westwood, Sallie (1988) 'Workers and Wives: Continuities and Discontinuities in the Lives of Gujarati Women', in Westwood, S. and Bhachu, P. (eds) *Enterprising Women: Ethnicity, Economy and Gender Relations*, London, Routledge.

Westwood, Sallie and Bhachu, Parminder (eds) (1988) *Enterprising Women: Ethnicity, Economy and Gender Relations*, London, Routledge.

Wheelock, Jane (1990) *Husbands at Home: The Domestic Economy in a Post-industrial Society*, London, Routledge.

Wight, D. (1992) 'Impediments to Safer Heterosexual Sex: A Review of Research with Young People', *AIDS Care*, 4, 11–23.

Wight, D. (1993) 'Constraints or Cognition? Young Men and Safer Heterosexual Sex', in Aggleton, P., Davies, P. and Hart, G. (eds) AIDS: *Facing the Second Decade*, London, The Falmer Press.

Willis, Paul (1984a) 'Youth Unemployment: A New Social State', *New Society*, 67, 475–7.

Willis, Paul (1984b) 'Youth Unemployment: Ways of Living', *New Society*, 68, 13–15.

Willmott, Peter and Young, Michael (1960) *Family and Class in a London Suburb*, London, Routledge & Kegan Paul.

Wilson, Elizabeth (1977) *Women and the Welfare State*, London, Tavistock.

Wilson, William J. (1987) *The Truly Disadvantaged: The Inner City, the Underclass and Public Policy*, Chicago, University of Chicago Press.

Wilton, Tamsin and Aggleton, Peter (1991) 'Condoms, Coercion and Control: Heterosexuality and the Limits to HIV/AIDS Education', in Aggleton, P., Hart, G. and Davies, P. (eds) *AIDS: Responses, Interventions and Care*, London, Falmer Press.

Witherspoon, Sharon (1988) 'Interim Report: A Woman's Work', in Jowell, R., Witherspoon, S. and Brook, L. (eds) *British Social Attitudes Survey: the 5th Report*, Aldershot, Gower.

Wood, Richard (1991) 'Care of Disabled People', in Dalley, Gillian (ed.) *Disability and Social Policy*, London, Policy Studies Institute.

Worsley, Peter (ed.) (1987) *The New Introducing Sociology*, (3rd ed.) Harmondsworth, Penguin Books.

Wright, Fay (1983) 'Single Carers: Employment, Housework and Caring', in Finch, J. and Groves, D. (eds) *A Labour of Love: Women, Work and Caring*, London, Routledge & Kegan Paul.

Yeandle, Susan (1984) *Women's Working Lives: Patterns and Strategies*, London, Tavistock.

Young, Michael and Willmott, Peter (1957) *Family and Kinship in East London*, London, Routledge & Kegan Paul.

Young, Michael and Willmott, Peter (1973) *The Symmetrical Family*, London, Routledge & Kegan Paul.

Zinn, Maxine B, and Eitzen, D. Stanley (1990) *Diversity in Families* (2nd ed.) New York, Harper & Row.

Author Index

Subject Index

Note: page numbers in *italics* refer to information to be found only in tables and figures.